WITH GOD ON OUR SIDE

WITH GOD
ON OUR SIDE

ONE MAN'S WAR AGAINST
AN EVANGELICAL COUP IN AMERICA'S MILITARY

Michael L. Weinstein and Davin Seay

Thomas Dunne Books
St. Martin's Press ✎ New York

THOMAS DUNNE BOOKS.
An imprint of St. Martin's Press.

www.thomasdunnebooks.com

www.stmartins.com

ISBN-13: 978-0-312-36143-3
ISBN-10: 0-312-36143-2

First Edition: October 2006

10 9 8 7 6 5 4 3 2 1

Mikey Weinstein would like to dedicate this book to his beloved wife, Bonnie, and his courageous children, Casey, Curtis, and Amanda.

Davin Seay would like to respectfully dedicate this book to his friend and fellow traveler, Ken. And, as always, Diane.

CONTENTS

ACKNOWLEDGMENTS

The authors would like to acknowledge, with utmost gratitude, the following individuals, without whose assistance, advice, courage, and inspiration, the book would not have been possible:

Bonnie Weinstein, Casey and Amanda Weinstein, Curtis Weinstein, Alice and Gerald Weinstein, Diane Seay, Reverend MeLinda Morton, Pam Zubeck, Dr. Kristen Leslie, Cecilia Peasley, and David Antoon.

Also, Steve Aguilar, Reza Aslan, Richard Baker, James Barash, Bryce Batchman, Jim Belshaw, Lexi Bennett, Donnie Blanks, Rob Boston, Howard Bragman, Sam Bregman, Jackie Bregman, James Carroll, Julie and Jessica Christian, William Clark, Dave Cowan, Cara Degette, Matt Dorf, Steve Dotson, Rabbi Malka Drucker, Thomas Dunne, Don Epstein, Marty Esquivel, Sam Fairchild, Jay Fawcett, Gene Fidell, Rabbi Art Flicker, Kathy and Paul Gregory, Bob Herres, Stan and Cindy Hill, Mal Hormats, Mala Htun, Pedro L. Irigonegaray, Steve Israel and his congressional staff, Oren Jacoby, Michael Josephson, the entire Jucknies family, Richard Katskee, Bud Kauderer, Ari Kayne, Ron Kennedy, George Keys, Dale Kildee and his congressional staff, Pat Killen, Dick

Klass, Patrick Kucera, Carly Lindauer, Jay Lindsey, Eric Loman, Herta Long, Anne Loveland, Barry Lynn, John McShane, Patricia Madrid, Mike Messina, Andrew Meyer, Lou Michels, Beth Newburger, Bobbi and Lloyd Patterson, Jeannie Patterson, Burnie Peters, Rachel Query, Steve Rabinowitz, Erza Reese, Mike Reith, David Rosen, Julie Rosenthal, Millie and Stanley Rosenthal, Dick Scholsberg, Richard Schwartz, Rabbi Joel Schwartzman, Susan Seligman, Smita Singh, the Sipos Family, Jason Spindler, Eric Svetco, Doug Turner, Rabbi Barry Weinstein, Burt and Carolyn Weinstein, David and Candy Weinstein, Myra and Jerry Wells, Ambassador Joseph Wilson, Evy Woods, Patrick Worms, and Ken Zangara.

And the countless unnamed individuals who, at considerable personal and professional risk, stepped forward to speak truth to power. You know who you are.

WITH GOD ON OUR SIDE

✲ 1 ✲

A FAMILY TRADITION

On July 29, 2004, Mikey Weinstein took advantage of an unpatrolled stretch of I-25 just outside of Santa Fe to open up his fire-engine-red, five-hundred-horsepower Viper GTS, punching through a glorious desert panorama bathed in bright sunlight.

Dense and compact, his shorn, bullet-shaped head fit snugly on his shoulders and his warm brown eyes set on stun, Weinstein radiated an unsettling mix of composure and coiled spring tension that fit well with his choice in automobiles. He'd bought the car specifically for its prowling, muscular profile, a conspicuous symbol, not of midlife angst, but of a decision he'd made back in 1998 when his wife, Bonnie, was first diagnosed with multiple sclerosis. "That changed everything," he recounts. "In a heartbeat. We decided right then that we had to live for the moment. The focus wasn't going to be about growing old together and dandling grandchildren on our knees. We wanted to get as much out of each day, every day, as we could, to enjoy our lives now, because neither one of us really knew how much time we had left together. We didn't want to take a single minute for granted."

Not that Weinstein is in the habit of letting much of anything slip by. With a taste for plum wine, chocolate pancakes, hard-core punk and metal rock, and profanity, he fueled himself on outsize emotions and unassailable convictions. His practiced ease with the perquisites of power echoes in his resonant baritone, which, no matter how impassioned, is restrained, measured. A quintessential soldier; a high-profile attorney; a self-starting entrepreneur—for all the high points of his skill set, what he seems most palpably to relish is his role as a rogue operative, a dangerous underdog who describes himself as "unpredictable, mercurial, and peripatetic." A man who habitually led with his jaw, feeling deeply, without reserve and sometimes to his detriment, Weinstein had a lifetime allegiance to honor, duty, and service, shot through with a rebellious streak, a fierce integrity, and the impressive ability to balance all the contradictions that define him.

There is, for starters, the incongruity of his nickname, stuck to him since his teenage years because of a resemblance to the stocky, pugnacious toddler in the famous Life cereal commercial, that, even now at fifty-one, five feet eight inches, and 178 pounds, still lingers.

But the dissonances and disconnects of the man reach down further. "There's only a couple of things I've tried to do in my life that I've completely failed at," he will say with a laugh. "One was being a Grateful Dead fan. I thought it would be cool and I gave it my best shot, but I had to face the fact that, to me, they sucked. The other was being an atheist." In fact, Weinstein's almost primal Jewish identity runs up hard and often against any comforting spiritual certainty. "When I look at these mountains all around me or into the faces of my wife, sons, and daughter-in-law, I can't shake the unflagging sense that there must be, in a very Jewish sense, a Supreme Being. That's why I pray twice a day, every day, even though I'm still waiting to get an answer about how a supposedly loving God allows the murder of children in the millions in the Holocaust. I identify absolutely with my people and my culture, but I'm not always sure where I stand on the absolutes of my faith."

The paradox of an assiduously secular Jew who regularly prays is echoed by Weinstein's counterintuitive patriotism, a belief in America predicated on an obdurate appeal to its highest ideals. It's a stance all the more remarkable given his inculcation in martial codes of unquestioning loyalty to God, country, and commander in chief and bolstered by his time served as a legal operative in the Reagan White House, whose evocation of a "shining city on a hill" still serves to inspire his American pride of place.

Weinstein was intimately familiar with the I-25 interstate corridor running from his hometown of Albuquerque to the front gates of the Air Force Academy. The Academy is a little more than a hundred miles across the border between New Mexico and Colorado—through Raton Pass, not far from the Continental Divide and straight into Colorado Springs. Over the years, traveling to and from visits to his cadet sons and various Academy alumni events and college football games, he had clocked it out at precisely three hundred minutes, a time he seemed sure to beat as he wound up the Viper into triple digits.

He enjoyed the run, as much for the memories it evoked as for the stunning scenery along the way. The vast prairies on his right stretched east to Kansas and Oklahoma, while the southern spur of the Sangre de Cristo Mountains off to the west rose higher and became the Rampart Range as he pulled past Trinidad and Aguilar and Walsenberg, up through the bedroom communities that feed directly into Denver, farther north up the arrow-straight freeway.

His destination was, after all, ground zero of his formative life experiences, the place where the best things and the worst things that had ever happened to him were staged against a breathtaking backdrop of snowcapped mountains in a cloistered hothouse of high ideals and unsparing indoctrination. His destination that morning represented, in short, the crux of his history and the crucible of his character.

That history and the character it shaped are, in turn, deeply rooted in the American military tradition. His father, Gerald Weinstein, enlisted in the Navy in the aftermath of World War II to escape the abject poverty of his upstate New York childhood. He would go on to earn a coveted place at Annapolis, where he befriended another young midshipmen by the name of Ross Perot. Having already earned his pilot's license as a teenager, he switched service branches upon graduation from the Naval Academy, following that dream of aviation so common to his peers, and joined the Air Force. That trajectory accorded well with his son's own aspirations, and Mikey would in time follow him into that most elite wing of the armed forces.

"My dad ran the house like a military unit," Mikey recalls. "If someone called, you'd answer the phone by saying, 'Captain Weinstein's quarters, Michael Weinstein speaking.' He had a duty roster for every day of the week. My relatives thought he was a real martinet. But he wasn't. He may have been strict, but he was also a very loving man, a very caring father. I was groomed from the beginning for a career in the military, and I never questioned it. I never had a reason to. I was proud of what he had accomplished, and if that was what he wanted for me, then that was what I wanted for myself. But at the same time he was very risk adverse. I think it's a common characteristic of people who grow up poor. He loved the Navy because he could eat three times a day, and if it wasn't for a petty officer in his unit continually prodding him, he never would have tested for Annapolis. Throughout his career, he did all the right things and was very conservative politically, very right-wing. There was a time when I started realizing on my own that being an American meant we had the right, the responsibility, to express ourselves freely, even if it was in opposition to authority. My father loves this country and told me from a very early age that we owe a debt of service to this great nation. He gave something back and he expected me to give back as well."

Those same inviolate principles—duty and continuity and a constant call to high achievement—were passed along to Mikey's own sons. His oldest, twenty-four-year-old Casey, is a graduate of the Air Force Academy, where he met his wife, Amanda, also an Air Force Academy graduate, when they were both cadets. His youngest, twenty-two-year-old Curtis, has also followed the footsteps of his father, brother, and sister-in-law to the Academy, and there is a satisfying sense of completion to the story, a full-circle affirmation that the most powerful pole in Weinstein's life—his abiding belief in military service—props up a large and all-encompassing tent.

"Family is the most important thing I know" is his unsurprising asseveration, even as, characteristically, he has formed an inclusive new definition of kinship. "As I get older," he says, "I find that the lines between family and friends gets blurrier," describing his expansive southwestern-themed home in Albuquerque as a "way station" for young academy cadets a long way from their own homes, as well as a haven for graduates awaiting assignments from the nearby staging center at Kirtland Air Force Base. "Year after year they come down to cool their heels," he says, "and for a while anyway, we can offer them a sanctuary."

Sanctuary. It's a word that resonated as he slowed the Viper into the flow of commuter traffic that ran uninterrupted from Pueblo through Colorado Springs. Yet for all the serenity he lays claim to, there is something contingent and conditional lying just below the surface, a kind of cagey vigilance that keeps him perpetually on his toes. A man of precise and ingrained habits, who appends the exact time, day, month, and year to every phone message he leaves and who keeps careful count well into the consecutive thousands of his daily cardiovascular workouts "to the full point of physical exhaustion," Mikey Weinstein never seems truly at rest, or fully at peace. He can't help but carry his grievances on his sleeve, nor does he disguise the grim satisfaction he feels in having his worst fears confirmed. A man impatient with all inwardness and introspection, his ideals are untainted by doubt. His feelings channeled through steely disciplines, his self-sustaining energies at once exhilarating and exhausting, he is disdainful of any notion of destiny or fate or cosmic causality. Yet it's difficult to imagine how else he might explain the extraordinary confluence of man and mission that were about to collide.

★ 2 ★

THE CADET CHAPEL

Once past the city limits, Weinstein took a moment to admire again the breathtaking vista and postcardlike perfection of Colorado Springs and its bustling environs. True to their name, the Ramparts erect a towering edifice of pine-covered ascents, climbing to the tree line up the fourteen-thousand-foot summit of Pikes Peak. As a cadet over thirty-three years ago, Weinstein, struggling to juggle his grade point average, his military bearing, his athletic performance, and his sanity, had scant opportunity to soak in the scenery. Enmeshed in the gears of a system designed to demolish his identity, ego, and self-regard, and then recast it in an elite leadership mold, Weinstein recalled a time when these mountains seemed to loom over him like the walls of an isolated prison, blocking any possibility of escape.

But that was then and this was now, when he could look back with something close to fondness to that time in this place and the processes that taught him how to accomplish more than he ever thought possible, savoring once again the pride he felt at surpassing his greatest expectations.

Since that time, little had changed within the 18,500-acre expanse of the Air Force Academy, although the adjacent town now sprawled across the valley in every direction. Malls and industrial parks and mushrooming housing developments crowded the boundaries of the Academy, peering over the high fences that guard the airfield and the Falcon football stadium, both tucked beneath the mountain shadows. In the distance, behind a high security perimeter, he could make out the low profile of the cadet quarters and, beyond, the declivity called Jack's Valley, where, as part of their initial basic cadet training, cadets are subjected to simulated combat privations. Ahead, the North Gate opened to a broad winding avenue up an incline to a scenic overlook surmounted by the enormous wingspan of an indigo-hued B-52 bomber, mounted in all its glory as a potent icon of the lethal technology this place has entrusted into the hands of its men and women graduates.

In fact, a technological texture is woven into every aspect of the Air Force Academy, in its architecture and curriculum and historical raison d'être. It's a faith in supersonic superiority; of science as the bulwark of national destiny; of exquisitely calibrated human beings trained to fly and fight faster, higher, and with more deadly accuracy than ever before in the annals of human warfare. It is an institution founded on the strategic exigencies of the Cold War, when airpower was perceived as the first and most formidable line of defense against godless communism, and it's a doctrine that endures to this day, even as our enemies have taken on new, more amorphous forms.

The Army and Navy air corps had, after all, proven their terrifying mettle over the Third Reich and the countless Pacific atolls of World War II, and after a proportionately titanic struggle in the halls of Congress and the Pentagon, the Air Force was duly constituted as coequal branch in 1947. It was Dwight Eisenhower, then president of Columbia University and head of the Service Academy Board, who concluded that the country's need for qualified pilots and their myriad support personnel could no longer be met solely at West Point and Annapolis. The decision was given impetus by the rapid development of jet aircraft, necessitating a whole new kind of airman, wedded to his machine by preternatural intuition and Mach-speed responses: a bionic blend of flesh and steel and outrageous velocity. From its inception, the Air

Force was envisaged as the razor's edge of America's might, and at the Academy that edge would be honed to hairbreadth tolerances. It was to be, in the words of then President Eisenhower's Air Force Secretary Harold Talbott, the "living embodiment of the modernity of flying."

Throwing the full weight of his heroic stature behind the institution's establishment, Eisenhower shepherded through the bill authorizing construction and signed the Air Force Academy Act on April 1, 1954. A site-selection committee that included Charles Lindbergh and Lieutenant General Hubert Harmon (later the Academy's first superintendent) had previously whittled a list of 582 locations down to three: Alton, Illinois; Lake Geneva, Wisconsin, and Colorado Springs.

The city fathers of the bucolic central-Colorado town would campaign relentlessly for six years to win the glittering prize with clunky slogans such as "Where Study Reaches Peak Efficiency due to Fine Climate and Surroundings." Founded in 1871 by Civil War general William Palmer as a rebuke to a reprobate mining town nearby, Colorado Springs stayed assiduously dry until the end of Prohibition and was known primarily as the spot where "America the Beautiful" was composed by Katharine Lee Bates in 1893. Here, electrical pioneer Nikola Tesla built his 12-million-volt "Tesla coil" in 1899, even as the town was becoming a resort destination for passengers on the Denver & Rio Grande Western Railroad and the discovery of gold at Cripple Creek sent the local economy soaring.

Whatever drew the site committee to this midcontinental locale would resonate with other military planners, and Colorado Springs, along with the surrounding El Paso County, eventually played host to three Air Force bases, an army fort, and, buried deep within the granite bowels of Cheyenne Mountain, the nerve center of the North American Air Defense Command (NORAD).

But its "fine climate and surroundings" would in time attract more than armed forces location scouts. Beginning in the midsixties, with the arrival of Nazarene Bible College, founded to "glorify Jesus Christ as Lord by preparing adults to evangelize, disciple and minister to the world," Colorado Springs had become a magnet for evangelical, charismatic, and fundamentalist churches, colleges, ministries, businesses, and outreaches of every description, earning, in the process, the sobriquet the Protestant Vatican. Within a five-mile radius of the Academy grounds can be found the headquarters of Officers' Christian Fellowship, the International Bible Society, Youth for Christ, The Navigators, Fellowship of Christian Athletes, Christian Booksellers Association, Hoops for Hope, Every Home for Christ, Worldwide Discipleship Association, Singles Ministry Resources, Music Evangelism Foundation, National Church Growth Research Center, Christian Camping International, Covenant International, Spiritual Growth Ministries, Fellowship of Christian Cowboys, and nearly a hundred others. Topping the list are such heavy hitters as the New Life Church, with a massive sanctuary decked in the official blue and silver colors of the Academy. New Life was founded by Ted Haggard, president of the 30-million-plus-member National Association of Evangelicals and, according to *The Wall Street Journal*, "one of the nation's most politically influential clergy." Haggard's Christian clout is exceeded only by that of Dr. James Dobson, with his forty-nine-acre Focus on the Family media empire strategically situated across the interstate from the Academy. Focus on the Family's ties to the Air Force are such that when the headquarters was inaugurated in 1993, the Academy's renowned parachute team, the Wings of Blue, dropped onto the opening ceremonies to present Dobson with "the Keys of Heaven." Such cross-collateralization is hardly surprising in the supercharged spiritual atmosphere surrounding the school. The Colorado Springs–based International Bible Study, for example, distributed copies of the New Testament subtitled *Our City, God's Word* and splashed on the cover was a photo of the Academy's instantly recognizable Cadet Chapel.

Weinstein was in sight of that same towering edifice now, cruising past a cluster of low-slung buildings fronting a parade ground and nestled among a well-tended copse of ponderosas. He spotted the Cadet Field House in the distance, where the Academy's Sports Hall of Fame is displayed, and beyond, Harmon Hall, seat of the Academy's vaunted Honor Court and not far from Sijan Hall, a dormitory named after the Academy's sole Medal of Honor winner, a martyred Vietnam War pilot, Captain Lance Sijan. An astronomical observatory is hidden in the trees, and just visible beside the eight-hundred-thousand-volume McDermott Library is the massive 1.7-acre Mitchell Hall mess, where over four thousand cadets can eat in a single seating. Behind this squat, sharp-angled ensemble is the Barry Goldwater Visitor's Center, named in honor of one of the Academy's most fervent supporters (and himself a major general in the Air Force Reserve) and situated above a wooded ravine opening onto the alpine expanses of Pike National Forest.

Yet for all its sweeping vistas, the Academy's architectural assembly has a claustrophobic feel, a relic of a modernist aesthetic that has not withstood the test of time. For an institution dedicated to the lofting glories of manned flight, "slipping the surly bonds of earth to touch the face of God," as Ronald Reagan would famously put it, stubborn earthbound horizons define the Academy's layout. It cleaves closely to the ground, hugging the landscape's contours, seeking safety in the hunkering sight lines and evoking a bomb-shelter profile that touches on the paranoiac Cold War context of its creation.

"We want our structures to be as efficient and as flexible in their design as the most modern projected aircraft," enthused Secretary Talbott before awarding the commission to Skidmore, Owings & Merrill Associates, one of three hundred architectural firms vying for the project. The resulting exaltation of glass, steel, and concrete, fused in expressed structure and unadorned geometric grids, has since been hailed as "the final triumph of the International Style." It bespeaks a brutalist utility that earned its fair share of criticism at the time, even as it explicitly articulated the mission and mind-set of the newly minted academy. *The New York Herald Tribune* lauded the design, singled out as "a lightning rod for conflicting values in postwar society," remarking, "Just as West Point with its medieval fortress-like appearance symbolizes the traditions of land warfare, so does the sharp-lined Air Force Academy represent the newest and swiftest military science."

Should anyone miss the freighted symbolism, actual jet fighters were subsequently mounted in the four corners of the Terrazzo, a large sunken plaza of Italian stone that forms the heart of the campus. There, cadets muster beneath the Academy Code—"We will not lie, steal, or cheat, nor tolerate among us anyone who does"—inscribed on the Honor Wall and watched over by an F-15 Eagle, an F-4 Phantom, an F-105 Thunderchief, and an F-16 Falcon, all poised on plinths in attitudes of eternal vigilance.

What triumphantly breaks free of the hulking bulk of this space-age Elysium and at the same time transforms the Academy into the state's most popular tourist destination, with over a million visitors a year, is the colossal Cadet Chapel. It is in its seventeen spiked crenellations—said to represent "the twelve apostles of Jesus Christ and the first five Air Force chiefs of staff"—that the institution's strange mix of hubris and devotion is most blatantly revealed. "As modern airmen brush wings with infinity," trumpets the chapel's promotional literature, "there is an increasing awareness of an ordered universe, a Divine Designer. The limitless vistas of the Space Age challenge our spiritual resources as well as our technology."

Like the bared teeth of a huge celestial saw, the chapel does indeed achieve the soaring presence that was the stated goal of the school's founders, simply by towering 150 feet above the grounds and, in its bone-white rigidity, defying the natural splendor of the nearby Ramparts. It has been described as the largest university cathedral in the world.

Inside its thirteen-hundred-seat main sanctuary, the so-called Protestant Chapel, an A-framed expanse is bathed in the vermilion light of inch-thick stained-glass tracery and hung with the forty-six-foot burnished-aluminum Soaring Spirit Cross. At the same time, the chapel's steely, jagged silhouette crushes the feeble ecumenical spirit that had mandated the installation of a five-hundred-seat Catholic church and a hundred-seat synagogue in its deep basement, along with a pair of All Faiths Rooms, where miscellaneous creeds are presumably espoused in a setting with all the majesty of converted janitor's closets.

Whatever the beliefs of those who initially enter the Academy's gates, the triumphalism embodied in the Protestant Chapel is, literally, a sharply pointed dogmatic declaration, overwhelmingly asserted in the gleaming structural facets of its hundred tetrahedrons, its polished nickel-silver altar, and the 4,334 pipes of its sonorous organ. "Make me an effective instrument of Your peace," reads the Cadet Prayer, asking God that they might "rise above human frailty." It is a theology fully articulated in the thrusting design of this famous sanctuary.

But there is also a sort of chicken-and-egg quandary to the dense aura of religiosity that hangs over the Colorado Springs region, for which the Cadet Chapel has long stood as a potent signifier. Was it this monument to America's Christian calling, erected in an era when that calling seemed especially in peril, that drew a plethora of evangelical missionary organizations like a beacon? Was it some trace element of the abstemious General Palmer's dream of a righteous resort for clean living that set the tenor of the town? Or was it simply the grandeur of the mountains, imperially rising from the plains, that put its citizens in mind of eternal rewards and punishments?

It never occurred to Mikey to ask. The landmark church had long since become a barely noticed backdrop to a place where what mattered most was to believe in himself. A scholar who had called the chapel "one of the great monuments of an era that seems so near to us in time but in other ways appears to belong to a past almost beyond recall" was speaking of its role as a Cold War totem. But the words might well apply to Weinstein's own distracted view as he took the final turn down Academy Drive and pulled into the parking lot of Doolittle Hall, where a small crowd had already begun to gather. The summer sun glanced off the chapel spires rising against a sky turned deep blue in the seven-thousand-foot altitude. He lowered his visor to block the glare, shifted down, and glided into a spot near the open door, where a sign greeted honored participants of the Air Force Academy's First Annual Graduate Leadership Conference.

3

A HISTORY OF HONOR,
AND OF SCANDAL

Ostensibly an opportunity for illustrious graduates to be updated on the latest accomplishments and innovations at the Academy, the Leadership Conference had, from its launch, a single overriding, if unspoken, objective. The 174 distinguished "Zoomies," as graduates are often called, included former Air Force generals, cadet wing commanders, and a select group of graduates who had excelled in the private and governmental sectors. Together, they represented the best of the best, culled from as far back as the inaugural class of 1959. Over the three-day confab they would be treated to the equivalent of a high-end spin session, including a jaunt out to Jack's Valley to watch the newest crop of basic cadets be put through their grueling paces. It was, on the face of it, a de rigueur exercise in building alumni goodwill, hosted by the Association of Graduates (AOG), among whose stated purposes was to "record, preserve and enhance" the institution's heritage.

Weinstein was a part of that heritage. His tenure at the Academy had been distinguished by achievement of the highest order, following up a stellar high school career that included being elected senior class president and earning three varsity letters in tennis, as well as playing base-ball and football. He secured three prestigious Presidential Nomina-tions and appointments to the Air Force Academy, Annapolis, and West Point. At all three, he had been a recruited Division One intercollegiate athlete. After his first semester as an Air Force Academy cadet, he earned a place on the Superintendent's List—an Academy version of a college dean's list representing excellence in both academic and mili-tary achievement—and would continue to do so for the next seven straight semesters. He had been a player on the Academy's intercolle-giate tennis team and graduated with honors in the class of 1977.

As a cadet, he eschewed the chance to become a pilot because "it bored the hell out of me. I knew immediately after my initial flight train-ing that I wasn't cut out to be a pilot," he recounts. "I decided to study law. Looking back, I think my decision was influenced very strongly by my Jewish heritage. The law was what protected us, what kept us free. And, anyway, I was good at writing, good at arguing. It became a very strong conviction during my last year at school and even after I graduated and was assigned to Keesler Air Force Base in Biloxi, where I went through combat communications school. Since the Air Force doesn't have a law school per se, I applied on my own and was accepted to several, ul-timately choosing the McGeorge School of Law at the University of the Pacific in Sacramento. I was transferred to McClellan Air Force Base in California as the chief of the secure systems branch of the 2049th Communications and Installations Group, and shortly afterwards began my legal studies. It was all part of an obscure Air Force program called Excess Leave, where they allow you to live on the base, make you pay rent without getting an Air Force salary, and give you unpaid time to go to school, so I had to borrow a lot of money from my parents and in-laws."

After one year at McGeorge, studying at night, Weinstein finally qualified for the full-time, paid Air Force law school program and earned his juris doctorate degree in three years. He would go on to be-come a judge advocate general, assigned to Holloman Air Force Base in southern New Mexico. "I got a chance to do it all," he continues. "I was a prosecutor, a defense attorney. I did union negotiations, walk-in divorce counseling. Basically I was a legal jack-of-all-trades and the Air Force and its members were my only clients. I really loved the work, the variety, and the chance to meet so many different kinds of people. I remember one case I had concerned an evangelical Christian who was seeking conscientious objector status based on his beliefs and I was asked to do an analysis of his argument. He was very devout and had even gone through the trouble of learning Hebrew to better study the Bible. We had talks together and he'd tell me that I was definitely heading for hell unless I accepted Jesus as my only Lord and Savior. That was part of the reason I eventually supported him in his case. He obviously wasn't trying to impress me or sway my opinion and, to me, that was proof enough that clearly he was completely committed to his beliefs, no matter what I might have thought about them. In the end he was excused from military duty, based in large part on my official legal evaluation of his C.O. claim."

After a year as a JAG, Weinstein got what he calls his "big break." "The Air Force was concerned about the breakup of AT&T," he recounts. "Talk about a company inextricably entwined with the government: We had telephone guys from AT&T on the beaches at Normandy. They were looking for an Academy graduate with a communication background to be their first chief of telecommunications law at a special command at Scott Air Force Base in St. Louis, and I fit the bill."

Weinstein spent the next year traveling around the country, briefing Air Force commanders and their staff on the coming divestiture and what it would mean to their communications cost and combat mission capabilities. "In the process my name got around," he says. "I got to be known at a corporate level as the Air Force's lawyer, and it was in the interest of all these new telecom companies to cooperate with me and my client, the Air Force, one of its biggest customers." His notoriety would, in late 1983, lead to a call from the office of David Stockman, the renowned budget director for the Reagan White House, which eventually hired him to oversee at the White House level many of the same complex legal issues evolving from deregulation as he had handled for the Air Force. "The problem was," he continues, "the Air Force didn't want to let me go. They eventually threw up all kinds of bogus roadblocks, including their contention that I still owed them time from back when I was studying law. I had to threaten to sue to finally get them to cut me loose completely after winning my case before the Air Force Board for Correction of Military Records."

Weinstein's three-year tenure at the White House was marked by a steady upward climb, moving from the Office of Budget and Management to assistant general counsel in the Executive Office of the President of the United States, White House Office of Administration, where, during the Iran-Contra investigation, he helped to coordinate the administration's response. "I learned a lot about public relations during those hearings and that very public investigation," he remarks. "Stonewalling; slow rolling; plausible deniability: I got to be a veritable expert in the field. I also got acclimated to spheres of power and influence that gave me a lot of confidence in my ability to move and motivate people. It was a very heady, rarefied atmosphere."

In the aftermath of Iran-Contra, Weinstein was quietly offered a far more senior position in the White House Office of Administration. "But by that time," he recalls, "I really wanted to get out. My family was growing and I needed to make some money. Working in the White House is often referred to as a 'trampoline job.' You bounce from there into something lucrative in the private sector. But it's not entirely true. You have to be good at what you do, no matter what your résumé says."

Weinstein was. After a stint as a senior attorney at both a Washington-based and a New York City law firm with international clients, he was tapped by his father's old Annapolis classmate and close friend, H. Ross Perot, to become general counsel at the newly created Perot Systems Corporation. "Let's just say Ross is a very rewarding and demanding man to work for, a man who has always been there for me and my family over the last fifty-plus years." Weinstein subsequently moved into a string of start-up, midrange and large private and public sector high-technology businesses, including a private investigation firm that went after deadbeat dads. He would eventually return to the information technology services industry, this time in the capacity of director of business development for Department of Energy programs.

Yet through it all, his connection to the Academy abided, as did his pride in a family history that exalted martial prowess and hard-won combat honors. "My father is a Distinguished Graduate of Annapolis and was on active duty in the armed forces for twenty-nine years," he recounts. "One of my cousins, Malcolm Hormats, flew Spitfires in the Battle of Britain and was one kill away from ace status before he got shot down over the white cliffs of Dover, surviving and continuing to fly. Another worked on the trigger mechanism for Fat Man and Little Boy at Los Alamos. I had an uncle who fought as a sailor in World War One and another, Jerry Wells, in World War Two who flew thirty-five combat missions in the Pacific theater as a tail gunner in a B-24. He was shot down, too."

"I would like to tell you how genuinely proud I am to have men such as your son in my command," Lieutenant General George Kenny wrote to the airman's mother, "and how gratified I am to know that young Americans with such courage and resourcefulness are fighting our country's battle against the aggressor nations."

Weinstein's wife, Bonnie, also brought a distinguished fighting legacy into the family. "Her father flew two hundred combat missions in Korea," Weinstein continues, "and her brother-in-law, another distinguished Academy graduate, was the first pilot ever to land a C-141 during a SCUD attack in the first Gulf War."

Yet, even Weinstein's enormous pride in his extended clan's record of service doesn't fully explain his fierce love of the military. To do that, it would be necessary to trace his history, from his birth at Kirtland Air Force Base, not far from his present home in Albuquerque, the oldest of three sons of Gerald and Alice Weinstein. What followed was a long sequence of postings—Sandia, Wright-Patterson, Holloman, Kirtland, Washington, D.C., and Vandenberg—characteristic of the rootless wanderings of many armed forces families. It's because of that lack of a true home turf that the military itself becomes the only constant in a life of constant upheaval, when most tours of duty last no more than a few years in any one place. In return for this quasi-nomadic existence, a support system feeds, houses, and cares comprehensively for its own with a guarantee of lifelong security all but unknown in the civilian world, which can evoke an ambivalent blend of loyalty and resentment. "You're taken care of from cradle to grave," Weinstein observes, "as long you go where they tell you, do what they say, and never ask too many questions."

The Air Force had been the backdrop to every key event in Weinstein's life, and those of his children. He was married to Bonnie two days after his graduation from the Academy, in the first Jewish ceremony ever held at the cavernous Protestant Cadet Chapel, the only place large enough to handle the overflow crowd. His son Casey would propose to his future wife, another outstanding cadet named Amanda Baranek, two days before their own graduation, presided over by President George W. Bush, before a crowd of friends and family gathered to celebrate the event in Colorado Springs at the famed Broadmoor Resort. On that occasion, emotion choking his voice, Weinstein read aloud a passage from one his favorite books, *My Losing Season* by Pat Conroy. Describing the author's last days at the legendary Citadel military college, Conroy's words perfectly described for Weinstein the rite of passage he, his son, his future daughter-in-law, his brother-in-law, and his father had completed.

"I thought I was the luckiest man on earth," it read in part. "I carried The Citadel inside me, and I knew it was not just a college in South Carolina I had gone to, and I have never pretended it was. It's a civilization and a way of knowledge, a paradox, a bright circus of life, a mirror and bindery of souls, a hive of sweat and hard work, a preparation for the journey, a trailblazer and road map, a purgatory, and an insider's guide to the dilemma of being alive and ready for anything the world might throw your way."

But whatever else the Academy was on that bright summer morning, it was also in trouble. Strolling toward the AOG's purpose-built headquarters at Doolittle Hall—named for the famous squadron commander who had boosted Allied morale in the dark days after Pearl Harbor with a daring night raid on Tokyo—Weinstein couldn't help but reflect on a bit of unintended irony in the form of a statue of the winged horse Pegasus erected in front of the building. In his cadet days, it was said that if your girlfriend touched the statue and it took flight, it meant she was still a virgin. In all his time there, he had never seen the horse fly, but the legend now seemed to take on another, ominously appropriate significance as he and his fellow alumni took their seats in the auditorium to hear firsthand the Academy administrators account of the incendiary sexual scandal that had lately rocked the institution.

Allegations of widespread sexual assault had first surfaced in early 2003 and had quickly escalated into charges of a systematic cover-up. There were estimates that nearly 20 percent of all women cadets— primarily freshmen and sophomores under twenty-one (fourth-class and third-class cadets)—had been victimized, occasionally being blackmailed after accepting alcohol from upperclassmen. The situation, it was maintained, was generally known among Academy and even Air Force brass, with complainants often threatened and expelled on charges of the same fraternization that had led to the rape incidents in the first place. A number of the accused male cadets were, on the other hand, allowed to graduate with honors despite multiple accusations.

With this major stain on the Academy's own honor, not to mention a mounting public relations disaster, the Air Force quickly went into maximum damage-control mode, initiating a plethora of working groups and ongoing inquiries, including an in-depth probe by the Air Force Office of Special Investigations. The Pentagon-mandated Fowler Commission, chaired by former Florida representative Tillie Fowler, unearthed disturbing evidence that, since legislation establishing coed enrollment had first been passed in 1975, the Academy had yet to fully come to terms with the integration of women into its ranks: one in five male cadets felt females had no place among them.

By the time the Zoomies had gathered at Doolittle Hall, the Air Force had snugly circled the wagons, issuing a lengthy report from its inspector general's office, blaming, by name, eight administrators, by then mostly retired, for the "culture of silence" prevailing at the Academy and handing down a laundry list of proposed changes, including eliminating alcohol consumption, prohibiting consensual sex, and limiting access to online pornography. Much of the impact of the report was subsequently lessened by Air Force Secretary Peter Teets's recommendation, in a memo to his boss, Defense Secretary Donald Rumsfeld, that none of the implicated officers be prosecuted since they had all acted in "good faith."

With what would, in hindsight, take on positively prophetic resonance, Teets had expanded on his rationale to leave well enough alone. "Any mistakes or misjudgments," he had hastened to explain to Rumsfeld, "are mitigated by the complexity of the issues," even as he went on to acknowledge that "the record of missed warning signs is disturbing." Beneath the obfuscating bureaucratese, a stringent code of loyalty had snapped into place. Even if the hapless administrators had been made scapegoats for a hidebound mind-set within the Academy, there was, ultimately, no one to blame. Tradition dies hard; harder still when those tasked to kill it are committed to its preservation.

The Academy, meanwhile, wasted no time in trumpeting its successful resolution of the scandal, spearheaded by this gathering of influential alumni. But an even more deeply rooted subtext for the Academy's elaborate self-absolution was, in fact, a long history of scandal that began in 1965, when 109 cadets were expelled for cheating. Two years later, additional academic deceit was uncovered and yet again in 1972 and in 1984. What this recurrence might have had to do with the strangely self-fulfilling phraseology of the school's honor code, with its insinuation that there are those "among us" whose behavior will not be tolerated, is open to speculation.

Yet despite all these dismaying precedents, what was settled beyond question in the hearts and minds of the graduates gathered in Doolittle Hall was an implicit faith in the institution itself: its ideals, its ethos, and the part it had played in transforming their lives and assuring their futures.

Simply put, the United States Air Force Academy has, from its inception, offered its chosen few one of the most complete, comprehensive, and contemporary educations available in America or the world. A significant part of that education is dedicated to the all-but-academically-abandoned notion of character building, a hugely complex, highly selective process precisely calculated to weed out the weak and single out the strong. Its ability to motivate, its power to transfigure, its capacity to inspire, are enduring testaments to its methodology, integrating the entire human being in all his or her physical, emotional, intellectual, and—in the faith and fervor it evokes—spiritual components. "Even the best Ivy League university stresses book learning," Weinstein asserts. "The Academy program is built on four pillars: academic, military, athletic, and, in many ways the one stressed most, character building."

No one knew the Academy's legacy better than those called together on that July afternoon, most already having had a lifetime to appreciate what had been passed along to them here, and what they had carried with them ever since. Inculcated with the institution's stated core values—Integrity, Service, and Excellence—they had each undergone a test of moral fiber that carried with it the ever-present threat of falling short and the tantalizing promise of brilliant achievement. Of course, any description of life in a military academy runs up hard against the accumulated clichés of every film and novel that has ever tried to explain how, exactly, it all works. What's revealing about such attempts is the glossing over of the system itself, the essential paradox of a process that, by stripping away the last vestiges of individuality and autonomy, ends up producing world-class leaders who are able to think for themselves, to act and achieve and lead others to do the same.

That, at least, is the goal, but one that is always at risk from the very techniques it employs. Inculcating absolute obedience and unquestioning loyalty is an essential first step in molding those who will one day require others to follow their example. It is also just as likely to create the blindly compliant, those subservient to authority no matter how compromised or corrupted. That is the dynamic tension at the heart of the Academy structure, built into a hierarchy as rigid and complex as any Byzantine court ceremony.

Like most civilian colleges, the curriculum is divided into four annual terms, fourth-to-first class years corresponding to familiar freshman-to-senior designations. Fourth classmen are regularly referred to either as doolies (from the Greek *doulos* for "slave") or smacks (an acronym for Soldier Minus Ability, Coordination, and Knowledge). First-class cadets ("firsties") fill cadet officer roles, while second-class cadets act as noncommissioned officers. As in the active-duty Air Force, the squadron is the Academy's primary organizational unit, with each of forty squadrons consisting of approximately 100 cadets, supervised by a first classman—the cadet squadron commander—who reports to the squadron's active-duty air officer commanding. Four groups of nine squadrons each (expanding to ten in the fall of 2006)—the Cadet

Wing—is also under the auspices of first-class cadets and, while operational and support posts are filled by second- and third-class cadets, military training for each wing is the responsibility of the commandant of cadets, an active-duty Air Force brigadier general.

The Air Force Academy Candidate Book is remarkably candid about what a cadet can expect during his or her doolie year. "They will take away your freedom," it baldly asserts. "All of it. You will do everything they tell you to do, when they tell you to do it, no matter how irrelevant or trivial or silly the tasks seem. There will be no questioning of their orders . . . because they want you to get used to obeying orders that do not make sense. . . . They will place great physical demands on you. . . . They will require you to perform a host of tasks with incredible precision and detail. . . . You will be forced to do things that seem stupid."

That's not the half of it. Cadets are chronically sleep-deprived, deliberately driven to extremes of physical exhaustion, carrying a mind-bending academic load; the program is so structured that no one by himself or herself can hold up under the pressure. "You must reach out to your roommates and friends," the *Candidate Book* insists. "When things are black and despair is upon you, let those around you hear what the demons are saying. . . . They will help you slay them. And you will do the same for them when they are down. It is a mutual dependence that you and all your classmates must develop. That is how it is meant to be: that is how the system works." With the obvious and essential goal of unit cohesion, this baptism of fire is critical to the cadet's individual success and the Academy's institutional goals. Tampering with this support and survival network derails the entire regimen, a lesson learned by the enforced silence of the sexual assault scandal and shortly to be taught all over again.

Yet, for whatever comfort may be derived from the company of fellow sufferers, the *Candidate Book* ultimately cautions, "You will hear yourself asking, 'Why am I here?' 'Why am I here?' 'Why am I here?'"

Part of the answer may lie in the extraordinary and comprehensive education afforded those fortunate enough to earn a place at the Academy, and the competition for the approximately thirteen hundred spots available annually can make Ivy League admissions look like signing up for a night course at your local community college. Of the some thirty thousand-plus application requests that are received each year, only about nine thousand will carry through to the next step, at which point approximately three thousand go on to actively seek the nomination required for admission. Nominations are made by U.S. senators, representatives, the vice president—each of whom may have five nominated cadets at each Academy at any one time and may appoint up to ten candidates for each vacancy—or by the president, who appoints candidates from military families and who may have up to one hundred appointees at each Academy at any one time. This selection process, which is fiercely competitive, often requires extensive networking by the prospective cadet, with interviews and evaluations in front of congressional panels, before potential candidates are even considered for the Academy's actual screening process.

The Academy's initial selection is heavily weighted to physical fitness, beginning with the demanding Pilot Qualification (PQ) requisite, which, among other criteria, requires perfect eyesight: any surgical procedure to correct nearsightedness, until recently, was automatically disqualifying. Prospective candidates must also pass a demanding fitness test in order to gain physical qualification.

Academic achievement is the next daunting hurdle. Grades, class rank, test scores, and college prep courses are lumped together into an Academic Composite, and, historically, up to 95 percent of entering cadets have been in the top quarter of their high school graduating class, with up to 10 percent having achieved valedictorian, number-one rankings. Extracurricular activities are also a significant factor, including athletics, student government, scouting, and, according to the *Candidate Book*, "church activities."

Those who make the grade will have their entire education underwritten by the taxpayers, and as an added incentive to serious consideration, anyone dropping out before the start of the second-class academic year will owe the accumulated six-figure cost of their time spent at the Academy or have to serve a term as an enlisted airman.

Graduation confers a five-year obligation to serve in the Air Force (eleven years if a flying career is chosen) and a bachelor's degree in any of thirty-two majors, from such service-specific fields as aeronautical and astronautical engineering, military strategic studies, and space operations, to such specialties as behavioral sciences, political science, legal studies, and management. Even a minor in philosophy is offered. The core curriculum includes extensive courses in the sciences, mathematics, engineering, social sciences, and military studies. Staffed by a faculty of over five hundred, 75 percent of whom are active-duty Air Force officers, the school plays host to a number of high-level academic conferences, including the annual Academy Assembly, a major public-policy forum. The Cadet Summer Research Program features five-week stints at the Department of Defense and various military research facilities around the world, with applications to everything from the International Space Station to "smart" warhead technology. The Academy also offers an active postgraduate program, facilitating thirty-three Rhodes Scholarships for its top graduates to date.

Along with compulsory intercollegiate, club, or intramural athletics, the physical education curriculum emphasizes water survival, martial arts, combative sports, team sports, and "lifetime" sports such as tennis and golf. Intercollegiate athletes compete in the NCAA's Division 1-A and the Mountain West Conference, and the school has traditionally strong football, gymnastics, soccer, volleyball, rugby, and, most recently, basketball programs. Its men's boxing program is especially well-known, with nineteen national championships and a standing never below second place. Teams are named the Falcons, and Coach Fisher DeBerry heads an impressive football program that produced, among others, three-time Super Bowl–winning Dallas Cowboy Chad Henning.

With athletics an indispensable gauge of a cadet's standing within the school hierarchy, it's hardly surprising that attendance is mandatory for home football games, particularly when the opponent is the traditional intrastate rival, Colorado State University, and, above all, service academy rivals Army and Navy.

The cumulative effect, both of the Academy's emphasis on maintaining its high-flying virtues and verities, and of the substantial prestige conferred by its world-class education, is enormous pride, instilled in both the institution and the individual's place within its living tradition. That pride was palpable as Weinstein made the backslapping rounds at the Graduate Leadership Conference late-afternoon mixer to kick off the three-day conference. The sour residue of the recent scandal had already began to fade in the warm glow of comrades and classmates, some of whom he hadn't seen since graduation. Sexual impropriety may momentarily have dulled the luster of their alma mater, but the foundations on which it was built remained as strong as ever, anchored in the loyalty and élan they shared.

As part of the day's agenda, graduates would have the chance to mix and mingle with current academy cadets mustered in especially for the occasion and impeccably attired in dress blues that still bore vestiges of the original parade uniform designed by movie mogul Cecil B. DeMille at the request Air Force Secretary Harold Talbott. Among them, Weinstein's youngest son, Curtis.

Weinstein was especially anxious to see the nineteen-year-old, who had recently completed the Academy's arduous Combat Survival Training (CST), simulating precarious conditions behind enemy lines and staged in the extreme reaches of nearby Saylor Park, which for ruggedness and remoteness gave Jack's Valley the comforting aura of a mere picnic ground.

Much of a cadet's actual military training occurs during the summer, beginning just prior to their fourth-class year, when they are subjected to six weeks of the infamous Basic Cadet Training (BCT), otherwise known as "Beast." CST was a third-class follow-up, and the wilderness rigors Curtis had just endured—conducted in midsummer heat at an altitude hovering around eleven thousand feet—involved intense escape-and-evasion maneuvers over a number of days, hauling an eighty-pound pack. Rations were composed mainly of two rabbits and a chicken provided at the beginning of the exercise and eaten with a wooden utensil carved by each cadet. When the rations ran out, participants often subsisted on a mixture of rice and crickets. Required to report to preordained check-in points by the end of a day that regularly lasted until two in the morning, the cadets were pursued by roving cadres of upperclassmen, and the punishment for "capture" was to retake the course. It was, recalled Curtis, an experienced Eagle Scout, "the worst week of my life," and such was CST's severity that the program would be suspended the year after the ordeal of Curtis's class.

It was a trial no ordinary parent would wish on a child. Not that Weinstein was an ordinary parent, nor, for that matter, Curtis an ordinary child. Soft-eyed and phlegmatic, with the haze of late adolescence still hovering around his close-shaved head, Curtis Weinstein had followed his uncle, his father and older brother, Casey, into the Academy with the kind of aplomb that suggested a preordained path. Yet there was no trace of coercion in his decision, or the warping pressures often exerted on the youngest member of a high-achieving family. "I remember the first time I realized that I wanted to go," recounts Curtis, who was competitively selected to attend the Academy's rigorous prep school a year before his ultimate nomination and acceptance to the Academy. "It was in my sophomore year in high school and we were in Colorado Springs at a Falcons football game. I looked around at everyone cheering, feeling the excitement and spirit, and realized that this was where I belonged, that I was a part of it and it was a part of me."

It was a turning point, he continues, arrived at entirely on his own. "My dad always told me he'd be just as happy if I went to clown college," he insists, "and he said if I ever wanted to quit, he'd only ask two questions: which airline, and did I want a window or aisle seat for the ride home."

There is, in fact, something uncanny in the young man's prepossession and the need to control a self-confessed "wild streak" that, he says, is another of the primary reasons he chose to follow the family career path. "When my older brother, Casey, and I were at the Academy at the same time," he recounts, "I always felt grateful that he was there to keep me in line."

The degree to which Curtis was in or out of line would become a crucial consideration in the light of what was shortly to transpire. As Mikey caught sight of his son at the far end of the happily buzzing crowd in the reception hall, his initial relief at finding him hale and healthy—if rather sunburned and a bit thinner—turned quickly to concern as he approached and saw the brooding expression on the boy's normally placid face, his equanimity vanished beneath tight-lipped anger and a stiff-legged gait. Even before Mikey could frame the question, Curtis bent close and in a low voice, as if fearful of being overheard, asked if they could go someplace else to talk—someplace off the Academy grounds.

Curtis remained stubbornly silent during the Viper ride out the

South Gate and across I-25 to a nearby McDonald's, and it was in that silence that Mikey wrestled with the worst-case scenarios: a pregnant girlfriend, a drug problem, an infraction of the unforgiving Academy regulations and honor code standards? He had time now, too, to reflect on the pressure his son was under and wonder if, albeit unwittingly, he had positioned the boy squarely in the bull's-eye of expectations he couldn't meet. He was all too aware of the conventional wisdom applied to family dynamics: the firstborn who gains approval by excelling in everything; the second born who gets attention by acting up and acting out. Was it possible that whatever was happening behind Curtis's normally easygoing exterior was an overdue bid to get noticed?

They sat down in the harshly lit restaurant, the circus colors and canned music in jarring contrast to the apprehension Weinstein had held in check until this moment. "What is it, Curtis?" he asked at last. "What have you done?"

Curtis took a long pull of his soft drink and took a deep breath. "It's not what I've done, Dad." He looked Weinstein straight in the eye, and in that instant Weinstein felt the twisting in his gut loosen a little. His son's expression conveyed something reassuring: there was anger in his eyes, certainly, and even defiance, but nothing akin to chagrin or confusion. Whatever it was, Curtis had already faced it squarely . . . and considered the consequences. "It's what I'm going to do," he continued, his gaze never wavering.

"Tell me."

"I'm going to beat the shit out of the next guy that calls me a 'fucking Jew,'" Curtis replied evenly. "I'm going to beat the shit out of the next guy that accuses me, or our people, of killing Jesus Christ." He broke his stare at last, gazing out the window, his equilibrium restored by the simplicity and sincerity of his avowal. The clatter around them faded, replaced by a roaring in Weinstein's ears.

"I just thought," Curtis said, still looking out at the passing traffic, then turning back to his father, "that before it happens, you and Mom should know."

4

"THEY WANT YOU TO BE
IN HEAVEN WITH THEM"

It was a moment Weinstein would later compare to the jolting realization that your wallet is missing. Time and space telescope as your only thought is to recover what's lost. Whatever your previous preoccupation, it seems suddenly trivial as you retrace your steps to the last place where you had what suddenly matters most.

Of course, some things lost can never be regained, and in those first few moments he struggled to put his overpowering anger into a coherent context. It wasn't easy. Like all the best betrayals, this one operated on multiple levels. Cheating on your wife is one thing; cheating with her best friend, another. Absconding to Rio with her life savings is, exponentially, something entirely else. As Weinstein brooded in his motel room that afternoon, with the blinds closed, nursing a fifth of rum and a liter of Diet Coke, he struggled to precisely categorize what hurt the most about his son's revelations. "I just sat there," he recalls, "getting trashed, alone in the dark. I didn't want to talk to anyone. Slowly, through the drunken haze, I realized that, as angry as I was, I was even more embarrassed at what the Academy had become."

It was, on the face of it, an odd response, this initial sense of shame for the institution and its failure to live up to its ideals. But as evening drew on and Weinstein continued to probe his feelings, the emotion deepened, mixed now with something akin to guilt, as if, somehow, he had brought this on himself and his family simply by being who he was—finally and irrevocably Jewish.

Weinstein's fierce Jewish identity had been formed from early childhood in outraged response to the Holocaust. "Ever since I was six years old," he recalls, "and they first started telling me about what had happened, I couldn't believe it. I couldn't understand how my people just lined up and let themselves be led to the gas chambers of Treblinka and Auschwitz and Bergen-Belsen like sheep to the slaughter. I asked my parents and Hebrew-school teachers, but they couldn't explain it. I read everything I could get my hands on, about how over one-third of the six million who were murdered were children under twelve, like me. And I couldn't wrap my head around that. I still can't."

He pauses, searching for a way to express the highly charged memories that seem almost to overwhelm him, and the ensuing silence speaks eloquently of a man whose deepest feelings lie just below a calm, self-assured exterior. "I eventually came to the realization that the two most important historical figures in my life were Adolf Hitler and Jesus Christ," he continues at last. "Hitler because of the Holocaust, and Jesus because, in his name, it could happen all over again, like it has throughout the history of my people, over and over, in oceans of blood and tears. And I knew what some Christians said: that Anne Frank and those millions of children—and along with them Albert Einstein and Jack Benny and Dr. Seuss—were all burning eternally in a lake of fire, and that any Jew that didn't wise up, surrender, and bow the knee and confess that Christ was Lord would suffer the same fate. And I promised myself that there wasn't going to be any more burning." He thrust forward his left hand, bearing the large, gem-encrusted ring he has worn since his graduation from the Air Force Academy in 1977. Pulling it off his finger, he points to the inscription on the inside of the gold band: NEVER AGAIN. "I engraved that," he says with a grim laugh, "to always remind myself of what I went through as a cadet. But, of course, it's really about the Holocaust and what had happened to my people."

It's a contentious colloquy, long since internalized, which seems to occupy his every waking moment, a high-stakes battle with opponents whose arguments he has committed verbatim to his prodigious memory. "Fundamentalist Christians imagine that another Holocaust, a worse one, awaits not just Jews, but anyone who doesn't accept their particular belief in Christ." His pause now is for effect. "They quote John 14:6, where Jesus says that no one comes to the father except through him. But they ignore Acts 10:34, where Peter states that God shows no partiality and that any person who fears Him and does right is acceptable."

He takes a moment to collect himself, drawn along the rapid-fire line of his thoughts and feeling to a conclusion he has reached many times before. "I made a decision a long time ago," he says finally, "that I would never be one of those docile, pious Jews dressed in black, eating bagels and lox and trading jewelry in midtown Manhattan. I wanted to fight back. I would be a Warsaw-ghetto Jew; an Israeli Jew of 1948 and 1956 and 1967 and 1973; I would be a Judah Maccabee Jew, the ones who faced down Antiochus and his ten thousand howling Syrians on their armored elephants; the ones who stuck their Jewish swords into the bellies of the beasts, knowing they would be trampled and crushed in the process. I wanted to excel in competitive athletics and not actuarial tables. I wanted to carry on the fighting tradition of my people. My attitude was 'How dare you pigeonhole me, how dare you tell me that the only way I can be somebody is to sit in a room somewhere reading a pile of books on science and finance until they come and escort me off to the ovens.'"

There's a disconcerting edge to his declamation, an uncomfortable awareness of the self-loathing stereotypes in which he is trafficking, rubbing up against his stubborn rejection of all conventional notions of assimilation.

But Weinstein's Judaism is of a distinctive stripe, most significantly in its affirmation of his American citizenship. "I'm Jewish American," he insists, "not an American Jew." It's a distinction that, for him, makes all the difference. "This is a country of immigrants, but there comes a point when, no matter where you're from or how you got here, you stop being a guest. That's a place where a lot of the members of the previous generation of my family could never quite get to. I remember when we first moved out West. For my beloved mom and dad, it was like a dream of starting over, building a home on a fresh frontier. But at the same time it seemed to me that it was imperative for them never to unnecessarily rock the boat. But for me, from the very beginning, somehow it was always very different. I felt I had this drive, this responsibility to make my presence known, to make some uncomfortable and inconvenient noise, as an American and as a Jew."

There's a neglected nuance here that furrows his brow, a debt yet to be paid. "My parents were not boat rockers," he says at last, "but it was they who manifestly instilled this passionate drive in me. They also made sure that their three kids knew who they were and cherished the heritage that we shared. I had the first bar mitzvah in the history of Andrews Air Force Base when we were stationed there. But I also remember when they briefly considered changing the family name to West to smooth the way for us. It was my dad who decided against it. He said it didn't matter, that you could doctor your birth certificate, get plastic surgery, do whatever you wanted, but there would always be someone around to remind you that you were Jewish. My parents lovingly instilled pride in me for our Jewish faith, heritage, and culture. Indeed, for me it was a badge of honor of the highest order."

It was that honor that had turned, obscurely but implacably, to shame as he replayed Curtis's words over and over. Yet, just as surely, defiance rose again in his gorge, extinguishing his maudlin mood. This was, after all, just a new front in the same old battle, and as ever, he found himself spoiling for a fight.

But who was the enemy? Uncovering anti-Semitism in the U.S. military was hardly headline news. Credible evidence had long since made the case that, from World War I until at least the late sixties, virulent Judeophobia had infected the highest ranks of the armed forces, particularly in the Army. The allegations were verified, in large part, by secret files from the Military Intelligence Division (MID), declassified in the 1970s, which purported to document copious links between Jews, communists, and other enemies of the state, even citing the forged *Protocols of the Elders of Zion* to back the claims. "I am so thoroughly convinced of the reality of a Jewish movement to dominate the world," wrote one MID operative, "that I hate to leave a stone unturned." MID documents were ultimately utilized to fabricate a variety of bug-eyed conspiracy theories of Jewish world domination and helped to influence the refusal to admit Jewish refugees or bomb concentration camps during World War II, as well as to fuel postwar hostility—spearheaded by former U.S. Army chief of staff General George Marshall—to the founding of the state of Israel.

But that was the Army, with all its musky history of redneck dough-boys and mud-spattered mules. Under normal conditions it would have been difficult for Weinstein to accept that hard-core race hatred might actually have infected the ranks of the Academy. True, as at Annapolis and West Point, Jewish attendance had traditionally hovered somewhere around 1 percent of incoming cadets, but it wasn't about the numbers, was it? It was about being able to make the cut and keep the pace and finish the race, and implicit in the Academy's credo was the egalitarian principle that anyone with the determination and tenacity to win a place would find a place.

The truth was, from Curtis's very first words at that McDonald's, Weinstein had other inklings, darker and more ominous than simply re-cidivist military Jew-baiting. It was a suspicion grounded in events that had begun in February, as his eldest son, Casey, was preparing to grad-uate from the Academy, a momentous step for the twenty-one-year-old made more significant by the plan to propose to his girlfriend and fellow Academy classmate only two days before graduation ceremonies in late May and in front of an assembled crowd of friends and well-wishers at the Broadmoor Hotel.

Handsome and highly sociable, with a thatch of blond hair and his mother's clear eyes and pale complexion, Casey represented a new breed of cadet, one attracted to the Academy more for its prestigious academic program than as a sure step toward a thirty-year Air Force ca-reer. "I was never really sure that I intended to stay in the Air Force af-ter my five-year obligation was up," Casey explains. Like his father, he had also been invited to attend West Point and Annapolis and, unlike his father, had also been accepted at the Coast Guard and Merchant Marine academies. But he had chosen the Air Force Academy, because, he says, "I could see how good it had been for my dad."

Many among his classmates, Casey asserts, felt that, "the Academy was a stepping-stone, and a lot of us were willing to trade five years of dedicated service for the education we'd get and connections that came with it. My plan from the beginning was to eventually get into business and, from there, politics. I wanted to start off my career by continuing my families' tradition of military service to our nation, but I have a lot of other goals that I plan to accomplish outside of the Air Force."

Without the starry-eyed goal of a lifelong climb up the military career ladder, many new arrivals took a more jaundiced view of the Academy's emphasis on unquestioning loyalty and unswerving obedience. "There were things that happened that made us distrustful of authority," Casey admits. "I wouldn't say we were cynical, but we could see the faults and failures in the system. How you responded was up to you, and you had to walk a very fine line."

One of the first inequities Casey confronted, as a fourth-class cadet, had direct bearing on the observance of his Jewish heritage. "Every Friday we had mandatory physical training," he recounts. "The schedule interfered directly with Shabbat services and forced those of us who wanted to attend to have to pick and choose. It may not seem that big of a deal in itself, but you have to realize that unit cohesion was the most important building block of Academy life. Training together reinforced our sense of classmate teamwork and solidarity. Choosing to deliberately separate yourself from your squad for whatever reason sent a message that you had other priorities, and I regularly caught hell from classmates for going to Friday-night services."

The conflict was assuaged somewhat by a strong camaraderie among the Jewish cadets in Casey's class. "There were about twenty of us," he recounts, "and we really stuck together. We also had a rabbi who understood what we were up against and provided an outlet for us to express our fears and frustrations. But even so, it was very difficult to have to make that choice every week, knowing the consequences. No matter what you decided, it felt like you were betraying something significant."

When Casey, who had been recruited for the Academy's intercollegiate baseball program, was put under particularly direct pressure from his classmates, he stopped going to Shabbat services entirely. "Not long after that, the rabbi was transferred," he recalls. "At that point I really lost an important connection." He pauses, weighing his words carefully. "A spiritual connection."

That connection was further attenuated by what Casey describes as "the give-and-take atmosphere" of daily Academy life. "I'd get called a Jew by upperclassmen who were just giving me a hard time during training, yelling into my face, and I kind of took it in the spirit in which it was intended. There was a sort of invisible line that got drawn, and you could tell immediately when it was being crossed. During my first year, a classmate had had some problems with me and once passed me in the hall and muttered, 'Jew,' under his breath. I stopped him and made it real clear what would happen if he ever said that again. You could pick up a difference in people's attitudes right away."

It was considerably more problematic, however, to confront attempts by both his classmates and the administration to promote an altogether more pointed spiritual agenda, and Casey began to run up hard against persistent and aggressive challenges to his faith. "The entire school was required to attend inspirational-speaking events," he recounts. "They always had a Christian context, even when it was presented as a motivational message. I remember once when John Wooden, the famous UCLA coach, came to speak and used the time not to talk about basketball or teamwork or sportsmanship, but to quote from the Bible." Again he pauses, trying to mark out a fine line. "This kind of incident was normal. He came to talk to us as part of an officially sanctioned, mandatory event. Even more telling to me, however, was that almost all the cadets in the audience thought nothing of it. It was routine, expected. It was part of the consistent message we got directly or indirectly: 'This is important. This is part of what we're teaching you and you'd better pay attention.'"

While still a fourth classman, Casey began to encounter one-on-one evangelizing from his classmates. "If you're in the outside world, it's an entirely different matter," he insists. "You can tell the person to mind his own business or just walk away. There was no place to walk away from at the Academy, and in a real way, your business was everyone else's. We were all together, all the time, in close quarters, being told to trust and depend on each other as a band of brothers and sisters. There was no way to escape if your roommate or the guy next to you in formation was determined to introduce you to Jesus. And, even if you could get away or tell him to back off, what did that say about your team spirit and your allegiance to the squad and to your classmates? Some of these people were friends of mine. What was I risking by refusing to accept something so important to them?"

What he was risking quickly became a point of confusion and crisis for the young cadet. At the point of tears, he went to his history teacher, an Air Force captain and practicing Christian, for counsel and advice. "I needed someone to talk to, and I felt I could confide in him," Casey continues. "I had never had religion pushed in my face like that, and I didn't know how to respond. He told me basically that I had to learn to put up with it. 'They're doing it because they want you to be in heaven with them,' he said, and, the funny thing is, at the time it really helped me to hear that. At least it didn't seem so much that they were trying to turn me into something I never was."

The notion that the Academy experience turned young men and women into something they hadn't been before was, of course, integral to the institution's mission. But the dilemma Casey and others were faced with cut much deeper into issues of identity and integrity than they had ever bargained for. In this crucible, where character was cast in new molds, the pressure to conform was in constant tension with an only too natural insistence on individual autonomy. What was intended, from the first day, to prevail was the model of a new man or woman, weaknesses and limitations purged in a relentless purifying process. It was a powerful feat of human engineering that required the willing participation of those undergoing the transformation. "I may not have been considering a lifelong career in the Air Force," Casey asserts, "but I went to the Academy because I wanted to be of service to my country and I wanted to be successful. What I hoped to learn there was how to increase my effectiveness and my ability to execute."

What he was slowly discovering was that the Academy considered service and success to be contingent on spiritual conviction. As the official Cadet Prayer put it, "Make me an effective instrument of Your peace in the defense of the skies that canopy free nations." God, in short, would be every airman's indispensable copilot. That God is a notoriously nebulous concept, colored by a palette of discrete traditions, predilections, and experiences, has remained an unacknowledged contradiction at the heart of egalitarian America's warrior credo. It was a contradiction that a determined faction within the Academy and, to a hitherto unrevealed extent, the entire armed forces was determined to resolve one way or another. In the early spring of 2004, they seized upon a unique opportunity to advance their cause.

"The Academy was like a room filling up with gas" is how Casey describes it. "*The Passion* was just the spark." It's an apt analogy and one that could well apply to the whole country, when Mel Gibson's hyper-controversial crucifixion drama *The Passion of the Christ* finally opened. For months prior to its release, the film had generated enormous contention, as much for its sadomasochistic subtext as its depictions of Jews complicit in deicide. A cultural event of momentous import, *The Passion* would go on to earn nearly $400 million worldwide and expose a divide deeper than any red-state blue-state election return could ever plumb.

The extraordinary success of the Gospel According to Gibson, both commercially and as a tool of strident rhetoric on both sides of the debate, can primarily be attributed to its wholehearted embrace by the American evangelical community. The first major motion picture in history to be marketed directly, and brilliantly, to this enormous constituency, *The Passion* was, at first glance, a strange bedfellow for prevailing evangelical aesthetics. The rigorously Catholic iconography of its images, its historical resonance with the blood-drenched passion plays of pre-Reformation Europe, and its general emphasis on suffering and death were in stark contrast to the considerably sunnier, resurrection-weighted theology promulgated by many American evangelicals. Among other surprising revelations, what *The Passion* proved resoundingly was that Christian America was hungry for "entertainment" that spoke for and about who they were and what they believed.

But the film proved useful for another purpose, fast-tracked by evangelicals. The studiously contemporary, fully wired, and technically savvy megachurch movement had long held as a matter of faith that modern media provided the perfect means for mass evangelizing. They had, after all, been proving the point for decades through radio and television. All that prevented them from harnessing the persuasive power of big-budget movies, or so some of them had argued, was the implacable hostility of Hollywood's liberal/Jewish/homosexual power brokers. Gibson, in his crazed-renegade persona, had broken that stranglehold and had, his retrograde Catholicism notwithstanding, made the local multiplex the latest stop on the road to salvation. Within days of its American release on February 25, 2004, the evangelical grapevine was buzzing with accounts of spontaneous conversions before the third reel, and churches scrambled to corral every available unbeliever into the next screening. Study guides were distributed, group discussions were organized, and preachers actively endorsed the film's saving virtues from the pulpit.

The Passion had, in short, become a promulgating powerhouse, and within the cloistered confines of the Academy its persuasive potential was given full sway. For weeks prior to its release the school had been abuzz with anticipation and awash with promotion. Posters depicting the bloody but unbowed Christ, his thorn-crowned head set against an apocalyptic sky, began appearing on bulletin boards and posting sites around the cadet area, including the previously off-limits academic building, Fairchild Hall. In the cavernous Mitchell Hall cafeteria, promotions for the movie were splashed on the big projection screens hung over the heads of cadets during mealtime. Cadets sent out wing commander–approved messages, some with reviews of the movie, urging everyone to attend the screenings.

Since it was essentially the only building large enough to accommodate the entire cadet wing at once, Mitchell Hall had, in fact, been the scene of another common practice that demonstrated overweening religious influence at the Academy. "During Beast there were three church services a week, often organized and overseen by members of local, civilian religious groups." Casey explains. "Attendance wasn't mandatory, but they had a very effective way of persuading you to go. We'd all be eating dinner according to strict Beast protocols, for instance, and there'd be an announcement that a service was about to start. If you were one of the ones who chose not attend, you were required to line up and march out in formation. They called it the Heathen Flight."

The equivalent of a pagan perp walk, the Heathen Flight was a regular occurrence that ended up with the offending cadets back in their rooms, where they were required to sit with their doors open to be more easily monitored by eagle-eyed upper-class cadre. "It was an open invitation for them to barge in and 'train' us," Casey reports, using the Academy euphemism for all-purpose harassment. "This was our introduction to the Academy and the Air Force. We thought that this was the way it was. The Academy's philosophy for its Basics is to break them down to nothing, then build them back up. I always wondered why there were outside civilian religious organizations constantly at our services, and why there was such an emphasis placed on attending so many days per week. I eventually came to the realization that much of the outside religious influence at these services was a result of people trying to get in at the ground level and reprogram us from the foundation up. We were a captive audience in every sense of the word."

After four years of dealing with a variety of incidents that affected him or his friends, the tipping point for Casey came when cadets arrived for lunch one afternoon in mid-February to find a flyer announcing a special cadets-only screening of *The Passion* laid at every place setting. For many, it was an egregious intrusion that, by its implicit stamp of administration approval, simply crossed the line. "Later that day, one of my professors pulled me aside," Casey relates. "He asked me if any of this was bothering me. I don't think I really realized how much it was until it was put to me directly. We ended up talking for two hours. In the midst of our discussion, it struck me that we had to be secretive about voicing any dissent in the current atmosphere at the school. Both of us knew that raising any opposition could lead to alienation and damage to our careers. That was the reality we lived and worked in, and that was a pretty sobering realization, especially for a graduating firstie. But ultimately, it was about trying to leave the Academy a better place for other cadets, maybe freeing them from of some of the disturbing issues I had to deal with. I knew someone had to speak up, and that that someone was going to be me."

The opportunity to do so would come almost immediately, in the form of an e-mail sent out to the entire cadet wing under the auspices of the cadet vice wing commander and containing a *Passion* press release that specifically took issue with those who objected to the film's message. "I'd already had to back up a third classman who had gotten a lot of shit for complaining about the way *The Passion* was being shoved down our throats," Casey continues. "Now I had a chance to take this further up the chain of command."

The attempt to find someone answerable for what was quickly escalating into official sponsorship of religious propaganda got him nowhere. "When I finally met the vice wing commander and asked him directly about the e-mail," Casey remembers, "he kind of shrugged and smiled and said he hadn't really looked it over before approving it."

That response would become maddeningly emblematic of the bureaucratic maze that, in the weeks and months to follow, provided ample "safe harbor," for those who actively engaged in evangelical infiltration at the Academy. In a place where accountability and responsibility are layered with exquisite precision, it would become increasingly difficult to find anyone willing to admit that they were purposefully promoting the coercive conversion of recalcitrant cadets. "After hearing the vice wing commander kind of pass the buck," Casey concludes, "I started to realize what I was up against. I needed help. So I called my dad, who jumped on it immediately."

The Passion saga was replaying in Weinstein's mind as, the morning after his meeting with Curtis, he showered, dressed, and worked out, still slightly woozy from the night before, preparing for the morning's schedule of the Graduate Leadership Conference. It was a schedule he was determined to turn on its ear.

As he headed out of his motel room and into the thin, bright air, a quote suddenly came to mind, something he had heard somewhere before—something worth remembering, describing "the thirteenth stroke of a crazy clock which not only is itself discredited but casts a shade of doubt over all previous assertions." It was that chiming sound— in the equivocations of men and women in uniform, in their bland reassurance of business as usual and their rote recitations of cherished ethics and ideals—that he could swear he was even now hearing.

5

"SWORD OF THE LORD"

The crazy clock and its thirteenth stroke was a metaphor coined by the father of English parliamentarian and novelist A. P. Herbert, but the obscurity of the aphorism made it no less apropos to Weinstein's growing "doubt over all previous assertions" proffered by the Academy's power structure. And there were other, all-too-appropriate adages, as well, echoing in Weinstein's mind as he made his way back to Doolittle Hall that morning, stoking an already full head of steam. The words of another renegade Jew could, for example, have had particular resonance in the present circumstance. "Since we have the rare good fortune to live in a commonwealth where the freedom of judgment is granted to the individual citizen and he may worship God as he pleases," wrote the philosopher Baruch Spinoza from his precarious redoubt of religious tolerance in the Dutch Enlightenment, "and where nothing is esteemed dearer and more precious than freedom, I think I am undertaking no ungrateful or unprofitable task in demonstrating that not only can this freedom be granted without endangering the peace of the commonwealth, but also the peace of the commonwealth depends on this freedom."

Although he hardly knew it at the time, Weinstein was about to embark on a prolonged defense of that very principle, returning again and again to the bedrock conviction that, without the individual freedom of judgment to worship as one saw fit, or not to worship at all, the American commonwealth could hope for neither peace nor justice. That the stage on which this drama was to be played out would be the U.S. military—manifestly the most indispensable expression of that commonwealth—only served to underscore, for Weinstein, just how far that hope had already been eroded. "This was never a fight between Jews and Christians," he insists. "Sure, my Jewish background made this issue intensely personal, but I doubt I'd have felt any different if I was a Muslim or a Hindu or nothing at all."

Religious practice in the armed forces was hardly a new phenomenon. In the 1846 Mexican War, Roman Catholics were incorporated into the hitherto all-Protestant chaplaincy for the first time, as much to blunt implications of a sectarian war with Catholic Mexico as for any effort to address the actual religious demographics of the fighting force. In 1862, President Lincoln, at the request of the Board of Delegates of American Israelites, struck the word *Christian* from all regulations relating to the chaplaincy appointments, and during World War II, Greek Orthodox chaplains were allowed to minister to their flock in uniform for the first time. The Buddhist Churches of America were registered as an official endorsing agency for the first time in 1987, and six years later the Army saw its first Muslim chaplain.

These earnest attempts at pluralism were often contrasted with unsanctioned attempts to bring sanctity to the armed forces, from the revivalist fervor that swept both Union and Confederate camps during the Civil War, to various hectoring attempts to stiffen the moral fiber of troops during and immediately after World War II. GIs were returning from combat, according to a 1946 report from the Veterans of Foreign Wars, "physical, mental, moral and social wrecks, having been infected with venereal diseases" and "coddled by a complacent service attitude which encourages promiscuity." The situation was subsequently exacerbated at the dawn of the Cold War when, in 1945, President Truman proposed a one-year program of universal military training for all males over eighteen, a move vigorously resisted by evangelical churches. "We began to wonder what might happen to our youth removed from home and church influences," fretted the National Association of Evangelicals (NAE), "and subjected to the temptations for which military training camps are notorious."

The proliferating paranoia of the Red Scare, however, radically altered such attitudes by the early fifties, when the world, according to literature distributed by the Nazarene Service Men's Commission, was neatly divided between "the Communist dictatorships and the Christian democracies." The Nazarenes concluded, "The stricken nations are looking to the free world . . . we are our 'brother's keeper.'"

Aside from being a bulwark against godless communism, the military was perceived as a target-rich environment for missionary outreach. In 1959, the NAE asserted, "Fifty percent of all who pass through the military service have no religious background or church connection." The implication was clear. "This is the ripe harvest field in which our chaplains are working."

They weren't the only ones intent on reaping the souls of unsuspecting soldiers. Early in the decade, mainline Protestant denominations aggressively promoted annual "preaching missions" on U.S. military bases, and in 1952, the year the campaign was initiated, nearly a hundred weeklong events were launched around the theme "Christ Is the Answer."

Competition between liberal Protestantism and fundamentalist evangelicals for influence within the military was fierce, focused primarily on inserting as many chaplains as possible into all available postings. A battle quickly shaped up between the rival commissioning arms of various denominations, with the evangelicals fighting on two fronts against both mainline Protestants and Catholics. "Evangelicals must not fail the proportionately large number of men in the armed forces who are anxious that the New Testament gospel be preached," warned the NAE. ". . . Real evangelistic work must be carried on by our chaplains."

Evangelicals were also at the forefront of what author Anne C. Loveland in her pioneering study, *American Evangelicals and the U.S. Military, 1942–1993,* calls "an unprecedented religious and moral welfare program" instituted by the Truman administration, largely in response to a widespread outcry against drunkenness and immorality among Korean War conscripts. Dubbed Character Guidance, the program was in force throughout the fifties, and while ostensibly nonsectarian, the curriculum reveals a rigorous religious agenda, bristling with exhortations that "service to the nation is most effective only when religion becomes part of individual life," and that in the "covenant nation" of America, "public institutions and official thinking reflect a faith in the existence and importance of divine providence," with God as "the final source of authority."

The most effective wedge for the insertion of evangelicals into every rung of military life was the NAE and its influential chaplain-endorsing agency, the Commission on Chaplains, which worked tirelessly as a liaison for a wide array fundamentalist denominations, from the Assemblies of God to the Southern Baptist Convention to a full index of offshoot and splinter congregations. Notwithstanding the military's policy of allotting chaplaincies on a quota system designed to roughly reflect the religious affiliations of society as a whole, by the late sixties evangelical denominations were regularly exceeding their allotments.

The phenomenon mirrored, in part, the explosive growth of fundamentalist Christianity in America and, in part, the assiduous efforts of the NAE and its Commission on Chaplains to fill posts left empty by the Catholics, Jews, Orthodox, and others who were regularly failing to meet their allocations. In what Loveland terms a "quota juggling act," the NAE and others aggressively lobbied to fill chaplaincies left vacant by other denominations, resulting in a marked shift in the selection process weighted more and more to religious demographics within the military itself, where evangelical numbers continued to swell. This consolidation of power would result, by the late eighties, in the NAE Chaplains Commission's acting as the endorsing agent not only for established denominations but for hundreds of nonaligned individual churches.

By the midsixties nearly all the forty evangelical denominations listed by the Armed Forces Chaplains Board had met or exceeded their assigned postings. This influx of evangelizing chaplains would have an extraordinary effect of the spiritual tenor of the armed forces, especially in the wake of such mandatory programs as Character Guidance, which had imbued chaplains with hitherto unimagined authority. Loveland

cites a glowing article in a 1952 issue of *Chaplain,* the official publica-
tion of the Navy Chaplaincy, that focuses on religious instruction at the
Great Lakes Naval Training Center, where recruits regularly attended
lectures designed to "reinforce the moral and spiritual strength of Navy
men during the most impressionable period of their Naval career." The
"thorough, dynamic program of evangelism," concluded the story, presented "a vital religion that may never have been available to them in
civilian life." "Faith," another article in *Chaplain* asserted, "is an integral
part of being a good soldier," and it was to that end that chaplains were
provided extensive contact and increased influence at every level of the
military hierarchy.

Career considerations were another contributing factor to the flood
of evangelicals into the chaplaincy. "Pastors are taking a new look at
their military counterparts," wrote one observer, "and a significant number are leaving their civilian pastorate for service as a chaplain." The
subsequent rush by pastors into the armed forces was hardly surprising,
considering the steady paycheck, generous benefits, and comfortable
pensions provided by the government. But it wasn't only individuals who
were taking a "new look" at the military mission field. Evangelical
church support organizations began to bring their considerable proselytizing prowess to bear on the armed services, spearheaded by such entrenched outreaches as the Colorado Springs–based Navigators, the
Officer's Christian Fellowship, the Overseas Christian Servicemen's
Centers, the Christian Military Fellowship, Campus Crusade for
Christ, and the Full Gospel Businessmen. As the most established
among them, the Navigators had, by the mid eighties, a staff of over seventy dedicated solely to missionary work within the military, operating
active chapters in and around far-flung bases from Turkey to West Ger-
many to Spain. In the literature of their Military Ministry branch, the
Navigators singled out the Air Force Academy for special attention with
an ominous-sounding (if syntactically muddled) goal to "impact eternity
by multiplying disciples through spiritual generations."

It was inevitable, considering the concerted effort by evangelicals to
penetrate every echelon of the service, from the lowliest barracks to the
loftiest policy-making aerie, that there would eventually emerge a cadre
of Christian officers emboldened to openly profess their faith and use

the full influence of their rank to bolster the cause. Among them were such high-profile figures as Army general William Harrison, dubbed the Two Star Evangelist by the press in recognition of his status as one of the nation's first bona fide born-again celebrities. While he worked at the Pentagon in the early 1950s, Harrison's exhortations could regularly be heard on the *Word of Life* radio program, sponsored by the Officer's Christian Union, an organization he would later head. Steadfastly promoting an end-time doctrine, Harrison, while still in uniform, declared, "The second advent of Christ will include great wars with terrible suffering," a leading indicator that "the course of civilization is toward self-destruction." It was, to say the least, a peculiar conviction from a man sworn to uphold the peace and preserve civilization.

Another front-and-center fundamentalist was John C. Broger, whose more than two decades at the helm of Armed Forces Information and Education (AFIE) from 1961 to 1984 provided him, according to Anne Loveland, "a central role in the ideological indoctrination of armed forces personnel." A former radio evangelist, Broger was hired by the Defense Department at the height of the Cold War to provide what his mentor, Admiral Arthur Radford, called "Spiritual stiffening" of the troops in their battle against atheistic communism. Broger's view of that battle was quickly made clear: it was a fight that could not be won on the basis of "military manpower and production potential" alone. What was needed was "godly precepts and principles," and "strength and inspiration in godly righteousness." To that end he created the Militant Liberty program, consisting of what some observers at the time dismissed as "pseudo-scientific jargon and high-sounding clichés." It was nevertheless relentlessly promoted by the Defense Department, with Broger delivering briefings on its provocative precepts to war colleges and service schools around the country. The eventual refusal of the Pentagon to fully implement Militant Liberty hardly slowed the peripatetic evangelist's military career track: he was subsequently appointed director of AFIE, from which perch he delivered such pronouncements as "If the government is to be ordained of God, then spiritual and moral concepts must under-gird and relate to all political, economic, educational and cultural areas of national life."

Yet of all the emergent Christian cold warriors in the years before and during the Vietnam War, none wielded more influence and authority than Army general Harold Johnson. A survivor of the Bataan Death March and a Korean War combat veteran, Johnson was appointed Army chief of staff in 1964, four years after he had declared in an interview for the American Tract Society that "Christianity is the very foundation of military leadership." The four-star general would regularly deliver addresses with titles such as "Turn to God," proclaiming, "There is a special need for the soldier to understand the strength and purpose that can be provided by a deep and abiding faith in our Father through His son, Jesus." Only Christ, according to Johnson, could provide "the inner strength that is essential to meet the wide variety of conditions encountered in the environment of the warrior."

Johnson, in fact, considered the "environment of the warrior" to be his unique purview, as witnessed by his efforts to protect and preserve the explicitly Christian content of the Character Guidance program, in place since the end of World War II. In 1962, the American Civil Liberties Union had first lodged a complaint about the "religious indoctrination" inherent in the curriculum and succeeded in removing some of its more egregious First Amendment violations, such as the "One Nation Under God" lesson plan, with its stated objective of "leading the individual to a recognition of the importance of the spiritual element in his training."

Six years later, under Johnson's watch, Character Guidance once again came under attack from the ACLU, and the Army chief of staff took personal charge of the Pentagon's response. According to historian Anne Loveland, Johnson "saw nothing wrong with using the Bible in support of the program," and, more significantly, took a staunch stand in opposition to many mainline denominations, united in their criticism of the program's coercive character. Suffice it to say, Johnson at the same time aligned himself resolutely with the evangelical political forces, still smarting from recent Supreme Court decisions banning school prayer and for whom the attack on Character Guidance was another attempt to excise God from every social sphere.

The cumulative effect of men like Harrison, Broger, and Johnson on the prevailing military mind-set was ultimately to move evangelicals from the fringes of America's fighting forces squarely into the councils of power. Yet, for all their personal charisma and crusading zeal, it was implacable historical forces that best served to consolidate fundamentalist influence within the armed services. "It was Vietnam," remarks Anne Loveland, "which really turned the tide. As the war progressed, more and more mainline denominations spoke out against it and, in fact, became centers of organized resistance. That never really happened with evangelicals." Perhaps largely due to their stark view of human events as a titanic struggle between the forces of good and evil, evangelicals often subscribed to official rationales of the war as a necessary stand against the domino-tipping strategies of a godless opponent. Fundamentalist John Rice, editor of the fire-breathing *Sword of the Lord,* neatly summed up the bellicose attitude when he wrote that, in Vietnam, America was "carrying out the command of God." The sentiment was echoed by preacher Carl McIntire, who thundered, "It is the message of the infallible Bible that gives men the right to participate in such conflicts, and to do it with the realization that God is for them, that God will help them, and that if they believe in the Son of God, the Lord Jesus Christ, and die in the field of battle, they will be received into the highest heaven."

As the war continued to grind away at American conscience and consensus and the military increasingly became the object of the swelling antiwar movement's fury, a siege mentality took hold. In the us-against-them polarization that was splitting the nation, the armed services looked within itself to single out and promote those who would wholeheartedly support the savagely decisive conflict, and none were more vociferously vocal in their allegiance than the evangelicals, who had spent much of the last two decades securing positions within the ranks. "Should a follower of Jesus participate at all in the messy military business of killing people?" asked evangelical author Randolph Klassen. "Would Jesus? Would Christ carry a draft card? I am convinced He would. Does He want me to carry one? Of this I have no doubt."

But there was more at play than simple knee-jerk jingoism or even evangelical opportunism. Setting aside for a moment the fatalistic complexities of premillennial theology—in which Christ's return is delayed until man's cup of iniquity is filled to overflowing, and the death and destruction of war becomes a precursor to paradise—the interface of the military's historical identity and fundamentalist Christian rhetoric reaches much deeper.

The Bible, of course, is rife with martial imagery, from the scorched-earth conquest of Canaan, to David's stalwart stand against Goliath, to Paul's familiar Ephesians metaphors for the well-equipped Christian: "the breastplate of righteousness," "the shield of faith," "the helmet of salvation," and "the sword of the Spirit." Together they comprised "the whole armor of God," in which believers would sally forth to do battle against "the rulers of darkness of this world and against spiritual wickedness in high places." The Church Militant has been one of Christianity's most resonant and effective self-conceptions, from the time of the Crusades to the military orders of the Salvation Army, and, of course, the Christian Soldier in the durable old hymn, forever marching as to war, the cross of Jesus going before, their royal master leading against the foe. With the possible exception of athletic similes, it is the serried imagery of combat that is most often evoked from the pulpit, and while the warrior archetype may not answer to the often diffuse and inchoate longings that bring seekers to the foot of the cross, it seems especially well suited to the evangelical aesthetic of conquest and conversion.

Given this potent affinity, it's hardly surprising that fundamentalists found a familiar context for their exalted concepts of authority, duty, and sacrifice within the military and all but inevitable that the methods of war would be deployed in the Great Commission: to reach the whole world for Jesus in preparation for his promised return. It is a convergence that would, in turn, reach its apotheosis in *You the Warrior Leader,* a gung ho handbook for "applying military strategy in victorious spiritual leadership," published at the same time Weinstein was beginning to gird himself for a different kind of battle. Written by former Green Beret and current Southern Baptist Convention president Bobby Welch, *You the Warrior Leader* is as unequivocal a statement of evangelical militarism as could be imagined, an unabashed tactical manual on storming the barricades of unbelief with rousing rhetoric that evokes a kind of holy bloodlust for the trophies of triumphalism. "Fix Bayonets" commands the first chapter, broken into subheads variously titled "Scratching, Biting, Ear-Ripping-Off War Fighting," "Jesus the Warrior Leader," and "Making Hell Gun-Shy." In "The Quick and the Dead," a section dealing with battle-hardened evangelism, Welch seamlessly melds the urgency of conversion with a military leader's motivational role: "The Warrior Leader knows he must not only exemplify personal evangelism, he must never stop trying to get every Christian man, woman, boy, and girl to perform evangelism. Leaders must not allow those whom they lead to become disoriented and thereby fail to rescue family and friends from the devil and hell." In the chapter "Attack! Attack! Attack!" Welch asks, "Remember the Warrior Leader's Mission-Vision?" as he hammers home with steely-eyed determination his grand strategy for winning souls: "To develop victorious spiritual-war fighters who form a force-multiplying army that accomplishes the Great Commission."

It was precisely those spiritual shock troops that Mikey Weinstein was about to confront head-on at the center of America's military power structure.

⋆ 6 ⋆

THE PASSION OF THE EVANGELICALS

The morning briefing for the second day of the Graduate Leadership Conference passed for Weinstein in a red-tinged blur. "I was nauseated with fury," he recounts, "literally sick to my stomach. Curtis's words kept running through my mind, and I couldn't get away from the look on his face. It was as if he had somehow moved beyond fear into some kind of grim resignation to stand up for himself, for his people—or for any-one who is not in the majority—regardless of the consequences. I think the thing that shook me the most was realizing how serious his resolve was and, at the same time, how alone he must have felt. Without know-ing anything more than what he'd told me that afternoon, it was clear to me that he'd been pushed to the edge."

Only later would Weinstein get a complete debriefing from his son, who, even as he detailed the slurs and slanders that had become a rou-tine part of his cadet life, remained characteristically taciturn. "He's not a whiner," Weinstein asserts. "He's a tough kid, a high school wrestling champion and New Mexico Eagle Scout of the Year in 2002. He's the sixth member of my family to attend the Air Force Academy. If anything, he often holds things in deeply. I think that's all a part of his awareness that he's got to keep a tight rein on that impulsive, impetuous side of his personality. He tried keeping his feelings to himself, but there are some things no kid should be expected to handle on his own."

What became clear as Weinstein delved deeper into his son's grievances was that patterns of abuse had been established almost from the moment of Curtis's arrival at the Academy. "I can remember back to Beast," Curtis says, recalling the grueling six weeks of the Basic Cadet Training regime. "I think it's a very spiritual experience to begin with, the way that everything you thought you were gets tested to the max. A lot of times, out in the woods, we were put together in big tents, with twenty of us packed together like sardines. And there'd be some guy in there giving a sermon, talking about turning your life around, giving your heart to Jesus, and going to heaven when you die. At first I could sort of understand why they were doing it. I asked myself how I would act if I believed something like that so strongly and saw so many people around me tired, scared, and lonely and stressed out and looking for some kind of escape from what they were going through. But it also seemed as if they were taking advantage of the situation, like they were moving in on purpose just at the point when we were at our weakest and most confused. It finally got to where I had to say something, and when I did, they would more or less tell me that they were doing it for my own good. They wanted to save my soul. Mostly, all I wanted was to get some sleep. I'd ask them to take it somewhere else, and I think, right then, I kind of marked myself out as different."

Over the ensuing weeks and months the harassment became more specific, often taking on the theme of Christ-killing culpability. Curtis continues, "It got so I could tell the difference between the ones who had heard others saying it and just repeated it to be part of the group without knowing any better, and then the ones who were really out to cause some damage. The naïve ones I could try to talk to, to explain what was wrong with putting all that guilt from two thousand years ago on a whole group of people who had nothing to do with it. With the others, well, I just didn't feel that there was any place at the Academy where I could officially report this harassment. One of the cadets I tried to talk to about this turned out to be a very religious guy whose reaction to my complaint was, unbelievably, to invite me to a Bible study. After that, I just kind of kept it to myself. I learned to live with it, even though it was difficult because of the distance it could put between you and the rest of your squad. Some of the Christians in my class used to meet on the Terrazzo for prayer meetings, and there was one girl who used to take cadets off by themselves and pray over them. You'd get so you'd purposely avoid situations like that, which didn't help us feel like we were part of a team."

The resulting alienation extended beyond Curtis's fellow doolies. "A lot of the worst of it came from upperclassmen," he reveals, "especially in the gym and on the intramural field. To me it made sense, because we were trained to be really competitive in sports, and you could really feel the pressure in those situations to win at any cost. I remember once we were playing flickerball, which was big at the Academy, and we were beating some third classmen. One of them got pissed and called me 'Christ killer.' I told him I never killed anybody, and he said, yeah, but the Jews had; they murdered Jesus, and pretty soon there was a group of cadets around us, laughing and egging the dude on, and what I remember most was that no one, not even the cadets on my team, were backing me up."

The anti-Semitism at the Academy is, at first glance, curiously inconsistent with professed American evangelical alliance to Jewish causes, most especially their continued support of Israel. Yet, even aside from the age-old function of Jews as all-purpose scapegoats, this stubborn persistence of prejudice even in the face of fulsome fundamentalist lip service could well be attributed to other causes. Most significant among them were the millennial expectations that bound Christians to Jewish history in eager anticipation of the Second Coming.

Beginning in England in the early nineteenth century, evangelicals had been promulgating a variety of complex doctrinal propositions to explain the relationship between the Church Universal and God's Chosen People, as part of an attempt to link together their eschatological destinies. Prompted by such passages as Paul's discourse in chapters nine through eleven of Romans, in which he forthrightly announces that his "heart's desire and prayer to God for Israel is that they might be saved," what eventually took on the tongue-twisting handle of Covenantal Pre-millennial Restorationism would, through the efforts of immensely popular writers such as Hal Lindsey and Tim LaHaye (authors of *The Late Great Planet Earth* and the "Left Behind" series, respectively), devolve into a single overriding assumption: the return of Christ was dependent, according to a literalist interpretation of Biblical prophecy, on the final conversion of every last Jew to Christianity.

The resulting evangelical embrace of Jewish statehood and self-determination could also be felt as a smothering choke hold. The very condition for Jewish-Christian accord presumed the eventual extinguishing of Jewish identity, which, over the blood-drenched centuries, had stubbornly been defined by its resistance to Christian assimilation. And for nearly as long, evangelicals had been waiting patiently for Jews to "come around" and thus clear the way for the inauguration of Christ's rule on earth.

Was their patience wearing thin? While the cadet flickerball players on the Academy intramural fields could hardly have been expected to grasp the nuances of dispensational hermeneutics, the urgency and intensity of the missionary calling to which a growing number had responded may well have provided an additional incentive to eradicate the errors of non-believers by any means necessary. Add to that the highly charged atmosphere in the run-up to Gibson's *The Passion of the Christ*, and it seems likely that, within the Academy, labeling Jews as Christ killers was just another way of encouraging them to get with the program. "The first time they always ask nicely" is the way Weinstein puts it. "When that doesn't work, they go to Plan B. That's when women and children start dying."

But it was ultimately nothing more than sheer arrogance that most animated the intolerance for anyone outside the fundamentalist fold. Four years into an administration that owed its grip on power to well-organized right-wing-Christian political support and during which the constitutionally dubious "faith-based" agenda of religious conservatives had been advanced across a broad front, it seemed as if millennial prospects of every description were tantalizingly close to fulfillment. From a previously marginalized and frustrated constituency, evangelical Christians had become the single most powerful fraction of the electorate, thanks in large part to the assiduous sectarian efforts of many of the organizations perched just across I-25 from the Academy.

THE CULMINATION ON THAT DAY OF THE ALUMNI WEEKEND WAS TO BE THE presentation, by Colonel Deborah Gray, the Academy's vice commandant, of what was called a "climate survey," bullet-pointing various areas of ongoing interest and concern at the school. The droning recitation neatly wrapped up the smug aura pervading the campus, a business-as-usual satisfaction that looked beyond the recent scandals to a full restoration of the institution's good name. This impression, clearly meant to be taken away by the distinguished alumni, could not have anticipated the explosive new controversy brewing in their midst.

"It was right at the end of Gray's spiel that I just snapped," Weinstein recalls. "The last agenda item on the PowerPoint projection was something like 'An Apparent Insensitivity to Non-Christian Beliefs.' It was that 'apparent insensitivity' that really did it. The presentation concluded and everyone was heading out to the superintendent's house for a cocktail party, but just as Gray got out from behind the podium, I came up and really let her have it. Everything just poured out. It seemed like ten minutes total had passed, but when some friends finally pulled me away, they told me I'd been going at her for the better part of an hour. The only thing I really remember is at one point telling her that I wondered, in light of the sexual harassment scandal, if she'd call it 'apparent insensitivity' if I said she had fine tits and a nice round ass. To me, it was pretty much the same thing. Apparently it's okay if my kids are called 'fucking Jews' and accused of killing Jesus Christ? No, Debbie, you don't have an 'apparent insensitivity' to non-Christian beliefs here. Instead you have a lusty and thriving intolerance, objectively manifesting itself in numerous acts of unconstitutional prejudice and discrimination."

Gray, who had been part of the school's first coed class in 1980, apparently got the point and agreed to arrange a meeting with Lieutenant General John W. Rosa Jr., superintendent of the Air Force Academy. Affable and unassuming, with a career that had begun with a commission from The Citadel, Rosa was well into his tenure by the time he met with Weinstein on the Monday morning following the weekend graduate confab. He had been promoted twice in 2003, thanks to what was generally being spun as the Academy's successful resolution of the sexual imbroglio. But he would not survive the next major stain on the school's reputation.

"I had agreed to stay over another day to try and get some resolution," recounts Weinstein. "I went up to Rosa's office, where he and Colonel Michael Whittington, head chaplain for the Academy, were waiting." Whittington had been recruited to replace the previous senior chaplain, who, Mikey had heard, had been chalked off as collateral damage in the aftermath of the sexual assault scandal.

"By the time we all sat down," Weinstein continues, "I'd managed to chill a little, but by the end of the meeting I was having a hard time holding it together all over again. I remember telling Rosa what Curtis had said about hitting the next guy who called him a 'fucking Jew' and asked what his response would be if something like that were to happen. 'I wouldn't blame him,' the general had said, and I flat out told him that wasn't good enough. But I could see that we weren't getting anywhere. I left even more frustrated and angry than I'd arrived."

What wasn't "good enough" extended beyond the Academy's tacit toleration of religious coercion as revealed by a single cadet. Curtis's account had served only as the tipping point to a pattern of harassment that Weinstein had been made aware of ever since *The Passion* controversy had flared up earlier that year.

"Casey had come to me with stories about what was happening at the Academy, primarily focused on the film but also covering a lot of other areas of potential violation," Weinstein explains. "At that point I kind of took it in stride." He pauses, reflecting. "Look, I wasn't born yesterday. It would be obvious to anyone who spent any time around the Academy that there is a religious 'consensus' existing that is very much a part of the identity of the place. It was obvious that, as Jews, my kids and I were de facto outsiders in that regard, but I had always assumed, given the constitutional protections afforded us as Americans, that none of that really mattered. In this country, people can believe, or not believe, anything they want. And, when it comes to concepts as emotionally charged as faith in God, heaven and hell, salvation and damnation, and all the rest of it, it would be foolish not to expect zealots to occasionally step over the line. That's what the law is there for: to correct the excesses of individuals for the common good of us all."

At the same time, Weinstein is just as ready to acknowledge his own role as self-appointed guardian of what he considers the virtually sacred tenets of the First Amendment and related constitutional clauses. "I have a low threshold for any breach in the firewalls of power," he readily admits. "I always have. As a student of history, I know only too well what they can lead to, especially where church and state are involved. There's nothing new there: my whole life is a testament to keeping religion and government in their respective corners." As proof, he points to an early encounter with military brass over the use of taxpayers' dollars, not to mention Air Force laboratory space and equipment, to analyze the authenticity of a piece of the famous Shroud of Turin. "It was the late seventies and I was a lowly second lieutenant," he declares, "but I couldn't fucking believe that the U.S. government was countenancing the use of my taxpayer dollars for this bullshit. They ignored me, but that's not the point. Someone's got to stand in the breach, and apparently I was the only one available at the time. That doesn't make me a hero. I'm not a hero. Just a conscientious citizen with a long memory for human history."

Which is precisely the role he stepped into at the moment he began to get a clear picture of what was being tolerated and even promoted at his beloved alma mater. "I put the word out," he continues. "I contacted old classmates and people I knew who were still on staff in Colorado Springs. A lot of them were scared shitless to talk to me on anything other than an anonymous basis, which got my attention all by itself."

As revealing as their insistence on secrecy might have been, the information imparted by those he called his "Deep Throats" was even more eye-opening. "I listened to Jewish cadets like Mikey's son Casey and others discuss what was happening around *The Passion*," says one of Weinstein's sources inside the Academy. "They'd argue amongst themselves about what they felt and whether they should speak up about the situation. Most of them just wanted to let it go. They didn't want to be seen as 'angry Jews' and seemed to feel that as a minority within the overwhelming Christian majority, they had no choice but to take the abuse. It was the classic beaten-wife syndrome, where the victim is conditioned to think that their treatment is somehow normal, that they've brought it on themselves. At that point I had to step in and ask them in all sincerity if they thought that what was going on was right."

Subsequently contacted by Weinstein, the source, who acknowledges his role as "one of the guys on the inside," saw his responsibility as simple and straightforward. "Mikey was a taxpayer," he explains. "He had two sons at the Academy and he was an alumnus. He had the right to know."

The source continues, "At first, I tried to pacify him. I mean, he wanted to go to the press right away. I think, given half a chance, he would have nuked Harmon Hall. He was that mad. I tried to encourage him to be patient, to give the organization a chance and work up the chain of command. To his credit, he listened. The problem was, the chain of command was broken. Under a system of sheer structural incompetence, the problem itself was irresolvable. I mean, how can you make something right if you don't believe it's wrong in the first place?" It was now clear to Weinstein that the severely chronic constitutional problems at the Academy and, later, at the entire Department of Defense, were quite simply never going to be solved by the same minds that created them.

Even as he counseled patience, the source encountered "one unbelievable obstacle after another." He insists, "You have to put it in context. The Academy is smack-dab in the middle of one of the most religiously fundamental cities on earth with the possible exception of Mecca. Of course, evangelicals were going to have an undue influence. Add to that the fact that, for evangelicals, converting unbelievers is a mandate of their faith, and the notion of plurality and tolerance doesn't stand a chance. This situation is woven into the fabric of the institution. The only way to eradicate it was to drag it into the light of day, which is what Mikey wanted to do. Considering his personality, I consider it a minor miracle that he held out for as long as he did."

As for the source's insistence on anonymity, he acknowledges fearing for his job and his future, but at the same time points out his vital role "in the middle of everything." "I'm white and I'm a Christian. That makes me a poster child for the kind of individual the Academy is interested in. I've been at all the meetings. People say things to me that they shouldn't. And what I came to believe is that Mikey is fighting something bigger than religious intolerance at the Air Force Academy. This is going on throughout the military. It's systemic."

Notwithstanding the palpable atmosphere of fear he had immediately encountered, Weinstein did indeed allow time for the procedures and protocols of both the Academy and the Air Force to take their course. "I honestly wanted to believe that, once these abuses were brought to the attention of those who could do something about them, solving the problem would be like Tiger Woods sinking a two-inch putt. I had a kind of vestigial confidence, not just in the authority structure, but in the clear and unambiguous language of the Constitution these individuals were sworn to uphold. After all, it's right there in the plain language of clause three, article six, of the main body of the Constitution and in the free-exercise and no establishment clauses of the First Amendment, which categorically forbid the government from 'regulating, prohibiting, or rewarding religious belief as such.' And if that's not clear enough, you can take it from the Supreme Court, which says that the government can't 'coerce anyone to support or participate in religion or its exercise.' It was Justice O'Connor who said, 'Endorsement sends a message to nonadherents that they are outsiders, not full members of the political community, and an accompanying message to adherents that they are insiders, favored members of the political community.' I could go on. Believe me," Weinstein adds, tapping his forehead, "it's all up here. But why bother? The fact is, this is not some fine-grained legal argument and it doesn't take a legal scholar, or even an Air Force general, to figure out what it means and how it's implemented. I just assumed the usual suspects were up to their usual tricks and, once I blew the whistle, they'd be reined in and that would be that."

Blowing the whistle proved easier than he could have imagined. It was getting anyone to listen to the shrill alarm that proved to be problematic. "I started getting together information immediately," he continues. "Or, rather, information started getting to me. Once word got out on the grapevine, evidence started to flood in. By the end of April of 2004, I had a pretty good portfolio together."

Exhibit A in Weinstein's dossier was a paid advertisement appearing on the back page of the 2003 Christmas issue of the *Academy Spirit,* the school's official military-installation newspaper. The same ad, in various permutations, had, in fact, been a regular holiday occurrence over the entirety of at least the previous decade. Under its boldfaced headline, *Jesus Is the Reason for Our Season*, was the proclamation, *"We believe that Jesus Christ is the only real hope for the world. If you would like to discuss Jesus, feel free to contact one of us!"* The solicitation was signed by over two hundred senior Academy officers and their spouses, including sixteen academic department and deputy department heads, nine permanent professors, both the incoming and outgoing dean of faculty, the director of athletics, and fundamentalist football coach Fisher DeBerry. "There is salvation in no one else," the spread concluded, quoting from Acts 4:12, "for there is no other name under heaven given among mortals by which we must be saved." The entire effort was underwritten by an organization called Christian Leadership Ministries, a division of Campus Crusade for Christ.

"If someone wants to pay for an ad in a newspaper, that's their business," Weinstein avows. "When that newspaper is an official organ of the Air Force, housed on the grounds of the Academy, with six positions fully federally funded by taxpayers, then it becomes my business." Yet, aside from the question of blatant religious propaganda appearing in the widely read broadsheet of a U.S. military installation for over a decade, the solitication raised a far more significant issue, one that Weinstein would continue to evoke again and again as battle lines were drawn. "Think about it," he insists. "The names on that back page were some of the most important and influential authority figures at the Academy. If I'm a doolie, or even a first classman, what message is that sending me? Is the invitation to talk about Jesus, with the same people who hold absolute power over my life and my future, a suggestion, an order, or a none-too-subtle hint that my career could benefit by lining up behind their religious agenda? The people who signed that list either knew the impact their names would have, or they didn't—but they should have known. Either way, it was an abysmal and inexcusable abuse of their authority. In one fell swoop, their role at the Academy became a means to further their missionary objective."

As Weinstein dug deeper through the spring of 2004, he began to piece together a pattern of prejudicial behavior in many aspects of Academy life. A series of "brown-bag" lunchtime talks, well attended by department heads and senior faculty, featured such guest speakers as John Bolin, author of *Two Doors of Heaven: A Story of Your Future*, a book billed by its publisher as "a conversation-starter on evangelism." Another brown-bag lecture attraction: Hugh Ross, who used his weekly program on the Trinity Broadcasting Network to promote his quasi-scientific doctrine of "progressive creationism." "I found an announcement for another one of these events," Weinstein recounts. "The title of the talk was 'Why We Cannot Let You Have Your God While We Have Ours,' and there was a warning at the bottom not to remove the flyer, since this was an officially sponsored Academy event in coordination with something called Christian Leadership Ministries."

Ted Haggard's New Life Church was also front and center in the evangelical offensive, dispatching vans to transport up to two hundred cadets to Friday-night services and encouraging them to return to their quarters with flyers to help recruit new prospects. The megachurch's focus on the Academy reached to all levels of its huge congregation, with one New Lifer telling journalist Jeff Sharet that Colorado Springs itself was a "spiritual Gettysburg" in the battle between good and evil. "I'm a warrior for God," he is quoted as proclaiming. "Colorado Springs is my training ground."

Official Academy e-mail correspondence likewise bristled with exhortations to "do it all in the name of the Lord Jesus," "pray as if it all depends on God," and "delight yourself in the Lord," while prayers at mandatory meals were regularly concluded with an invocation of Christ's name. "It's remarkable," Weinstein observes, "that at precisely the same time this was going on, the United States Fourth Circuit Court of Appeals contemporaneously ruled that the Virginia Military Institute's officially sponsored Supper Time Prayer exacted an 'unconstitutional toll on the consciences of religious objectors.' It's as if the Academy was happily existing in a bubble into which reality never intruded." It was a view underscored by the statement of an anonymous Jewish cadet who spoke to Weinstein of having "no choice but to live and work in an environment that effectively professes that my faith is not the right one."

The same environment granted unprecedented access and influence to those whose faith fit the Academy's increasingly stringent criteria. Commissioning ceremonies for graduating cadets were regularly in off-campus churches, as well as the huge Academy chapel, while the same passes that were provided to Christian cadets wanting to attend services in town were denied to Jews, Seventh-day Adventists, and others professing no particular faith. "There's certainly an impression that evangelicals have here," remarked one staff member, "that the leadership is kind of on their side." It was an impression the administration did nothing to dispel. An April 2003 message endorsing National Prayer Day was sent to the entire school by Brigadier General Johnny Weida, commandant of cadets and, according to Weinstein, "a real piece of work—evangelical, imperious"—who had successfully lobbied to change the Prayer Day services from nondenominational to strictly Christian. "Unless we voiced some serious opposition, the service would be changed," Casey Weinstein remembers the Academy's rabbi telling the Jewish cadets. "We were informed the day before the change went into effect."

"Weida," Weinstein asserts, "was a walking and talking constitutional disaster and one of the leading causes of the problems at the Academy. He made no bones about his evangelical calling to convert the unbeliever and consistently blurred the line between his beliefs and his authority. Promoting the National Prayer Day was just the beginning. He also sent a letter to the entire cadet wing that declared that each and every one of them was 'accountable first to your God.' This goes a lot further than some vague violation of principle. It's a direct contradiction of the Air Force oath that explicitly swears primary allegiance to the Constitution and to the basic religious tolerance tenets of the long-established Air Force 'core values,' universally referred to as 'the Little Blue Book.' Simply put, Weida was trying to realign the loyalties of American fighting men and women, transforming us from a democracy to a theocracy."

The allegations continued to accumulate. An Academy bus driver refused to change the channel of a fundamentalist-Christian talk-radio station while transporting cadets, who, when they complained, were told to take it up with their "mommies and daddies in the ACLU." Falcons football coach Fisher DeBerry regularly harangued his team with fire-and-brimstone exhortations, fiercely insisting on the primacy of Jesus in every aspect of life, not least on the athletic field.

"Christianity isn't just about what you say," DeBerry would write in his book *For God and Country,* one of two volumes in among the baseball caps, jerseys, and coasters for sale at the Academy's gift shop. "It's shown in the consistency of how you live your life. . . . I feel that when I am called to speak to groups that it is God saying, 'Here is an opportunity to spread the word.' To that end I believe that a lot of our opportunities are spirit led."

There was apparently no greater opportunity for the colorfully outspoken DeBerry to spread the word than in the steamy locker room of the Falcons football team, where his go-for-broke evangelism methods combined an aw-shucks country-boy demeanor with a blithe disregard for even the appearance of plurality. "When I was three years old, I was drugged," the South Carolina native would joke. "I was drugged by my grandma to church." He would employ the same approach with his football players, who, by the mideighties, had been ranked as high as number four nationally and had become a formidable NCAA football force. The Falcons regularly dominated their archrivals Army and Navy, winning the coveted Commander in Chief's Trophy fourteen times in twenty-one seasons under DeBerry, a winning record the coach attributed directly to God's favor. "Religion is what we're all about," he would avow, and to underscore the connection between worship and winning, he had, in the final home game of the 2004 season, hung a banner in the locker room quoting the Fellowship of Christian Athletes' Competitor's Creed, reading in part, "I am a Christian first and last. I am created in the likeness of God Almighty to bring Him glory. I am a member of Team Jesus Christ. I wear the colors of the cross." The Kansas City, Missouri–based Fellowship of Christian Athletes had, in fact, inducted DeBerry into its Hall of Champions in recognition of his role as a "servant-leader who faithfully served Christ through the vehicle of the FCA." That service included a pledge to "present to athletes and coaches and all whom they influence the challenge and adventure of receiving Jesus Christ as Savior and Lord." The FCA's mission statement bore more than a passing resemblance to Bobby Welch's *Warrior Leader* template, which listed among "The Leader's Expectations of Those He Leads" a requirement that "they accomplish the Great Commission," with its characteristically evangelical blurring of distinctions between winning on the playing field, winning on the battlefield, and a colossal, winner-take-all contest for souls.

"Go to church tomorrow," DeBerry habitually told his players after every game. "Tell your mom and daddy that you love them, and remember who you are." Who they were, it seemed, were targets for a concerted campaign of conversion and religious reinforcement that eventually brought DeBerry to the attention of the national media, and not for his game-winning strategies. "This is our foundation and this is what we're about in Falcon football," DeBerry would insist when confronted with his evangelical excesses. "Religion is a part of life. Football, academics, military training—everything."

DeBerry's argument was a cagey appeal to the traditional connection between sports and spirituality, stretching from the late nineteenth century, when Yale professor Eugene Lamb Richards observed that the school's best teams comprised "the most moral and religious men," to those ubiquitous prayers for miraculous intervention on a Hail Mary pass. "Fisher's fighting a heck of a battle with the U.S. government," asserted Florida State coach and Fellowship of Christian Athletes colleague Bobby Bowden at the height of the DeBerry furor. "He happens to be a Christian and he wants his boys to be saved."

"Maybe if I was a Christian, I might want my boys to be saved, too," counters Weinstein. "But I'm not. I'm Jewish and I pay DeBerry's salary at a federally funded military academy, which gives me the right to insist that he keep his personal religious convictions to himself while he's on the job." After a thoughtful pause, Weinstein continues, "Look, if I was a Muslim, a Hindu, or an atheist, the principle would be the same. I have the right not to have my children cornered and coerced by Christians in positions of authority. DeBerry got into trouble later for implying that black athletes are better runners than white ones. Maybe they are. And maybe Jesus Christ is the Way, the Truth, and the Life. But it's not the coach's job to tell his players that. If anything, he's there to bring out the best in his team, regardless of race or religion. I wonder if the Falcons' white running backs felt the same as the team's few non-Christian players when they found out what DeBerry considered the criteria for success on the gridiron."

⋆ 7 ⋆

THE YALE PRACTICUM:
AN EXTERNAL REVIEW

Weinstein's initial flurry of information gathering had concluded by the late spring of 2004. Assembling the results in a bulging file, he sent it directly to General Rosa, the school's chief administrator.

"After that I got a little distracted," Weinstein admits. "Casey was getting set to graduate. President Bush was going to be the keynote speaker, but what really got us excited was when Casey announced that, on the day before the actual ceremony, he was going to ask his class-mate Amanda to marry him. Needless to say, it was a hugely significant juncture for the whole family." Captured on a home video, the proposal, with Casey on his knees in front of his intended bride and witnessed by a contingent of 150 of Weinstein's family and close friends at the Broadmoor resort, includes a touching moment when his mother, Bon-nie, draws her son aside and asks him in a whisper if he is really ready for this moment. The look in Casey's eyes conveys a mix of courage, de-termination, and sheer terror.

"We all went to Hawaii afterwards," Weinstein continues. "It was our time together and I put everything else out of my mind. As much as anything, it was a function of my confidence that the Academy would handle the problem. I'd done my duty by bringing it to their attention in a timely manner."

There appeared however, to be an attention deficit in the upper echelons of the school's administration. "It was only when I confronted them at the leadership Conference about what Curtis had told me that I found out the dossier I'd compiled had never made it to Rosa's office. Everyone sort of shrugged their shoulders when I brought it up, pointing fingers at each other in a classic bureaucratic runaround. It was infuriating, and not just because of all the research and hard work, not to mention the terrible personal risks taken by my sources, that had gone into bringing the situation to their attention. There were real human beings with dependent families caught up in the middle of this mess, and I was getting the feeling that these people were looking to me to make it right."

What Weinstein had no way of knowing—primarily because the Academy had buried the fact with the same finesse with which it had lost his evidentiary file—was that other wheels had already been set in motion by an audacious individual trying desperately to address the same situation that Weinstein had stumbled upon. Bringing the Academy's persistent pattern of evangelical intimidation to light had, up until then, been the single-handed mission of a remarkable woman, in deep cover within the very command center of the conspiracy.

First impressions would hardly qualify chaplain Captain MeLinda Morton to lead the charge against religious zealotry in the fishbowl atmosphere of what she calls "The Hill," shorthand for the Academy's elevated complex in Colorado Springs. With precise comportment and a soft, uninflected voice, Morton discovered an interest in theology at a Lutheran boarding school leading her, in turn, to a seminary education with an eye toward eventual ordination. "My family has a very strong military tradition," Morton, who is part Cherokee, recounts. "My father and many siblings served in the armed forces. I joined the Air Force and attended officer training through ROTC at a nearby university during my seminary years. I was seeking leadership training and experience in the military because I really valued that environment and believed that, with my ministerial education, I could help to meet the needs of military people."

Serving briefly as a flight navigator, she was subsequently stationed at Whiteman AFB near Kansas City, Missouri, and became missile launch officer for the Minuteman II arsenal of the 351st Missile Wing, one of the first of a female cadre to assume the posts of combat crew commander and flight commander within the Air Force's Minuteman II missile program. Morton next served in Space Command during the first Gulf War, doing orbital analysis employing high-powered GPS systems.

A line officer for ten years, she resigned her commission to complete her delayed dream of earning a Ph.D. in theology, serving as a parish priest even as she continued studying to earn a law degree at the University of Texas. "In the late nineties, the Air Force asked me to return to the reserves," she continues, choosing her words in a characteristically meticulous manner. "I thought it over and realized that there was still something I could offer the service, a way to very directly practice my calling and put my faith to work. I came back as a chaplain." A Distinguished Graduate of the Air Force's basic chaplain course, Morton returned to active duty and, in late 2002, assumed the post of one of four group chaplains among the sixteen chaplains assigned to the Academy. "I loved the work," she avows. "It was a unique assignment, focused intently on the cadets themselves. In essence, I was doing campus ministry, which gave me a chance to really meet the inner needs of bright, dedicated young men and women. It was an honor."

Within a month of her arrival, the sexual assault scandal broke wide open. "Most of the routine pastoral work I was doing at the Academy came to a screeching halt as soon as the revelations were made public," she explains. "There was an immediate and obsessive focus on dealing with this issue to the exclusion of almost all others, especially when it came to managing the media. The administration took any negative publicity as a critique of the Academy and its core values and set out to prove that they were serious about prosecuting rapists. Somebody's head was going to end up on a pike."

Unfortunately, the resulting witch hunt took time and resources away from those most directly affected by the violations: the cadets themselves. Morton: "In the frenzy to find someone to blame, the Academy ignored the actual survivors of abuse and harassment or worse, ostracized them, in some cases simply dismissing them from the school as a way to keep them at arm's length. In the meantime, I was overwhelmed with young cadets who had actually been assaulted, both male and female, lining up in front of my office for counseling. Along with a few of the other chaplains, we were the only ones they could turn to."

Morton's and her colleagues' response was, in fact, the fulfillment of a pastoral function long consecrated by military regulation. "In the civilian world," asserts Morton, "if you want to have a truly private conversation, it's probably best to make an appointment with your lawyer. Unlike that of doctors or priests, the privileges afforded attorneys and their clients can't be directly impinged upon. In the military, that protection is also extended to chaplains. I'm not obligated to reveal anything told to me in confidence as part of my professional duties, even if it's a four-star general who wants to know."

This unique shield of secrecy has played an invaluable role in social interactions throughout the armed forces. "On the outside, you may have an eating disorder, be addicted to porn, or be in the middle of an extramarital affair," Morton continues. "That's your business. In the military, it could get you court-martialed or, if you're an Air Force cadet, thrown out of school. The chaplaincy was intentionally designed as a buffer between those very human problems and the remedies that good discipline requires. Its usefulness has been recognized time and again and an almost sacramental place was created for this privileged communication. Of course, it's also my responsibility to provide ethical advice to commanders regarding any and all moral and morale problems, always with a realistic understanding of the mission of the troops and never singling anyone out by name. Chaplains must always balance their knowledge of the mission with the needs of the person seeking counsel, a very different mandate from any community-based counseling. We listen to and speak with the person, keeping in mind the specific demands of their military service and what they are saying about their ability to perform that duty. This is why it is so important that chaplains understand the military operational environment. It's a system that worked very well for a very long time."

That its efficacy was in peril became distressingly clear with the widening stress fractures of the sexual assault controversy. "For many years there was a fairly equitable distribution of Jewish, Roman Catholic, and mainline Protestant chaplains in every branch of the service," Morton explains. "The real influx of evangelicals came in the eighties and nineties, mostly at the invitation of like-minded believers who were already in the service and, of course, at the expense of many of the mainline progressive Protestant traditions. Indeed, these mainline Protestants are nominally liturgical in worship and confessional in belief, attending to certain historic statements of faith. As a result of this denominational imbalance, cadets of diverse religious background stopped seeking out chaplains for counsel and comfort, simply because they were afraid of being cornered into some kind of forced conversion. I've heard horrendous accounts of gay and lesbian cadets going to their chaplains to talk about their sexual orientation and being subjected to extemporaneous exorcisms to cast out the demon of homosexuality." The traditional mandate of the chaplaincy—to advocate on behalf of those who sought out succor, no matter what their beliefs—was being short-circuited by a surfeit of fundamentalists, bent on winning souls for Jesus by exploiting weakness, fear, and confusion.

The situation had reached a crisis stage by the time allegations of sexual misconduct at the Academy began grabbing headlines. "The necessity of finding someone to blame really opened the door wide to evangelical voices within the chaplaincy and the administration," Morton asserts. "Their message was simple and very appealing to those who were bewildered and fearful about what was happening around them: the sexual scandal, they claimed, was the result of a lack of sexual purity among the cadets and an absence of moral authority from the administration and teaching staff. The cadets were here because God had chosen them for a special purpose and the enemy was doing his best to subvert that purpose with sin and temptation. The problem was spiritual and the solution was in an unwavering commitment to a stern spiritual program."

The result, according to Morton, was a renewed emphasis on saving lost souls by the burgeoning evangelical faction within the chaplaincy, and, in direct response, an increased reluctance by the cadets to confide and confess to those placed among them for exactly that purpose. "Those few of us who were willing to talk and listen to the cadet survivors of sexual assault without our own agenda were inundated," says Morton, recalling summer of 2003. "And it soon became clear that we just didn't have the background to really deal effectively with the stories we were hearing."

To compensate, Morton began delving deeply into anything and everything she could find on the subject of pastoral care for sexual abuse survivors. "A lot of it just didn't make sense in our highly regimented environment," she admits. "You can't really tell someone to start a journal when whatever they write can be read at any time by their commanding officer. But then I found a book that really seemed to apply to what was happening around me."

The book was *When Violence Is No Stranger*, written a year before by Dr. Kristen J. Leslie, a professor of pastoral care and counseling at the Yale Divinity School and an ordained United Methodist minister. "So much of what had happened at the Academy fell under the description of acquaintance rape," Morton continues. "These young men and women studied together, worked together, combat trained together, ate together: they were taught to think and function as a team, which is exactly what made the sexual assaults so harrowing. It was a betrayal in the deepest sense of the word. Dr. Leslie addressed that betrayal and, more important, how to begin the healing process in a therapeutic setting."

An engaging and articulate Ohio native, Kristen J. Leslie was invited by Morton to visit the Academy on several occasions in late 2003. "She asked me to come out under what's called an Assess and Improve protocol to evaluate the school's entire pastoral care effort," says Leslie. "By the summer of 2003, there was a great deal of urgency behind the request, coming directly from the Pentagon, which was still reeling from the scandal and its fallout. Eventually I took six graduate students with me to assist in observing and reflecting back to the chaplains what we would see and hear over the period of a week. Our input would then be applied to helping to refine training in pastoral care. It was very specific and everyone seemed very open to our participation."

"The visit was timed with the Basic Cadet Training course that summer," continues Morton. "Dr. Leslie and her students went out to Jack's Valley and slept in tents like everyone else, shadowing the chaplains as they did their work. It seemed like a very good opportunity to see first-hand the quality of our care under very trying circumstances and we had regular debriefs with the twenty-plus participating chaplains to discuss what was being observed. For whatever reason, Colonel Whittington chose not to attend." Conspicuous in his absence—especially considering the upper echelon weight given to the Yale team's work—Whittington's lack of interest hardly came as a surprise to his subordinates. "Some of the staff used to have a saying," Morton reveals. "They'd tell each other, 'it's all about Wit.' It wasn't that he was lazy or incompetent. It was just hard for him to see how what we were doing would be a direct benefit to his career."

Whittington would come to regret the attitude, as Leslie and her students began methodically formulating and articulating their impressions of both the necessarily brutal training course and the chaplains charged with guiding the young cadets through its ego-annihilating rigors. In their "outbriefing," the group's final summation of their weeklong immersion in Academy precepts and practices, a generally positive impression was undercut with some very real apprehensions.

"With the proviso that, as outsiders, we had an incomplete understanding of the culture we were observing, there were three general areas in which we expressed reservations, or at least puzzlement," Leslie recounts. "The first was the treatment of incoming female cadets by the upper-class female cadres. They were especially harsh on the new appointees, and we wondered whether they were in some way trying to overcompensate in what was, by large measure, a male-dominated environment."

But it was the next two items on the team's list of concerns that clearly exposed what, up until then, had been both unspoken and taken largely for granted by both the Academy's staff and student body. "We noted an overarching evangelical emphasis in many aspects of the training regimen that didn't seem to jibe with the goal of unit cohesion," Leslie continues. "For example, during the high rope training course, which had an especially punishing physical requirement, we heard many of the trainers encouraging the recruits with comments like 'Be faithful' and 'Jesus will get you through.' We witnessed a midweek worship service when those who didn't want to attend were subjected to the

'Heathen Flight' and marched around the camp. Often, after a day's training, we'd float around the camp and see prayer meetings being held in tents. The tenor and terminology was always overtly evangelical, including repeated references to the cadets being called to the Academy to fulfill God's plan for their lives."

What was even more revealing was the response of the evangelical chaplains on hand for the outbriefing. "They seemed surprised that we even brought it up," observes Leslie. "Their attitude was generally that this was the way we do things around here, and if we didn't like it, it was because we didn't understand how important it was to bring this spiritual component to basic training."

That spiritual component was made explicit in a remarkable incident observed firsthand by the Yale team. In what might well have been the Academy's version of the traditional ghost story told around a campfire, chaplain Major Warren "Chappie" Watties regaled the cadets over a bullhorn in Jack's Valley with visions of their unsaved tentmates "burning in the fires of hell" if the Christians among them didn't do something, and quickly, to salvage their immortal souls. He ordered them to confront their nonattending classmates located in adjoining tents and evangelize them on the spot. Further, they were told that if they refused to be evangelized, the penalty would be the aforementioned "fires of hell." It's all too easy to imagine the impact of these words set against the grim struggle for survival that Basic Cadet Training had, by design, become for these young men and women. Isolated in a wilderness environment, many of them away from the comforts and security of home and family for the first time, they had relentlessly been drilled on the absolute necessity of team loyalty and interdependence. The notion that eternal punishment for one of their fellow cadets and classmates was entirely dependent on their ability to effect a religious conversion would have enormously amplified against a backdrop of towering mountains and primeval forests. Simply put, Watties had a captive audience in every sense of the term.

Later to be singled out for a Distinguished Service award as the Academy's "most energetic and effective chaplain" by the Military Chaplains' Association, as well as being named the 2004 Air Force Chaplain of the Year, Watties began his service career in the Marine

Corps in the late seventies, joining the Air Force Reserve in 1990 while employed as a principal at a Christian school. Assuming full-time duties three years later, he would go on to serve a stint in Baghdad in the Iraq War, boasting of baptizing troops in one of Saddam Hussein's swimming pools.

In measured scholastic language, the Yale team suggested that Watties's fire-and-brimstone homily "challenged the necessarily pluralistic environment of basic training," while its "overwhelmingly evangelical tone encouraged religious divisions rather than fostering spiritual understanding."

Submitted to Colonel Whittington in July, the project's After Action Report (see Appendix A) concisely framed the extent of evangelical encroachment in the character-shaping dynamics of the basic training regimen. "The Yale Practicum team observed consistent specific articulations of evangelical Christian themes," noted the report, under the heading "Challenges to Pluralism." "Protestant Cadets were encouraged to chant 'This is our Chapel and the Lord is our God.'" They were "encouraged to pray for the salvation of fellow BCT members," "regularly encouraged to 'witness' to fellow Basic Cadets," and "informed that God's plan for their life included attending USAFA." Written by Morton and Leslie, the report suggested that the Academy's Chaplain Service "reconsider the worship dynamics and Chaplain/Basic Cadet interaction" during training and focus on "aspects of ecumenical teamwork and developing an appreciation of spiritual diversity."

Spiritual diversity seemed to be at a premium within the confines of the Academy. When, several months after the fact, news leaked of his scarifying spiritual tactics, the Academy jumped to Major Watties's defense, insisting that his "messages and sermons were deemed to be appropriate encouragement to his congregation to share their religious convictions." Those convictions had, by direct implication, earned the official imprimatur of the institution. There would, it seemed, be no turning back.

★ 8 ★

PANIC IN THE AIR

In December of 2000, almost four years before Chaplain Watties's bull-horn-enhanced wilderness proselytizing, far from the dry dust of Jack's Valley, deep in the bowels of the Pentagon, U.S. Army Commander in Chief General Tommy Franks issued General Order 1A under the heading "Prohibited Activities for U.S. Department of Defense Personnel Present Within the United States Central Command." Its stated purpose: "To identify conduct that is prejudicial to the maintenance of good order and discipline of all forces in the USCENTCOM (U.S. Central Command)."

Promulgated primarily as a code of behavior to armed service personnel stationed in the Middle East in the aftermath of Desert Storm and the run-up to the Iraq War, General Order 1A expressly forbade such activities as the "sale, possession, transfer, manufacture or consumption of any alcoholic beverage; any controlled substances or drug paraphernalia and any pornographic or sexually explicit photograph, video tape, movie, drawing, book, magazine, or similar representations." And there, tucked amongst this catalog of common vices, in Section J of Part Two, was a single, straightforward command explicitly prohibiting "proselytizing of any religion, faith or practice."

The ramifications of Franks's directive had passed all but unnoticed in the wax-polished hallways of the Academy as Weinstein prepared to do battle with forces entrenched behind its frosted office windows. Only in hindsight, as the full scope of the institution's rigorous endorsement of fundamentalist Christian religion, faith, and practice became clear, did the glaring disconnect stand out in sharp relief.

"On a battlefield is precisely where a soldier might want to begin considering their [sic] ultimate values," Tom Minnery, spokesman for Focus on the Family insisted in the wake of the public disclosure of Section 2J. "To deny someone the chance to depend on God is a concern." It was an uncomfortable echo of an earlier statement by Minnery that the purpose of cadet training was "to make the ultimate sacrifice for their country, to meet their maker."

"Somebody please tell me, why is proselytizing acceptable over here but not in the combat zone?" Weinstein would respond, but what neither of them could have known then was that the Air Force Academy had itself become a de facto battlefield, an ideological combat zone that was quickly spreading to the entire U.S. armed forces. It was that reality Weinstein was about run up against hard, exposing a deep division in the fabric of American military life and, by extension, the consensus of the country itself.

Weinstein's war would be waged across a political and social landscape polarized by an almost ultrazealous fervor on both sides, with demonized enemies, crusader's zeal, and apocalyptic furies. If the new millennium was teaching America anything, it was that extremism, in the pursuit of an ideological agenda, was a law unto itself. America's citizens were living in an age of increasingly dangerous disagreement, vitriolic and vindictive. Yet, as Americans, they were also assured of the protections that shield them from their own excesses. Tolerance, the rule of law, and a Constitution that balances power and enshrines impartiality: when all else fails, these fire walls are there to hold back the heat of Americans' partisan passions, ensure their way of life, and safeguard their pursuit of happiness.

Except when they don't.

"In my conversations with General Rosa, the Academy's superintendent, I made it clear that I expected results," Weinstein recalls of the quickly accelerating events in the late summer of 2004. "Maybe it seems odd that an Academy graduate, no matter what his rank or role, would be in a position to dictate terms like that. But as far as I was concerned, I had them by the short hairs. What was happening at the Academy was wrong. It was vile. I knew it, and even if they didn't, they were sensitive to my willingness and capability to raise hell. In the aftermath of the sexual assault scandal, that was the last thing they wanted, and I knew that, too. In the end, I told him I'd hold off doing anything and give them time to fix the problem until Parents' Weekend, when families come up to visit the cadets during the Labor Day holiday. After that, all bets were off."

Typically, however, Weinstein would take a proactive approach in the interim. "It's hard to overestimate the sense of betrayal I felt," he explains. "I had, to the best of my ability, acted in good faith, making my concerns known up the proper levels in the chain of command. When nothing happened and, in fact, the situation got worse, it wasn't just that I lost faith in the Academy's administrative structure. It was that I couldn't help but wonder if there wasn't actually an active resistance to the necessary changes that had to be made. There was a show of cooperation and a total absence of follow-through. Based on those suspicions, I began building a case. It's the attack-dog lawyer in me."

A consummate networker, Weinstein had maintained extensive contacts throughout the Academy, the Air Force, and the entire Department of Defense, which he began actively tapping for insider information. "There was no shortage of friends and colleagues at all levels of the military hierarchy that were only too aware of what was going on, often to a fuller extent than I could have imagined," he continues. "They were experiencing it firsthand, and once word got out, they started coming to me on their own. My initial strategy was to prepare a legal brief with the skillful help of another attorney, my litigator friend Esteban "Steve" Aguilar, which would lay out both the constitutional issues and the individual incidents that were coming to me." Using the dossier he had put together during the *Passion* dustup as a starting point, Weinstein set to work as the sweltering New Mexico summer slowly cooled with the approaching fall.

The Academy was also buckling down, although internal divisions between hard-line evangelicals and those intent on putting out fires, such as General Rosa, the Academy's most senior military commander and its "university president," gave the effort a fractured focus.

"The Yale study was completed and Dr. Leslie and I put together a report that I delivered to Colonel Whittington personally in late July 2004," recounts MeLinda Morton. The After Action Report of the Yale Practicum Team clearly articulated the scope and objectives of the project: "Engage USAFA/HC (Headquarters Chaplains) in constructive and intentional discussions of pastoral care in a pluralistic environment, cadet ministry and worship events," as well as providing "resources to examine cultural influences prevalent in the cadet population."

"I took it outside administrative channels to put it directly into Whittington's hands," says Morton, "because I wanted to be certain he got it, that it would not get lost in the shuffle of office paperwork or be confused with any other report. At the same time, I made sure to convey to him that issues of religious diversity were being dealt with directly in the report. I had heard through the grapevine that Mikey Weinstein had already gotten deeply involved and I felt that the conclusions we had reached in the report, and the fact that we had even commissioned such a report at all, might go a long way to defusing the situation by demonstrating that we were already on the case. I laid it in front of him on his desk and, as far as I know, that's the last he ever saw of it."

Two weeks later, Whittington called a staff meeting of the entire Academy chaplaincy. "There was panic in the air," Morton recalls. "We were told that the school was facing a huge problem on a par with the sexual assault scandal and that we immediately needed to create a program that would forestall any suggestion of religious intolerance. The task was to take precedence over everything else, and results were expected immediately, if not sooner." As a measure of the urgency attached to the looming crisis, Whittington mandated the formation of a Tiger Team, an ad hoc working group with the power to recruit anyone deemed necessary to complete the mission. "All of this resonated even more given the fact that we were accustomed to Whittington making it clear that because he spent his waking hours trying to find ways to please the superintendent, it was our job to spend our waking hours trying to find ways to please him. That's pretty much a direct quote and, at the time, such statements seemed shocking. We had always considered our job to be to minister to the needs of the cadets. But, under the circumstances, it was obvious that our commanding officer was under a great deal of pressure from above." Weinstein's Labor Day ultimatum to General Rosa was apparently having its effect.

"Shortly after the Tiger Team was formed, I went back to Whittington," says Morton. Shortly afterward, she would become the chief chaplain's executive officer, strategically situated to observe the unfolding drama from the inside. "I reminded him again about the Yale study and stressed that the resources of the team that had worked with Dr. Leslie and me were at his disposal. A month later, I brought it up a third time. I truly believe that had he actually read the report, the Academy might have been able to deflect some of the accusations that were eventually made against it. The fact was, it was simply never upchanneled. In my opinion, that's dereliction of duty, pure and simple."

Meanwhile, work proceeded apace on the Academy's stopgap program to promote religious diversity. "It was called RSVP," continues Morton, "which stood for Respecting the Spiritual Values of All People. From the very beginning, it was a no-man's land. The team was comprised of a fairly representational mix—evangelical, Roman Catholics, and Protestant mainline—and what some of us felt had to be avoided at all costs was a finger-wagging lecture, blaming cadets for lapses real or imagined. We wanted to facilitate a dialogue, talk about the practical aspects of tolerance as it applied to successful team integration and, along the way, to find some more imaginative ways to get the message across, with film clips and other mixed-media approaches. Not everyone shared our perspective," she added drily.

Given the snail's pace of progress on RVSP, Labor Day and Parents' Weekend passed with only bland assurances to Weinstein that the new program was well along and shaping up nicely. "I bided my time," he concedes. "I knew they were getting something together, and it only seemed fair to give them their shot. I remained confident, which, in hindsight, I define as the feeling you have just before you realize the comprehensive enormity of the problem you're suddenly facing. I knew enough about military procedure to understand that there was no way to jump the queue. The ball was in their court and it would stay there as long as they deemed necessary." In fact, Weinstein himself had his hands full putting together his expanded brief on the situation at the Academy and its teeming legal ramifications. "I wanted to have something ready when the time came to go public," he explains. "A lot of this material had already been given to General Rosa seven months earlier. They weren't going to get the benefit of a heads-up this time."

The Religious Climate at the United States Air Force Academy, completed in late September by and for Weinstein and under the legal stewardship of fellow attorney Steve Aguilar, presented a cogent nineteen-page argument for what its title page termed "A Clear Violation of the U.S. Constitution." "From a legal point of view, even with the differences between military and civil law, it was all pretty straightforward," remarks Aguilar. "This was clearly a violation of the Establishment Clause, and whatever the nuances presented by the other side, that's what it remained: an open-and-shut case."

That case was bolstered with fifteen sections of supporting evidentiary documents, much of it from anonymous sources far too fearful to step forward on their own. Among the more disturbing allegations: a plethora of anti-Semitic slurs by cadets, including among other vulgarities the use of "fucking Jew," "filthy Jew," and "Christ killer"; a complaint lodged against the cafeteria staff at Mitchell Hall over reluctance to provide a Passover meal: wrote a Jewish cadet, "Our dietary requirements are religious obligations for observant Jews that the main cadet dining area is unwilling to accommodate. . . . Our meals tie our community together and often may be the only time when Jewish cadets are able to socialize and bond as a group"; an incident in which General Weida delivered a lunchtime message in the two-acre Mitchell Hall dining facility on religious tolerance in response to *The Passion* flap while New Testament passages unscrolled incongruously on giant video screens; an e-mail from several cadets with a request to discuss personal experiences of religious harassment with Captain Morton "under seal of privilege" and a specific request that their identities not be revealed to General Weida. "It was the first time I came across MeLinda's name," Weinstein would later remember. "I made a note of it."

"The authors of this paper seek to impel the command structure of the USAFA to vigorously enforce the First Amendment in all aspects of Academy life," wrote Weinstein, throwing down the gauntlet in no uncertain terms. "They seek an Air Force Academy...which never promotes or favors any single religious belief." He concluded with a quote from the 1987 Supreme Court decision in *Edwards v. Aguillard* striking down a Louisiana law requiring that creationism be taught in public schools alongside evolution. "A governmental intention to promote religion...may be evidenced by promotion of religion in general."

Tucking away the incendiary summary for future use, Weinstein turned his attention to an upcoming briefing scheduled by the Academy in the Arnold Hall ballroom on Election Day, November 2, 2004. The sole purpose of the event—for which attendance was mandatory for virtually the entire school's leadership, down to the senior cadet leadership level—was to unveil an early iteration of the RSVP program, even then still mired in the Tiger Team's conflicting agendas. "Of course, I wasn't invited," Weinstein recalls, "but it didn't matter. I was determined to get a look behind the curtain and had several of my moles—teaching staff and administrators who had already done so much to keep me in the loop—strategically placed in the hall that morning."

Some three hundred officers and senior cadets were corralled for the presentation, with General Rosa, Colonel Whittington, Colonel Gray, and a clearly disgruntled commandant of cadets, General Weida, perched on the dais. "My contacts were calling me periodically on their cell phones," Weinstein continues, "and at first things seemed to be going well. There was a tacit acknowledgment that they indeed had a problem and were addressing it, albeit with typically glacially paced bureaucratic dispatch. But it was also clear from the beginning that Weida was having a hard time holding it together, just by the evidence of his body language and demeanor, which was confirmed independently by several of my sources."

Also present in the hall that morning was Chaplain Captain MeLinda Morton, who had been recruited to help lay out the RSVP curriculum to the assembly. "It didn't go well," she acknowledges. "There were a lot of evangelicals in attendance, both from the cadet wing and the Academy's staff and administration. They were critical about the program to the point of scorn, making it clear they didn't like its tone, its content, or its direction and that, underneath it all, they didn't much like me either. Among the more fervent fundamentalists, chaplains were not considered to be very good Christians, especially those from a liturgical background."

Finally, after almost three hours, Morton recounts, the session was opened to a question-and-answer period. "Myself and another chaplain began taking prepared questions from the floor, but we were quickly superseded by Colonel Whittington and Colonel Gray, who seemed intent on managing the exchange. An issue was raised about whether it would be appropriate for Bible studies to be held in the squadron assembly rooms, where cadets regularly gathered to unwind and socialize, watching television or playing Ping-Pong."

At the podium, Whittington, doing his best to toe the Academy's freshly minted accommodationist line, suggested that there were, in fact, already spaces designated to the chaplaincy for just such a purpose. Even as he was speaking, Weida jumped to his feet and brusquely elbowed him aside. "Whittington was cut off at the knees," Morton recounts. "General Weida announced in no uncertain terms that Bible studies would continue in the squadron assembly rooms. Period."

"What became clear at that point," Weinstein remarks, "was that there was a power struggle going on at the highest levels of the Academy, and no one was quite sure who was winning. The fact that General Rosa, as superintendent, literally sat quite idly by while Weida essentially laid down religious-expression policy suggests more than just tacit endorsement. It was a clear indication that institutional authority itself was shifting. The evangelicals had spent a long time and lot of energy establishing their base at the Academy. They weren't about to give it up without a fight. At the same time, Rosa and others were desperately trying to stave off another sexual-scandal-style upheaval. I could feel the tension over the phone line, and for the first time, I think, I realized the full magnitude of what I was dealing with."

✶ 9 ✶

CIRCLING THE WAGONS

While Weinstein, hot-wired into the struggle for supremacy being played out in Arnold Hall, may have apprehended the breadth of evangelical infiltration at the Academy, it was Captain MeLinda Morton who would plumb its depths, only to emerge breathless and battered, with her Air Force career in tatters.

What had begun in good faith as an effort to more effectively respond to the elemental American virtue of religious diversity had became a grim struggle for dominance as the RSVP deliberations grew more contentious with each deadlocked day that passed. "It was difficult," Morton admits. "The evangelicals on the team made a concerted effort to impede progress at every turn. Between the time we started work in August of 2004, with the highest priority to expedite the process, to the final submission in mid-March of 2005, the RSVP program went through seventeen separate revisions." Morton singles out as the main obstacle to progress Chaplain James Glass, an Academy classmate of Weinstein's, who was later represented in a legal motion filed by Focus on the Family's litigation surrogate, the Alliance Defense Fund, alleging any curb on prayer or proselytizing would violate his free speech rights. "He insisted that the word *intolerance* never be used in the program," Morton recounts, "and that no Christian should be portrayed as biased or prejudiced in any way. We virtually got down to fighting over punctuation marks."

Even as the beleaguered program was being patched together, what Morton calls "a dog and pony show" had been staged a month before the Election Day showdown in Arnold Hall, primarily for the benefit of two-star General Charles Baldwin, Air Force chief of chaplains, who flew out from Washington for the occasion. Blue-eyed and thin-lipped, with a deceptively mild demeanor, Baldwin was a 1969 graduate of the Academy and later flew HH-53s as a rescue helicopter pilot. He earned a master of divinity degree from Southern Baptist Theological Seminary in the heart of the Bible Belt, and he eventually returned to serve at the Academy's Cadet Chapel before becoming chief of the Air Force Chaplain Service. In that capacity he took a place on the Armed Forces Chaplains Board, advising the secretary of defense and Joint Chiefs of Staff on religious and ethical issues.

Baldwin was less in the mood to offer advice than to issue peremptory commands when he met with Morton and other members of the RSVP Tiger Team at the Academy in October. "We got pretty bloodied," Morton remembers. "It was becoming increasingly clear that we wouldn't be getting any support from our superiors as long as we insisted on presenting religious diversity without a Christian bias." Evincing an almost paranoid vigilance for protecting the sole authority of his evangelical view, Baldwin asked repeatedly why, in the RSVP material, "Christians don't ever win." "We had included a clip from *Schindler's List,*" says Morton, "and he demanded we remove it because it made 'Christians look like Nazis.'" The scene was eventually replaced with one from Mel Gibson's Vietnam saga, *We Were Soldiers*, while use of the Native American film *Smoke Signals* to convey aspects of Native American spirituality was deemed inappropriate by Baldwin, who sniffed, "What does this have to do with spirituality?" "Every level of the hierarchy was imposing the official evangelical stamp," Morton insists, no more so than after an especially fractious follow-up presentation early in 2005 that became known by the RSVP team as Black Tuesday.

That evangelical stamp would come to seem more like a brand, a mark of the abject failure of the RSVP program not simply to educate cadets, but to break the fundamentalist stranglehold on any and all military religious doctrine at the Academy. During nearly nine months of relentless undermining, RSVP had been transformed into what Morton and a handful of others had hoped it wouldn't.

"It had become all about legality," Morton explains. "As with the sexual assault scandal, the strategy was to circle the wagons and litigate their way out. The original intent of RSVP was for it to evolve over time, to have an RSVP2 and RSVP3. Instead, they locked in this finger-wagging lecture on rules and regulations and declared victory. The program was instituted, as is, on March thirtieth, 2005, and by the end of May of the same year had already been taught to over four thousand cadets."

"The Academy asked me to vet the RSVP program in early March," recounts Yale's Kristen Leslie. "It immediately became clear to me that they had entirely missed the point. The onus of blame for intolerance had been placed on the cadets who, in the Academy system, were the ones with the absolute least power. The real problem arose from those in a position to impose their views: the administration and staff." As part of her continuing connection with the school, Leslie and a second team of graduate students were invited back to Colorado Springs to evaluate the improvements ostensibly made since their last visit. "The difference was like night and day," she recalls. "It wasn't that the influence of evangelicals in the chaplaincy and cadet wing had in any way changed, but that, instead of being regarded as an asset, we were treated like pariahs. There was a palpable tension when we were around, and we got the distinct impression that we were being handled."

Handling cut both ways. "After the November fiasco, with Weida, among others, drawing a line in the sand, I sadly realized it was a waste of time to wait for the Academy to fix itself," Weinstein reveals. "By the next day I had made a key initial contact with the press." After a thoughtful pause, he smiles. "I have to admit there was a certain resigned satisfaction in going public. For so long, this thing had been kept under wraps and I'd gone along with it, thinking all they needed was time to make it right. Now, I was all about turning over some rocks to see what crawled out. There was a sense of righteous comeuppance and justice knowing I was about to make their worst nightmare come true."

He was, at the same time, cognizant of the jeopardy such exposure might cause his son Curtis, who, as a cadet at the Academy, could conceivably be open to retaliation in any number of direct or indirect forms. "I contacted him before I made a move," remembers Weinstein, "and he was unequivocal in his support. I think, as a family, we had already crossed the Rubicon; the point of no return. We were poised and ready and willing to take on the consequences together."

Weinstein's choice to break the story was *Colorado Springs Gazette* reporter Pam Zubeck. A Kansas native with tenacity and a well-honed instinct for the heart of a story, she had come to the paper in 1993 from the *Tulsa Tribune,* worked her way from the city hall beat to *The Gazette's* police desk, scoring exclusives that resulted in criminal convictions and administrative policy changes, reassignment of personnel, and an investigation by a congressional panel. She would eventually become the paper's chief military reporter, a key posting in a town inextricably entwined with its income-generating armed service installations, Fort Carson and Peterson Air Force Base, along with the sprawling Air Force Academy, Northern Command, and NORAD. Her coverage garnered a distinguished-reporting award from the Association of Military Reporters & Editors, along with honors from the Colorado Press Association.

"Pam was confidentially recommended to me by a dear friend, a classmate who had been following developments at the Academy," Weinstein explains. "She had already picked up the scent of the story when I approached her, and I knew from the start that, in bringing this to light, I would have to adopt a crawl, walk, run strategy. What better place to throw down the gauntlet than in pages of the newspaper delivered to the doorstep of every true believer in Colorado Springs?"

Although not originally assigned to cover the Air Force Academy, Zubeck was handed the file on the sexual assault scandal in February of 2003, several weeks after the news had broken nationally, and, over the next several months, filed a string of scoops that put her, and kept her, far out ahead of the competition on the story. "In a very direct way, the religious controversy at the Academy was a continuation of the sexual scandal," she asserts. "I think it could be said that while the Academy realized it had a problem, it had no idea how to deal with it." It's a conjecture echoing MeLinda Morton's contention that the ignominy attached to rape allegations emboldened the school's evangelical cabal to advance their militant agenda of stern spiritual discipline. "They were able to make a compelling case for stiffening the moral fiber of the cadets," Zubeck confirms.

By the summer of 2004, the reporter had already begun to pick up rumblings of trouble brewing at the Academy, particularly in the wake of the unchecked endorsement of *The Passion of the Christ* and the arrival of Kristen Leslie's Yale team. "I didn't move sooner because the rumors themselves were so vague," Zubeck recounts. "But by the fall it was clear that something was going on. In October, I put in a request at the Academy to see any complaints that might have been filed over religious discrimination, but they didn't get back to me for a while."

Then, Zubeck got belated word of a report delivered by General Rosa in Washington, D.C., to the Academy's Board of Visitors during which, in an early and halting attempt at spin, he made reference to unspecified religious issues at the school.

"I was a little miffed," Zubeck admits with carefully couched understatement. "We're a small paper. Obviously we didn't have a stringer in Washington to cover the event, and it ended up in *The Denver Post* and on the AP wire, even though it wasn't given a lot of play by either. But I didn't want to get scooped again on this story." Shortly thereafter, she received a call from Weinstein. "I was scheduled to attend the Military Reporters and Editors Conference that weekend," she continues, "but I cut it short so I could meet with him. It was a snowy Sunday when we got together in Colorado Springs, he and I and someone from the Academy who didn't want his name used. He handed me some documents, including a lot of e-mail traffic. A few days later, the Academy finally coughed up the files we had requested. There were fifty-five official complaints. We had enough to run a story." The complaints released to Zubeck were, in fact, the tip of the iceberg, skimmed from literally hundreds of e-mails and letters Weinstein had gathered on his own initiative from aggrieved cadets and graduates and duly submitted to Chaplain Whittington and Colonel Gray.

On November 18, 2004, under the headline "Air Force Academy Faces Faith Bias Allegations," Zubeck made public for the first time the broad strokes of what was going on behind the Academy gates, quoting Weinstein as an anonymous graduate, provocatively asserting, "The fish stinks from the head, and the head of this fish is [Superintendent] John Rosa and [Commandant] Johnny Weida." What would soon become a familiar litany of abuses followed, from Weida's wild exhortations, to numerous Heathen Flight incidents, to Curtis's allegations of anti-Semitic slurs.

Yet, what was most revealing about Zubeck's piece was in between the lines of the Academy's official response, a decidedly schizoid amalgam of grudging admission, staunch denial, and bald-faced stonewalling. At the same time Rosa acknowledged that no substantive action had taken place in response to the fifty-five complaints, he blandly assured Zubeck in an interview that he had told the cadets, "Regardless of what you believe, you're all part of the team." Further probing elicited the response that "we realize we have issues. We're working hard on them." But the superintendent could only be pushed so far. "I get complaints every day about something," he snapped. "I could chase myself down a rathole." While announcing that the school had already launched a sensitivity-training program for staff and cadets—a reference to the tumultuous November 2 set-to at Arnold Hall—he went on to characterize as "not mean-spirited" such behavior as the use of racial invectives, seeing it as simply the product of a misguided upbringing. While promising to remove the blatantly evangelical Christmas solicitation from the back of the *Academy Spirit,* he declined, in the same breath, to comment on Weida's well-documented rhetorical excesses.

In the ensuing months, Zubeck would write a steady stream of stories, covering the mushrooming controversy from various angles, including the wide-ranging response of alumni and further embarrassing revelations regarding Falcon coach Fisher DeBerry's gung ho Christian cheerleading. In a disingenuous attempt at religious pluralism, DeBerry had taken to praying to the "Master Coach" instead of directly to Jesus, even as he insisted in an interview with Zubeck that "I don't think you can separate religion from normal, everyday life. Football, academics, military training—everything. . . . Religion is a part of life. It's what we're all about here."

On such gusts of windy sentiment, the storm continued to gather. "There is an anti-Christian bigotry developing," Focus on the Family's Tom Minnery would subsequently charge. "We fervently hope that this ridiculous bias of a few against the religion of the majority—Christianity—will now cease." "The motto the nation's cadets are trained to defend is 'In God We Trust,'" avowed a spokesperson for Colorado Springs Republican representative, Joel Hefley. "Religion does have a place at the Academy."

So it would seem. Among the fresh revelations uncovered by Zubeck was the school's sanctioned flag-folding ceremony, a ritual rife with Christian symbolism, equating the raising of the Stars and Stripes at reveille to "a symbol of our belief in the resurrection of the body."

"We didn't get a lot of help from the Academy," Zubeck recounts. "Most the information came to us from other sources." She cites as an example a number of religious-discrimination complaints filed by cadets outside the Academy's purview at the offices of the Freethinkers of Colorado Springs, a minuscule enclave of stubbornly secular humanism in the city's fundamentalist hothouse. "One might get the impression that the Academy was scrambling," she resumes wryly. "Even as the story got bigger, their public affairs department was asking us why we were bothering to cover it, that the problem had already been taken care of. But they kept sending mixed signals. It was announced that they were hiring an expert to look into the problem, then suddenly they weren't." The specialist in question was universally admired California ethicist and radio talk-show host Michael Josephson, who had previously been hired to do a "climate study" in response to the sexual scandal, as well as to provide an overall evaluation of the school's character-development curriculum.

In early 2005, Josephson was again approached, this time with a no-bid contract, to appraise the escalating religious crisis. "He had made some useful observations and suggestions," Morton recounts, "but almost anyone who comes from outside a closed system like the Academy can only provide so much insight. In the end, that can make them appear to be nothing more than a rubber stamp, endorsing whatever the official line might be. Josephson has a very close relationship with General Rosa. Some people questioned that." It could well have been that that appearance of collusion—unwitting or otherwise—as well as the unseemly implications of a $93,000 no-bid deal, which eventually scuttled Josephson's involvement.

On the other hand, says Josephson, "Some people which suggest that it was the religious right that kept me from moving forward. I can't go that far. What I will say is that what I was proposing to do represented a threat. There were individuals who wanted things to be just as they were and were not all interested in formulating new guidelines, which would, in all likelihood, have been more restrictive."

Before he departed, however, Josephson had formulated his own, nuanced impressions of the Academy's pervasive atmosphere. "At the time I was evaluating the character-development program," he explains, "I had identified a pervasive feeling of cynicism about the whole system. At a certain level, cadets seemed to consider it all a game, in part because the honor code system had become so hidebound and legalistic. But when the religious issue came to the fore, what I saw was quite the opposite: an excess of zeal and self-righteousness. The single most significant question that I was never able to satisfactorily answer was how, exactly, such a high percentage of the leadership at the Academy had become so adamantly evangelical. It was remarkable and, I think, unique to any comparable institution. Of course, the fact that Colorado Springs surrounded the school created a huge comfort zone. Within that zone, it was only natural to find plenty of support for very overt expressions of Christianity. For the evangelicals at the Academy, there was simply nothing wrong with vocally expressing one's faith. In fact, any attempt to limit that expression was seen as an attempt to make them less of a Christian and, of course, was resented and actively opposed."

Resentment and opposition were becoming endemic within the Academy's halls of power as Zubeck kept up a steady stream of investigative pieces into the early months of 2005, earning the enmity of the evangelical establishment in Colorado Springs. "They hate me," she declares. "After a while they just shut me out completely, especially Focus on the Family. They wouldn't respond to my calls for comment and informed the paper that I was excluded from the pool of reporters they would talk to. Since they wouldn't deal with me, I was never sure what their actual grievance was and only learned secondhand that it was directly related to my coverage of the Academy."

Zubeck would eventually be transferred off the Academy beat. "It was a little hard to let go," she admits. "The place had always been a rich source of stories, not least because it was an incubator for the next generation of military leaders."

The reporter's diligence in cracking the school's code of silence virtually guaranteed that her scoop would quickly find its way out of the cloistered environs of Colorado Springs. "We all knew that, sooner or later, this was going to show up on the national radar," Weinstein recalls. "After I gave the story to Pam Zubeck, I didn't hear much from the Academy one way or the other. You got the feeling they were all up there waiting with bated breath for the other shoe to drop."

When it finally happened, the reverberations could be heard across the country, around the world, and with profound echoes in Weinstein's hitherto tranquil world.

☆ 10 ☆

GOING NATIONAL

"It was in early February of 2005 and we were at the wedding of Casey's longtime Little League and high school baseball buddy in Las Cruces, New Mexico, which, of course, is Spanish for 'the crosses,'" recounts Weinstein, alert as always to ironies intentional or otherwise. "I got a call on my cell phone. It was ABC's *Good Morning America*. They wanted me on the show. That was really the beginning. The ground had already been soaked with kerosene. I was just the match."

It's one of his favorite metaphors, used again and again to describe his catalytic role in bringing the Academy to account, a vivid image that nonetheless hardly does justice to the pivotal role he played in the skirmishes, ambushes, and full-scale battles that would unfold in the months to come. In fact, Weinstein would almost single-handedly ignite the controversy, fan its flames, and throw fuel on the fire, becoming the public face of the growing debate and the fierce emotions that fed it.

Never one to suffer fools in any guise, Weinstein would fearlessly cross the line between the political and the personal, ratcheting up the rhetoric to match the peril he perceived. It was a bravura performance, playing on everything from his bulldog demeanor to his practiced skills in legal reasoning. He was a formidable opponent, never ceding the offensive, relentlessly excoriating his evangelical enemies, and pushing the issue into the spotlight by the sheer force of his personality. Weinstein ran the constant risk of becoming immolated in his own intensity.

A telling example of his take-no-prisoners tactics would occur late that same year, in an escalating e-mail exchange with New Life Church pastor and evangelical front man Ted Haggard, president of the 30-million-member National Association of Evangelicals. The two had previously met in nationally televised debate forums, and Haggard, with the skewed bonhomie of the professionally affable, sent his adversary a holiday missive, poking fun at religiously oversensitive political correctness by wishing him "a gender neutral celebration of the winter solstice holiday, practiced within the most enjoyable traditions of the religious persuasion of your choice, or secular practices of your choice."

Responding in kind, Weinstein wished Haggard a "wonderful New Year," but couldn't resist a dig of his own, writing, "I keep waiting for you to invite me up to your New Life enclave to finally give *my* side of this bloody thing to your dominionist pals and followers."

Professing shock at Weinstein's "bloody thing" terminology and his characterization of Haggard and his allies as "dominionist," the pastor fired back a lengthy riposte, asserting, "I think I have a higher view of adults to manage freedom of religion, speech, and the press. I don't believe government supervision is necessary except in extreme cases." He then went on, unbidden, to cast their differences, with a scolding tone, in stark sectarian terms. After asserting his view that "both Christian and Jewish leaders would be wise to unite," "become friends," and "work together," he launched into an extensive talking points memo of recent anti-Semitic incidents and concluded, "I find it difficult to defend Jewish causes around the world and, at the same time, have men like yourself trying to use increased government regulation to limit freedom here at home."

A nerve was squarely hit and the blood-boiling battle was joined. "How *dare* you try to assert that I and my supporters are making it *more* difficult for *you* to fight global anti-Semitism," Weinstein fumed. "You exhibit a boundless hubris in trying to posit that, because we take a firm stand against you and yours, we are, thus, endangering *your* noble national and international efforts to 'protect' me, my family, my people and what—all of the rest of world Jewry, too? *Shame* on you for that! 'We' don't depend upon Ol' Ted to be our worldwide protector . . . perhaps someday you'll see me as something other than solely a Jew."

"Mikey, Relax. Take a deep breath," Haggard responded before promptly releasing the entire exchange to the press, leaving out Weinstein's plea to suspend the e-mails and have a phone conversation "like civilized human beings." It was a move Weinstein called "infantile in the extreme." "He wants to turn it over to the press?" he asked rhetorically. "Let's rock and roll."

The rocking and rolling had, in fact, been going on for the better part of 2005. The wedding-day call from *Good Morning America* was in direct response to a February 5 piece in *The New York Times*, which had finally picked up the scent Pam Zubeck had been following for months. With a byline by Mindy Sink of the paper's national desk, the story, under the headline "Cadets Embark on Basic Training in Religious Tolerance," was the first nationwide account of the Academy's growing evangelical impasse, "a problem with religious intolerance on campus where 93 percent of the 4,000 cadets are Christian."

Rife with the de rigueur equivocations from Rosa and others in the Academy administration (including Whittington, who insisted that reported incidents were not from "a single group"), the piece detailed specific allegations from Stephanie King, a twenty-two-year-old senior ("first class") cadet identified as Jewish by the *Times*, who alleged that one born-again instructor invited students to after-class discussions of Christianity, while another tutored in an office festooned with a "humongous crucifix and a basket of prayer cards."

"Stephanie was actually a Christian convert to Judaism," Weinstein recounts. "After the *Times* piece, she evidently came under a lot of pressure from her family and apparently others, and backed away as fast as she could. Like so many others, she understandably got scared and intimidated."

The national media was anything but. "After the *Times* story, the floodgates opened," Weinstein continues. "Even though I wasn't mentioned in the piece, it was easy enough to connect the dots, and *Good Morning America* was just the beginning."

The segment on the top-rated program aired on February 19 and included an interview with Curtis taped at the Academy. "Of course, there was an Academy public affairs officer standing on the other side of the camera," Mikey reveals, "but Curtis did an excellent job, just by telling exactly what happened in his own words."

"The day before the national airing of the show on ABC," Curtis recounts, "I got an e-mail from the CQ—cadet in charge of quarters— ordering me to report to her desk immediately. I went down there thinking I was in some kind of trouble, and when I arrived, there were a bunch of other cadets hanging around. The CQ had seen the promos for the show being pitched by Diane Sawyer and Charles Gibson and asked me why I had gone on television and what my problem was. I said that I was tired of being told that my people had killed Jesus, and she shot back, 'Well, they did.'"

In the ensuing days and weeks, Mikey Weinstein would appear on the prime-time news and analysis programs of all four major networks, every major cable network, on scores of talk-radio shows, and in the editorial pages of newspapers across the country and as far-flung as Australia and India and Great Britain.

Stepping into the spotlight came naturally to the gregarious and highly motivated scrapper. He'd had previous experience with national media when, after his Air Force and White House tenure, he'd launched his own business, Find Dad, Inc., a hybrid detective and collection agency that sought out deadbeat fathers behind on their child support. "I appeared on *Oprah* and *Maury Povich*, and Disney, among many other national television appearances" he explains. "I had a feel for it going in." His entire family, in fact, was getting used to living in a media fishbowl. A camera crew and reporter from NBC's *Dateline,* with Tom Brokaw, one of a hundred media requests had been de facto guests at Casey and Amanda's wedding celebration, chronicling the event as part of an early story on the mushrooming scandal and featuring forthright interviews with the Weinstein family. *Time* magazine also sent a photographer to the wedding for a story that ran the following week on the scandal titled "Whose God Is Their Co-Pilot?" Bringing his

legal acumen to bear, even as he eschewed the use of any prepared remarks, Weinstein was matched with an array of evangelical talking
heads in debates that often grew rancorous, due, at least in part, to his
characteristic inability to soft-pedal his scorn, even in the face of various and assorted sacred cows.

"It took me a long time to finally figure out how to penetrate the
evangelical cerebellum," he explains. "At some point a question would
inevitably arise: The legal issues aside, why was I so hostile to Christianity? After all, Jesus Christ was the Prince of Peace and the Lamb of
God. How could I be against peace and lambs? So I would tell them
that I lived in New Mexico, home to many Native Americans. I asked
them to imagine a little Navajo or Apache boy watching a John Wayne
movie. He's not cheering when the cowboy kills another Indian. I knew
what Jesus said: it was right there in John 14:6: 'I am the way, the truth,
and the life: no man cometh unto the Father, but by me.' The problem is
if you don't cometh to him, he's going to have to hurt you, really badly,
like light you on fire for all eternity. That doesn't leave us who have
doubts about who he said he was with too many viable options."

As the demands for interviews, editorials, and speaking engagements
grew, so, too, did the pressure on Weinstein to maintain what amounted
to two full-time jobs. "I was working for an information technology services company as the director of business development for the Department of Energy," he explains. "I was paid for access and influence,
which pretty much meant that I had to keep my contacts up-to-date on
an ongoing basis, and I did so. But I was also having to fly around the
country, on my own dime, to do shows and spent a lot time on the
phone or face-to-face with journalists. It was a lot to juggle, especially
considering that the company was, of course, interested in developing
contracts with the military. But I didn't let that stop me, and knock
wood, to their credit, they didn't either."

By the summer of 2005, Weinstein's do-it-yourself publicity campaign
was threatening to overwhelm him, and he enlisted both a national public relations firm and a speaker's bureau to help manage the traffic.

"He's not the kind of client that needs a lot of coaching," says Matt
Dorf, partner in the tony Washington, D.C., public relations firm of Ra-
binowitz/Dorf, and Weinstein's chief public relations strategist. "He has

no problem staying on message. If he were a politician, he'd be a dream candidate."

It's a curious contention, considering the degree of animosity Weinstein would generate as his efforts escalated. "Mikey's certainly a lightning rod," Dorf admits, "but it's got less to do with his personality, as assertive as that might be, than what it is he's saying. When you confront people who believe that they speak for God, you're setting yourself up to be reviled."

As the scope and intensity of Weinstein's media exposure continued to accelerate, so too did the flood of letters, e-mails, and phone calls from all over the world from those who had experienced firsthand the unconstitutional biases and pressure he was bringing to light.

"It was incredible," he reveals. "People were coming out of the woodwork. I felt as if I'd taken on the role of reporter, historian, therapist and vigiluante all at once. Many of these stories came with a lot of pain attached to them, a lot of fear, a lot of anger, and more than a little hope that justice would be done and punishment meted out. I did what I could, lending a sympathetic ear, putting individuals in touch with others who'd had similar experiences, and building my own network at the same time."

But all the attention his high-profile campaign was gaining him and his cause, came with a personal cost. Weinstein had assiduously prioritized his life with family at the top of the list, but his war with the Academy sometimes reached uncomfortably close to home. "We're very much a family corporation," he observes. "We designed it that way, with a clear division of labor, but, under the circumstances, we were forced to reevaluate our priorities."

"It's all-consuming," admits his wife, Bonnie, "and I'd be lying if I said there weren't moments when I felt like I'd lost him. But there's a term pilots use in the Air Force. It's called 'flying high cover.' That's what I tried to do for my husband."

With a core of stalwart determination to support her husband and family sweetened by a gracious temperament, Bonnie Weinstein knows well the unquestioning allegiance that is essential for a wife in any successful military marriage. Her father, himself an Air Force pilot who had completed two hundred combat missions during the Korean War, had brought up his daughter to respect and abide by the strict codes that ruled not only the professional deportment of those serving in the military, but extended deeply into family realms as well. From early childhood she had an inbred understanding of the unspoken structures and strictures surrounding her. "I'm hardly a shrinking violet," she asserts, and the proof of that statement is evident in her frank and unflinching appraisals of assorted hard truths and bottom lines. But at the same time, she is fully aware that her natural outspokenness could never be permitted to undercut the loyalty necessary to maintain a relationship often dependent on the whim of a vast and faceless bureaucracy. In the military, that's the way it's always been.

Born on Keesler Air Force in Biloxi, Mississippi, she spent a nomadic childhood typical of any armed services offspring, bouncing from Athens, Greece, to the Los Angeles Air Force Station and, finally, Colorado Springs, where, as a teenager, she dabbled in the arts before setting her sights on an Air Force career as a nutritionist.

She was sixteen, blond, poised, and already statuesque when, with a girlfriend in tow, she attended Monte Carlo Night, an Academy mixer, with the express intent of "finding some real men." Meeting a young cadet, she went out with him for several months. "We called it 'backwards dating,'" she explains. "Since the cadets weren't allowed to have cars, the girls were the ones who picked them up and drove them back." Her fledgling boyfriend's classmate was Mikey Weinstein, who eventually called her, suggesting that, since his roommate was now dating one of *his* former girlfriends, it was only right that they, in turn, switch partners as well. "I hung up on him," she recalls.

Nothing if not persistent, Mikey eventually won her over, and six months later the two were engaged. "It was a long engagement," Bonnie comments wryly. "Cadets, of course, weren't allowed to marry before graduation, and so we waited for twenty-six months until he was finished with his Academy education." It was a delay not without difficulties. "I knew he loved me," she continues, "but I sometimes had the feeling that the camaraderie he had with his fellow cadets, especially his classmates, took precedence. It took me a while to understand how much that was a part of being at the Academy."

The reality of Weinstein's passionate Jewish identity was another element to the impending marriage that took some adjustment. "I was raised Presbyterian," she reveals, "and I can't say my family was entirely happy about my choice of a husband. My grandmother, whom I was very close to and admired enormously, once said that, as much as she respected Mikey as a person, she just wished he wasn't Jewish. That was the first time I ever remember talking back to her. When we announced our engagement, my father told me that he had no reservations about the religious differences, but my mother's response was to tell my dad 'Speak for yourself,' and abruptly walk out of the room. Later that day she drove me to work. It was a very quiet ride. A rabbi later told us that we would be neither fish nor fowl, and a pastor said that, unless I was careful, Mikey would swallow me up."

It was not an unreasonable caveat, considering the force of Weinstein's personality, and after their marriage at the Academy's Cadet Chapel, the first Jewish ceremony ever held in the huge Protestant sanctuary, the young bride began to consider anew the consequences of her commitment. "A lot of Mikey's intensity was wrapped up in his Judaism," Bonnie continues. "There could have been a clash from the beginning. For me, religion has always very much been about unity and cohesion. Those traditions and that continuity are a big part of what holds a family together. Our religious traditions were very different, and Mikey was adamant about his principles. From the very beginning he made it clear that he really did not want to have a Christmas tree or Easter baskets in the house. He was concerned about my reaction to that preference. I was fine with that. It was something I understood going in, but I wasn't sure what would replace it."

With a dogged determination every bit the equal of her husband's, Bonnie nevertheless saw more in their cultural divergences than a mere contest of wills. "The fact is that at age thirteen I realized that I just didn't believe a lot of what I was being taught in church," she reveals. "Things like the Trinity—Father, Son, and Holy Ghost—simply didn't ring true to me. From that point on, church became a place I went with my family, to be together."

The prospect of unity was also what prompted the young bride to take a serious look at the ancient precepts of her husband's faith. "I started studying Judaism," she continues. "And what I found there answered a very deep need I've always felt, not just for tradition and continuity but as a way to approach God that I could understand and embrace." With characteristic resolve, Bonnie continued her studies even as Weinstein began active duty as an Air Force officer and the young couple were successively transferred from Biloxi to Sacramento, California. A year to the day after their Academy wedding, she was formally initiated into the faith, an event celebrated by another marriage ceremony, this time in full Jewish accordance, to celebrate their new bond of a shared birthright. The bond grew steadily stronger over the years, with Bonnie maintaining a Jewish home and becoming involved in synagogues wherever they were stationed. After moving back to New Mexico in 1994 she became very active in the senior leadership of Congregation B'nai Israel, their Albuquerque synagogue, where she was named Woman of Achievement for 2005.

"I take my Judaism very seriously," she asserts. "It's a part of a strong and unwavering belief I've had in God since childhood, in spite of my disenchantment with the church. It's true that Mikey played a big part in my desire to study Judaism, but I certainly didn't do it just to please him. This was a crossroads I came to on my own, part of a lifelong spiritual journey." It's a journey that also included a study of the kabbalah, the medieval Jewish mystical texts. "It taught me that through the trials of life the soul returning to God will be stronger, and that a strong soul, during its time on earth, will have a positive effect on other souls."

Even as Bonnie confesses that her husband's intractable conflicts with Christian fundamentalism have left her "at odds" with her lifelong belief in a benign creator, she remains firm in her conviction that tribulation is the crucible of spiritual growth. It's an assurance all the more remarkable given her ongoing battle with multiple sclerosis, first diagnosed in 1998. "After that we kind of drew in as a family," she explains. "It became very much about us. Before that, he was the breadwinner and I was the lead parent. Having MS has given us a new appreciation of what we mean to each other as people, as partners. At first I refused to discuss it, hoping maybe it would just go away, but eventually I had to face the reality that MS was a major fork in the road. What it never became is an excuse. I've been careful never to make MS an issue. We deal with it as we need to.

"What Mikey's doing is important," she concludes, "and not just for its social and political impact. I think he's showing a way to understand that, if God exists, he works through all sorts of people in all kinds of situations. It's not about going to the right church and having the right set of beliefs. It's about learning from the lessons that life throws in your way and helping your fellow human beings irrespective of their personal religious perspectives or lack thereof."

★ 11 ★

A CHAPLAIN DISMISSED

Weinstein's media blitz took an exponential leap in mid-March when, at the urging one of his secret sources at the Academy, he put in a call to Captain MeLinda Morton. "I had no idea there was someone in the belly of the beast fighting the good fight," he says. "We talked about thirty seconds before I realized that, however much I was invested in this fight, MeLinda was actually on the front lines with the gunsmoke in her face." During that initial conversation, Morton mentioned Dr. Kristen Leslie's work the previous summer, and the incriminating findings that had resulted. "I stopped her right then and there," Weinstein recounts. "It was the first I'd ever heard of the Yale report, and it was stunning to discover that, the whole time, the Academy had been sitting on an official document that backed up the very foundation of what I'd been saying."

Immediately sensing the potential impact of that document, Weinstein contacted Dr. Leslie and obtained a copy. "The first thing I realized was that, if it was going to be useful, I couldn't release it to the press as the 'After Action Report of the Yale Practicum Team.' So I shortened it to 'The Yale Report' and gave it first to Pam Zubeck."

From the wedding of
Mikey Weinstein and
Bonnie Patterson, at the
United States Air Force
Academy Chapel on
June 3, 1977. (PHOTO
COURTESY OF WEINSTEIN
FAMILY COLLECTION.)

President Ronald Reagan shakes hands with Mikey Weinstein at an impromptu
White House birthday party for the president in February 1987. (OFFICIAL WHITE
HOUSE PHOTOGRAPH.)

Casey Weinstein, photographed upon his graduation from the United States Air Force Academy, June 2004. (PHOTO COURTESY OF WEINSTEIN FAMILY COLLECTION.)

Casey Weinstein and Amanda Baranek at their graduation parade at the United States Air Force Academy, June 2004. (PHOTO COURTESY OF WEINSTEIN FAMILY COLLECTION.)

Casey and Curtis Weinstein, September 2003. (PHOTO COURTESY OF WEINSTEIN FAMILY COLLECTION.)

Curtis Weinstein at the United States Air Force Academy Preparatory School, August 2002. (PHOTO COURTESY OF WEINSTEIN FAMILY COLLECTION.)

Curtis Weinstein at the United States Air Force Academy. (PHOTO COURTESY OF WEINSTEIN FAMILY COLLECTION.)

Dr. Kristen J. Leslie of the Yale University Divinity School (and a board member of the Military Religious Freedom Foundation) testified before the Subcommittee on Military Personnel of the House Armed Services Committee, June 28, 2005. (PHOTO COURTESY OF GUS SPOHN.)

MeLinda Morton (left), chaplain at the United States Air Force Academy (2002–2005), and Dr. Kristen J. Leslie during a break in testifying before the House Armed Services Committee. (PHOTO COURTESY OF GUS SPOHN.)

David Antoon, retired U.S. Air Force colonel (Academy class of 1970), decorated Vietnam War combat pilot, and board member of the Military Religious Freedom Foundation. (PHOTO COURTESY OF DAVID ANTOON.)

Sam Bregman, the lead litigator in Mikey Weinstein's federal lawsuit against the United States Air Force. (PHOTO COURTESY OF SAM BREGMAN.)

Esteban "Steve" A. Aguilar, Sr., attorney who conducted the first independent legal analysis of the constitutional issues plaguing the Academy, titled "The Religious Climate at the United States Air Force Academy: A Clear Violation of the U.S. Constitution," September 2004. (PHOTO COURTESY OF ESTEBAN A. AGUILAR, SR.)

The Weinstein family (top row, left to right): Casey, Bonnie, Mikey, and Curtis; (bottom row, left to right): Amanda Weinstein, Jerry Weinstein, Alice Weinstein, and Amber Stearns. Albuquerque, June 2006. (PHOTOGRAPH BY STEVE MOST.)

Curtis Weinstein and Amber Stearns, Albuquerque, June 2006. (PHOTOGRAPH BY STEVE MOST.)

Casey and Amanda Weinstein, Albuquerque, June 2006. (PHOTOGRAPH BY STEVE MOST.)

Bonnie and Mikey Weinstein, Albuquerque, June 2006. (PHOTOGRAPH BY STEVE MOST.)

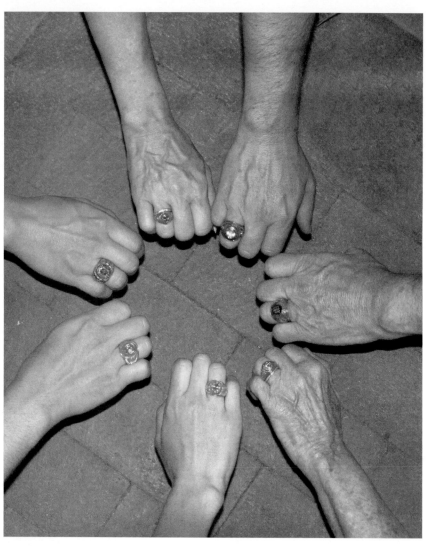

A circle of military academy rings from three generations of the Weinstein family. (PHOTOGRAPH BY STEVE MOST.)

In a subsequent story in the *Gazette,* Zubeck conducted a follow-up interview with Dr. Leslie, obtaining the clearest statement to date of the depth of the Academy's predicament. According to Leslie, "They're contending that the chaplains, within the power given to them, have the right to promote one particular notion of a Christian doctrine. In a pluralistic environment where you have multiple-faith traditions, there still needs to be room for mutuality of consent, and in the Academy there is not—even among Christians."

"The Yale Report" quickly became the focal point of the media's ongoing interest in the mushrooming issue. "Just the name *Yale* gave us a lot of credibility," Weinstein asserts. "Suddenly, I wasn't some loose cannon trying to bring down a revered American institution with wild accusations. Now there was real authority behind what I'd been trying to tell everyone."

The veracity of that authority was very much in the eye of the beholder. Following the release of "The Yale Report"—with Dr. Leslie appearing on *60 Minutes II* and CNN special report, as well as giving numerous interviews with *The Washington Post, The New York Times,* and others—Focus on the Family leapt into the breach with a story titled "Architecture of a Smear" on Citizen, their "Family Issues in Policy and Culture" Web site. Under the subhead "The Yale Liberal," writer Stephen Adams dropped such bombshells as Dr. Leslie's endorsement of a 2000 declaration calling for religious communities to endorse same-sex marriages. The declaration, Adams continued, "was the creation of Dr. Debra W. Haffner. Abstinence education leaders recognize Haffner as the former chief executive officer of their biggest foe—the Sexuality Information and Education Counsel of the United States, which is the nation's most aggressive, and successful, promoter of anything-goes sex education in American schools."

That anything-goes attitude seemed to have leaked into Adams's coverage of the controversy as well, reaching beyond guilt by association to identify those intent on "eliminating all expressions of faith in the American military" as "a Yale Divinity School professor who's protested the military and a newspaper in the Air Force Academy's hometown that was more than willing to report the Yale professor's allegations."

No-so-veiled references to Dr. Leslie's antiwar activities and Pam Zubeck's reportage at the *Gazette* notwithstanding, the most intriguing element of Focus on the Family's coverage came in an interview with Lieutenant Katie Veseth, a former cadet, who maintained that indeed "a strong Christian environment permeates the Academy. But the neat thing about it," she added, "is that such environment is cadet-initiated." She went on to recall memories of "Spirit Hill," an on-campus locale where students gather for nightly prayer. "These kinds of action are not forced in the least bit by officers," she insisted, before allowing, "We might have gone a little overboard on talking about Christ rather than acting like Christ."

"The intolerance came from the officers, not the cadets," Dr. Leslie retorts flatly. "Pointing out that there were fervent Christians among the cadets is beside the point. They would have been in no position to enforce their views without being encouraged and facilitated by the Academy staff and administration. By the same token, the efforts of Focus on the Family to malign me for my associations had nothing to do with the issue. Their intent from the beginning was to discredit the report."

"The fact that the report originated from Yale in the first place totally nullified it in evangelical eyes," Weinstein concurs. "To them, the Yale Divinity School is merely a hotbed of hedonism and secular humanism. It's one of the reasons they've created their own educational systems, their own political machinery. It's like a nation within a nation. It's no wonder the recommendations in 'The Yale Report' never saw the light of day. They were deliberately ignored or even hidden by the Academy's power structure."

While Kristen Leslie suffered the slings and arrows of outraged evangelicals, MeLinda Morton was facing the wrath of those who held her future in their hands. "Once Mikey started getting a lot of national media attention, there was an air of panic at the Academy," she recounts. "The evening before the report was released, I got a call from the public affairs office asking if I knew anything about it. I told them I'd helped to write it, but I was a little surprised they were asking me for a copy, since I assumed that Whittington had forwarded the report up the chain. The fact that the superintendent's office did not have the report seemed to indicate that Whittington had never passed it on. They asked me to provide a copy. Trying to be a good executive officer, I said I'd have to clear it with Chaplain Whittington. 'You can do whatever you want,' I remember them saying, 'but you better hurry. By tomorrow this thing is going to be all over the press.' It was around that point that the spinning really began.

The Academy issued a statement characterizing the report as simply a 'data point' in an overall culture-and-climate evaluation. Shortly afterwards, I was approached by Chaplain Whittington, who point-blank asked me to back him up by agreeing that the report was not only insignificant, but erroneous. I refused. That pretty much sealed my fate."

As the crisis ballooned, Morton found herself in the midst of a frantic effort to control and contain the damage. "They appointed an inspector general to look into specific allegations against General Weida, the Academy's commandant of cadets. As far as I was concerned, any thorough investigation would have revealed a full-scale cover-up. Whittington appeared in the press saying that he had polled all the Protestant chaplains and that none of them recalled the events we had referenced in the report. A week afterwards, General Baldwin returned, called a meeting of all the chaplains, and harangued us for forty minutes about how we were one big family that could tolerate no disloyalty in our ranks. The implications were clear enough, but in case they weren't, he went on to tell us that the pastoral care practices questioned in 'The Yale Report' were perfectly acceptable to both himself and the entire Air Force chaplaincy. I remember, at some point, Chaplain Baldwin exchanged a congratulatory high-five with Chaplain Jim Glass, who had written a letter to the editor of the *Gazette* critical of Dr. Leslie. The whole occasion was deeply disheartening. It was clear that this was not just a rogue evangelical element within the Air Force. There were very powerful people, with a lot of institutional Pentagon clout, behind this. I think that was the first time I really understood that change from the inside was going to be impossible."

Chaplain Captain Morton should perhaps have come to this recognition several weeks earlier, when it was peremptorily announced that, after her current tour of duty, she would be transferred to a distant Air Force base on Okinawa. As a staging area for Middle Eastern combat operations, the move increased the likelihood that Morton could be deployed to the war zones of Iraq and Afghanistan. "I had nothing against a remote island in the far reaches of the Pacific," she asserts, "but it did seem to me as if the timing was more than a little suspicious. After everything that had happened around the RSVP program and 'The Yale Report,' I think it was pretty clear to the powers that be what side of the fence I was on."

While Morton says that she "fully expected to be rotated," a duty assignment to the Air Force equivalent of Siberia was not exactly what she was expecting. "I had actually been told that my term at the Academy would be extended," she recounts. "Obviously, someone had pulled the plug on that."

She was, in fact, already circling the drain. "The day after our meeting with Baldwin, I was fired as Chaplain Whittington's executive officer, but instead of telling me face-to-face he informed me by e-mail. I thought that was about as clear a sign as I could have gotten, but I was wrong. Over the next few weeks he refused to give me a new assignment. It was really a very petulant response to what was perceived as a lack of trustworthiness on my part. Since I had, in effect, betrayed the chaplaincy, I was being left to twist in the wind." Perhaps sensing the brewing storm, both General Rosa and Colonel Whittington would shortly announce accelerated dates for their respective retirements.

With the handwriting writ large on the wall, Morton moved quickly, obtaining nationally recognized legal counsel and, taking a cue from Mikey, followed up on a contact with CNN who had previously requested an interview on the developing story. "My only interest at the time was to open up the loop at the Academy to some outside scrutiny," she recounts, "and I knew that, without a knowledge of the very rarefied atmosphere that existed there, a journalist wouldn't know where to begin."

By early May, Morton's interest in "opening up the loop" had prompted a momentous decision. "I had a leave coming up," she says. "I was going to go to New York, but before I left I let the Academy know what I was about to do. There's a regulation that requires anyone who talks to the press to inform their superior officer, so I called Chaplain Phil Guin, who was second-in-command, and told him I was about to go public."

Guin, who had an adopted family of eight special-needs Korean children, pleaded desperately with Morton to back off. "Emotions were running high," she concedes. "My own included. I'd been on call pretty much twenty-four/seven for as long as I could remember. I was exhausted, but I also knew that I'd done some of my finest work and that, as a pastor, I had been fulfilling my calling. Whatever happened from that point on, I could at least take comfort in that fact that, through all the politics and power struggles, I had never involved the cadets. I never traded on my relationship with them. I tried to stay true to myself as a chaplain and an Air Force officer, but mostly as a Christian, with a duty to stand up for the oppressed."

Within the first week of May, Morton had done interviews with *60 Minutes II*, CNN, and *The New York Times*. "They fired me," Morton later told *The Washington Post,* referring to her precipitous removal as Whittington's executive officer. "They thought I should be angry about these outside groups who reported on strident evangelicalism at the Academy. The problem is, I agree with those reports," she says, adding, "I may be toast."

As the story hit national headlines, General Baldwin began frantically calling Morton. "It was evening," she continues. "I talked to my attorney and we agreed that I should call him back at seven-thirty in the morning, at the beginning of the duty day." By then, Baldwin had apparently altered his tactical approach. "Through his office, two conference calls were set up and he backed out of them both. I got the impression events were getting out ahead of them."

Indeed they were. "When I got back to the Academy, I was completely persona non grata," says Morton. "It was a rigorously enforced regimen of silence and isolation. In the meantime, Mikey had clandestinely visited General Rosa at his residence at the Academy, pushing hard to have me appointed to his personal staff to advise on matters. The general's primary concern, of course, was to quiet the press down, and since Mikey was making all the noise, it was in his interest to placate him."

The ensuing meeting underscored the headless-chicken response of the administration in bizarre fashion. "He wanted to have the meeting at his house," she recalls, "which seemed odd on the face of it, especially when he told me that he couldn't have it at his office, since there were too many people who would see me coming and going. I wondered who, specifically, the highest-ranking officer at the school might be afraid would spot us together." Arriving on a rainy afternoon at the superintendent's spacious quarters, Morton was greeted by Rosa's wife. "We had a pleasant conversation, but when Rosa finally showed up, he invited her to sit in on our meeting. Considering that I had every reason to expect a rather contentious encounter, the situation was odd in the extreme. It seemed as if Mrs. Rosa might have been there to elicit sympathy from me, or maybe to just deflect some of the tension."

"You look like hell," was Rosa's opening gambit, followed by a rambling monologue, complaining of the "damned inconvenience" caused by the ongoing brouhaha and Morton's recent press offensive. "He waved around a copy of a regulation forbidding press contacts outside the public affairs office, but then assured me that no one had ever been prosecuted for it." Increasingly erratic, Rosa went on to reassure Morton that her Air Force career might still be "salvageable," if they could come to some accord. "He asked me what I wanted," she says, "and I told him that I could perhaps best be of service by staying at the Academy and helping fix the mess they'd gotten themselves into. At that point I was sort of yanking his chain, just to see where it would get me. I knew better than anyone his sincerest hope was that I would disappear off the face of the earth."

Doing his best to hide his dismay, Rosa promised to get back to Morton. "The fact was," she recalls, "even though I made the offer, I knew that meeting was the last nail in the coffin. A week later I handed in my resignation."

For Weinstein, the face-off in the presence of the undoubtedly bewildered Mrs. Rosa also had an air of finality. "I had also previously met with General Rosa in secret at his quarters as part of a last-ditch attempt to come to some understanding," he asserts. "My bottom-line prerequisite was that MeLinda not only be protected but that she be put in a position of real authority to deal with this horrendous problem. After the two of them had gotten together, he came back to me fully expecting that I would call off the hordes of press hounds. I told him it didn't work that way. Eventually he did offer her a spot on his staff. It was an untitled position that could last as little as a day, depending on the results of an investigation the inspector general had launched on the troubling circumstances behind her transfer to Okinawa. It was all too little, too late. She'd made up her mind and I fully supported her. What a travesty! If the Academy could produce graduates with half as much selfless integrity, loyalty, and character as MeLinda Morton, this nation could have avoided much of the turmoil that surrounds this unconstitutional issue and this institution, this bloody, dangerous impact upon our nation's entire armed forces."

Morton's resignation only added more fuel to the fire of the metastasizing controversy. "I was fired," she told the press matter-of-factly, and before long her words were echoed in the halls of Capitol Hill. "So here we have not just a refusal to deal with inappropriate abuse of people on religious grounds," thundered Representative Barney Frank of Massachusetts, "but punishment of a very brave officer, a woman of integrity, a chaplain, a member of the clergy, who in pursuance of her faith and her obligations and her understanding of the Constitution refused to say something that she thought untrue about the report." It wouldn't be the last time Congress weighed in on the issue.

With Morton on her way out, Weinstein considered the last channel of conciliation with the Air Force to have irrevocably been closed. "MeLinda was an absolutely superb officer who genuinely cared about the cadets whose spiritual well-being she was charged with nourishing. I know that as long was she was in uniform, she never stopped trying her best to find a way to effect real change within the power structure. If the Academy and, to a larger extent, the Air Force itself had given her the opportunity, availed themselves of her commitment and expertise, and given her real clout, we wouldn't be anywhere near where we are today. But the fact is, MeLinda Morton didn't meet the evangelical criteria for what a Christian should be. And that made her, de facto, the enemy."

Even as Morton began taking stock of the shattered remnants of her Air Force career, Weinstein was absorbed in recruiting new allies for the next stage of his all-out assault on an evangelical entrenchment at the Academy and beyond, the strength of which he was only now beginning to fully assess. "MeLinda's experience was a wake-up call," he reveals. "It was clear to me that I was going to need all the help I could get."

Back during *The Passion* flare-up in February of 2004, Weinstein had contacted Americans United for Separation of Church and State, the Washington-based advocacy organization founded in 1947 and in recent years headed up by Church of Christ minister Barry Lynn. Celebrating, according to its mission statement, "the rich religious diversity of the United States" and seeking a nation where "all people may peacefully pursue the truth as their consciences dictate," AU, with its considerable legal resources, would have been a natural partner in Weinstein's cause.

"Initially, I couldn't get arrested there," he admits ruefully. "I'd called them about what was happening with Gibson's film at the Academy, and I got put on hold a lot. Eventually they put me through to what seemed like a law clerk, very earnest but completely ineffectual. I finally just gave up and pushed on by myself."

Things changed markedly after Weinstein reached higher-ups at Americans United and was able to spend some time outlining the scope and abuses at the Academy. "We deal with an enormous volume of inquiries," says Richard Katskee, assistant legal director for the organization, by way of explanation. "Often we're dealing with two dozen calls a week, all from people who have witnessed or experienced religious encroachment in government at every level. We're obliged to investigate every incident to determine what action to take, and often it's nothing more than a letter to a school board or mayor's office whose city hall lawn might have a religious display. Other times it's more significant. Because of the workload and the fact that we're obliged to look into every claim and complaint, we pick our battles very carefully."

Among those battles: evolution vs. creationism and the impact of faith-based initiatives on constitutional establishment clauses. "But what was happening at the Academy was in a special category," Katskee claims. "Because the military is, by nature, a coercive environment, a necessarily separate set of rules applies. Government employees simply don't have the same rights and privileges as private citizens. They have to meet a wholly different standard."

The failure to meet that standard became increasingly clear to Americans United as Weinstein made his media rounds. "*The Passion* was one thing," Katskee explains, "but our view was that this was happening primarily among the cadets. What we discovered when we took a closer look was that the message coming directly from much of the command-structure teaching staff and administration was that the right religious attitude, or at least the willingness to go along with the prevailing evangelical consensus, was a key to success, the path to power. We encountered the same mind-set, in fact, at West Point and Annapolis, although, for some reason, not at the Coast Guard Academy."

AU had gone out of its way to reconnect with Weinstein and made its resources available in a coordinated effort to address the issue at the highest levels. Carrying its investigation forward, it encountered an early iteration of the legal argument that evangelicals would later make the centerpiece of their counterattack. "The contention was that proselytizing and conversion were central tenets of their faith and, therefore, to inhibit those activities was to impinge on the freedom of religion. They never seemed to understand that the military was an institution whose command and control structure could not support such activities, and, because they never got it, none of the solutions they proposed were effective."

But Katskee goes further, albeit gingerly. "I can't say there was an intentional strategy on the part of evangelicals at the Academy to capture the hearts and minds of those who would then go off and fight their holy wars, although it's not an exaggeration to point out that Colorado Springs is not just the epicenter of Christian fundamentalism, but for wealthy, well-organized, and politically powerful groups who have made no secret of their agenda. It's also a fact that there was no better place to inculcate a belief system than a place where young men and women are being systematically stripped down and rebuilt, with a special emphasis given to their belief system. It's also a fact that those who came out of the military often went on to assume leadership roles in civilian life. These individuals would be useful to any organization with a sense of worldwide mission."

Weinstein, of course, was on a death-march mission of his own, one that would be aided considerably by the legal team at Americans United, who undertook an independent investigation, largely assisted by Weinstein, beginning shortly after *The New York Times* story in February. "We followed up every lead we were given, and Weinstein gave us a lot to go on" Katskee continues. "The deeper we dug, the more we uncovered." By mid-April, modifying their letter-writing approach to suit the gravity of the circumstances and working closely with Weinstein, Katskee, aided by his staff of four attorneys and a pair of overworked clerks, began putting together an extensive report, which, before the month was out, would land on the desks of Secretary of Defense Donald Rumsfeld, acting Air Force Secretary Michael L. Dominguez, Generals Rosa and Weida, and others at the Academy and the Pentagon.

A concise recapitulation of virtually all of the evidence and testimony gathered by Weinstein, Zubeck, Morton Leslie, and others over the previous year, the "Report of Americans United for Separation of Church and State on Religious Coercion and Endorsement of Religion at the United States Air Force Academy," nevertheless ran to fourteen single-spaced pages. Citing the "egregious, systemic and legally actionable violations of the Establishment Clause of the First Amendment," the report was laden with legal citations comprising a pocket history of the relentless battle to maintain the separation of church and state, from a ruling that forbade public hospital chaplains from proselytizing patients, to an injunction against a school board ending its meeting with a prayer in the name of Jesus, to a constitutional finding that no public official can take any action that "has the purpose or effect of endorsing religion."

A damning indictment, all the more compelling for its tight legal reasoning, the report stacked one court decision after another up against extensive documentation of the Academy's slack enforcement of the Constitution it had been created to protect, support, and defend. It repeatedly called attention to the "open, notorious and pervasive nature of the violations." The list included a program attended by senior Academy officials that identified "secularism and pluralism" as a specific threat to "the followers of Jesus" conducted astonishingly in seminar rooms contiguous to RSVP classes where "secularism and pluralism" were being taught as foundational tenets of required military religious tolerance. It also brought to light a bizarre system of code words initiated by General Weida to motivate and activate evangelical cadets. "At a Protestant chapel service during Basic Cadet training," the report revealed, "General Weida told the attendees the New Testament parable of the house built on rock—a metaphor for building faith on the firm foundation of Jesus. General Weida then instructed the cadets that, whenever he used the phrase 'Airpower!' they should respond with the phrase 'Rock, Sir!' thus evoking the parable. General Weida advised the cadets that, when asked by their classmates about the meaning of the call and response, the cadets should use the opportunity to discuss their Christian faith."

"It was very gratifying, and at the same time very painful and sobering, to see everything laid out in one document," Weinstein remembers. "For the first time, I think, I really had a way to grasp the enormity of what was going on. The weight of the evidence, and the legal precedent, were unassailable. It was clear the Academy and the Air Force were going to actually have to do something. The question was, what?"

☆ 12 ☆

THE BRADY REPORT

The correct answer to Weinstein's rhetorical query would have been obvious to anyone who has ever encountered a massive bureaucracy with its back against the wall; within three days after the Americans United report became public, the Air Force announced the formation of a blue-ribbon "task force" to look into the allegations and quell the furor.

"You got the impression they were going to refight D-day," says Weinstein. "A task force evokes the image of a swarming, around-the-clock hive of eager staffers, ferreting through mountains of evidence, single-mindedly dedicated to getting to the bottom of the snafu, no matter how much it costs or how long it takes. But this was an organization at odds with itself: there was a cabal within the command structure intent on undermining whatever steps might be taken to bring about change. By the time this doomed attempt actually saw the light of day, it had gone from high-profile task-force status to a lowly briefing from a headquarters review group, charged with nothing more, they insisted, than evaluating the climate at the Academy, just as it would any other Air Force installation."

Major General Baldwin announced the inquiry with some fanfare on May 5, even as he was excoriating MeLinda Morton and other Academy chaplains for challenging the status quo. Spearheading the effort would be Lieutenant General Roger Brady, deputy chief of staff, manpower and personnel, for the Air Force, under whose purview the problem ostensibly lay. Entering the service in 1969 through the University of Oklahoma's ROTC program, Brady had served in Desert Storm as director of operations, Air Mobility Command, providing support in a raft of operations including Noble Eagle, Enduring Freedom, and Iraqi Freedom. Himself an experienced pilot, Brady had logged more than three thousand hours flying everything from T-37 "Tweets" to the C-5 behemoth.

Navigating through the choppy skies of the fast-expanding Academy crisis would require an entirely different skill set, however, one that depended heavily on the perception of total impartiality. "What everyone conveniently forgot to mention," says Weinstein, "was that Brady was a born-again Christian. I only found out when he let it slip to one of the key contacts that I had insisted he talk to. It was typical of the ineptitude with which the Air Force approached the whole question of religious bias in its ranks. In one fell swoop, by putting Brady in charge, they destroyed the credibility of the task force, or the headquarters review or whatever they were calling it that week. They had put a born-again Christian in charge of investigating the degree to which born-again Christians were allegedly violating the Constitution at the Academy. Didn't anyone pick up even the mere appearance of a conflict of interest or related impropriety? Of course, in a perfect world, it wouldn't matter what religion Brady or anyone else was. But it was clear enough that the Academy was far from a perfect world."

Despite the obvious bungling out of the starting gate, the Air Force made a conspicuous show of serious intent. "At the core of our airman ethos is respect," declared acting Air Force Secretary Michael Dominguez at a briefing on the eve of the report's release. "Respect is what enables us to do our job defending freedom. Instances of disrespect, no matter how unintentional or limited . . . are incompatible with what we do for this nation."

"Unintentional" and "limited." These words would come to comprise the leitmotif of the Brady report (see Appendix), which, Dominguez went on, "shows our challenges are more about improving sensitivity to the needs of all groups, and less about intentional discrimination."

"It was all bullshit," Weinstein bluntly asserts, "a combination of 'boys will be boys' and 'kids say the darnedest things.' It called upon all senior members of the Academy to behave in a noncoercive, sensitive, and reasonable manner. Let me tell you something. It's impossible to be noncoercive, sensitive, and reasonable in a typical military context. The whole system is designed to instill complete obedience no matter how big an asshole your superior officer might be. It's like claiming that a male prison guard can have consensual sex with a female prisoner. That's simply not possible. If you put on a uniform, you are, de facto, putting yourself under a rigorous, often unforgiving command structure."

Notwithstanding the cognitive dissonance generated by a branch of the armed services desperately embracing the kinder and gentler vocabulary of political correctness, the Brady report made a virtue of its scope and diversity. There was much ado about the twenty-seven focus groups and sixty-nine individual interviews, including a private face-to-face meeting between General Brady and Curtis, who refused to name those involved in the anti-Semitic incidents whom the Academy might well have wanted to scapegoat. "To me, it would have been a betrayal of one of the most basic tenet of the cadet code," Weinstein insists. "Loyalty." Conducted by a sixteen-member panel, both civilian and military, and including representatives from the Navy, which was shortly to face its own religious tempest, the investigation went immediately wide of the mark. "We did interviews with several people who were not at the Academy when we were," Brady blithely assured the press corps. "These included Chaplain MeLinda Morton; Dr. Kristen Leslie of the Yale Divinity School; and Mr. Mikey Weinstein, a 1977 graduate of the Air Force Academy who has expressed considerable concern."

The remark displayed General Brady's hitherto unknown flair for irony. "We were the last people they talked to," Weinstein fumes, "and we should have been the first. They only had a brief perfunctory phone conversation with Dr. Leslie, and they talked to MeLinda Morton literally an hour before the report was closed. As they were putting together their whitewash, I was getting word from my sources about just how far they were absolutely *not* prepared to go. I suggested in a press interview that their vaunted investigation of the evangelical choke hold on the Academy was the equivalent of setting up lawn chairs and sipping mint juleps. It was only then, after I made a stink about their methods in the electronic and print media, that they finally contacted me, MeLinda, and Kristen just to cover their asses. It was as if they suddenly realized they had some boxes they'd forgotten to check off."

During the final stages of the inquiry, Weinstein began to field none-too-subtle hints of the impeding report's hidden agenda. "I got a call from the token Jew on the team," he recounts, "a rabbi who they'd shipped over from Korea. He suggested to me they were doing a terrific job all things considered, and that perhaps I would like to dial down the invective."

Not a chance. "They were scared shitless," Weinstein insists. "The whole reason they'd launched this pathetic probe in the first place was to get me and others off their backs. They weren't interested in fixing the problem. They just wanted it to go away." Proof of the assertion would be underscored by an e-mail sent to 4,200-plus students on May 31, 2005, the day before Academy commencement ceremonies, by cadet wing commander Nicholas Jurewisc, which featured twenty-two attachments rife with religious references, including thirty-eight separate evocations of the Almighty, seven Old Testament and nine New Testament quotes, along with smattering of truisms from, among others, Mother Teresa, Muhammad Ali, and Marcus Aurelius. "The more things change . . . ," Weinstein observed, letting the back end of the aphorism dangle. The administration, by now pathologically gun-shy, issued a statement a week later describing the e-mail as "appropriate according to Academy regulations."

But evangelical impetus, once under way, proved difficult to stop or even slow. "I think their real attitude toward the issues we were raising," Weinstein asserts, "was reflected in the fact that, while they were ramping up their charm offensive, Johnny 'Jesus Rocks' Weida was being publicly put up for a second star. You can imagine the chilling effect that had on anyone considering stepping forward to Brady's crew with information about evangelical pressure tactics at the Academy." In any event, Weida was, at least temporarily, passed over for the promotion, a stinging career setback for which Weinstein and his crew took some of the credit. "I hit the roof when that intended promotion was announced," he says, "and by that time, the press was keeping a pretty good running tally of my grievances. I expressed shock and horror and they quoted me accordingly."

Weinstein's knack for generating ink was in this case enhanced, at least nominally, by a new ally that had belatedly rallied to his battle cry. "I had contacted the Anti-Defamation League in Denver in the aftermath of Curtis's revelations," Weinstein recalls, "and they ambled down to the Academy a few months later. After taking a look around, they announced that General Rosa was doing the best job he could under difficult circumstances and that we should all be patient and wait for the wheels of justice to turn." That attitude was in marked contrast to that of the ADL New Mexico office, which, according to Weinstein, had been "a strong, creative, and robust ally from the beginning."

Yet, by and large, the ADL, which had in recent years come under attack for its accommodationist stance on a variety of issues, took a wait-and-see attitude toward Weinstein's allegations, an approach that infuriated him. "This was right up their alley," he avers. "But I think they'd gotten a little too cozy with the people they were supposed to be scrutinizing. I spent a lot of time on the phone trying to coax them into action, and it wasn't until the end of the year that they finally came out with a general statement expressing grave concern about the power of the religious right. It was definitely half a loaf."

The venerable Jewish antidiscrimination association—founded in 1913 in part to end "ridicule of any sect or body of citizens"—had, however, stepped forward with Weinstein to condemn Weida's proposed promotion. At the same time—in what turned out to be an even more significant development—the ADL would provide General Rosa with a platform to directly address the crisis at the Academy. The results would send the whole controversy spinning off into an entirely new dimension.

On June 3, speaking to the executive committee of the league at a meeting in Broomfield, Colorado, just north of Denver, Rosa at last owned up to the actual dimensions of the conflict raging within the Academy's well-secured perimeters. "As a commander," he told the group, "I know I have problems in my cadet wing. I have issues with my staff and I have issues in my faculty—and that's my whole organization. It keeps me awake at night." He went on to reveal that he had admonished General Weida for his National Prayer Day e-mail missive before making the day's most jaw-dropping admission, acknowledging that "if everything goes well, it's probably going to take six years to fix it." Presumably referring to "fixing" evangelical entrenchment at the Academy, the job was one that Rosa would conveniently pass along to his successor. Even as Abe Foxman, the ADL national director, reported that he had "walked away with the feeling that the man is committed to solving the problem," Rosa was on the verge of accepting the presidency of South Carolina's legendary military college, The Citadel.

"My response to Rosa's statement at the time was that it was too little, too late," Weinstein says. "But the truth was, it broke the whole story wide-open. Here, for the first time, was the most senior commander and administrative officer at the school not only admitting, at long last, that there actually *was* a problem, but that it was one so deepseated, so systemic, that it was going to take more than a half decade to fix. It was a watershed moment." In the wake of Rosa's bombshell, Weinstein publicly called for a change of leadership at the Academy. "That was before I knew he was on his way to the Citadel," he says. "I guess ultimately I got what I was after, but I found it very peculiar that Rosa would deliver this unvarnished appraisal a little more than two weeks before it was officially announced that he was leaving the Academy. He always insisted that he took the job because his wife, who was recovering from cancer, wanted 'to be closer to her family back East.' I respect that, but the timing was certainly opportune for him, as well. In the end, I think of him as a sort of tragic figure, caught up in something that he couldn't control or contain, but that he knew was destroying the institution he had been called to lead."

Rosa would later tell Pam Zubeck at the *Gazette* that one of the conditions he laid down for accepting The Citadel's offer was that he could stay at the Academy long enough to complete the "unfinished business." "That would be my druthers," he said, before providing himself with a tried-and-true excuse to anyone familiar with the buck-passing bureaucratic tendencies in the military: "But the Air Force makes that decision."

Rosa did, in fact, stay long enough to usher in the vaunted Brady report, billed at the time as the Air Force's comprehensive response to any and all religious inequities at the Academy. Yet, as exhaustive as the report might have been—running to a hundred pages, with numerous attachments and addenda, including a handy glossary of Air Force acronyms—it seemed intended, to a significant degree, to placate and gain the approval of a single unstinting critic: Mikey Weinstein.

"Shortly before the report's official release, Brady flew out from Washington and came to my house," Weinstein remarks. "He showed up with his entourage in an Air Force staff car from Kirtland and gave me his best hail-fellow-well-met tap dance. I asked him if he'd like something to drink, and he suggested a mint julep. It was downhill from there." Whether to mend fences or to establish due diligence, Brady's visit quickly ran aground on the general's insistence that, among other issues, Johnny Weida's and Chaplain Major Watties's antics, which had been at the center of so much of the recently concluded investigation, did not constitute a breach of existing Air Force regulations or constitutional provisions. "I replied that they certainly did," Weinstein recounts, "and we traded chapter and verse until it became clear that we were getting nowhere."

Not long afterward, Rosa himself made an appearance at Weinstein's front door, an aide in tow, to present a freshly printed copy of the Brady report, twenty-four hours before its very public release. "I thanked him," Weinstein remembers, "but it was pretty awkward. I think he half-expected me to sit down, read through the whole thing, and sign off on it then and there. So I kind of glanced through it and almost immediately a passage from page eleven jumped out at me like a tarantula on a wedding cake."

The paragraph in question referred to the campfire excoriations of Chaplain Watties, identified only as "an ordained minister endorsed by the International Church of the Foursquare Gospel, an Evangelical, Pentecostal denomination." Referring to the after-action memorandum of the Yale team following their Basic Cadet Training observations in the summer of 2004, the Brady report singled out three incidents in Watties's watch that were "considered inappropriate": the chanting of "This is our chapel and the Lord is our God"; the cajoling of his Christian cadets to witness to "unsaved" cadets; and, of course, the lurid "burning eternally in the fires of hell" warning, which Watties subsequently denied. "While these comments," the report intoned, "if they were made, may be considered offensive or unnecessarily strident by some, they are not uncommon expressions of Foursquare Gospel doctrine."

"'What about this, John?'" Weinstein remembers asking Rosa. "'What's this shit?' He kind of shook his head sadly and said that it was deeply troubling to him, as well. I took that as the first cue that the report wasn't going to be all they'd advertised."

The meeting ended in terse pleasantries at the front-door porch, with Rosa lamely bemoaning the insubordination and intransigence of some of those within the bureaucracy he headed. At that point, Bonnie Weinstein, who had been listening silently, finally snapped. "I know only too well that the military is a vertically encrusted hierarchy," she recounts, "and that all of Rosa's excuses were just a way to avoid taking responsibility. So, since no one was stating the obvious, I told him myself that, in my humble opinion, this whole situation was completely and utterly his fault. He was a hundred percent to blame. 'You have a total of six stars on your shoulders, John,' I said to him. 'If you tell someone to do something, they will do it. This whole thing could have been cleared up with a simple and direct order from you. But you never gave that order and that's a failure of leadership.'" As Rosa and his aide stood aghast, she turned on her heels to attend to the day's chores.

Visits from ranking general officers were not the only attempts made by the Academy to placate their adversary. In a bizarre turn, Weinstein would receive a pair of personal notes, one on official Academy letterhead, directly from General Weida. "The bizarre and incredibly condescending thing was that they were both written out solely in Hebrew," Weinstein explains. "I don't read Hebrew, but it was obvious that Weida saw me primarily as an obstinate Jew and must have assumed that all us Jews can read the mother tongue. I immediately placed a call back to him and suggested he tell me what he wanted to say in English. I even copied both notes and hand-wrote my own replies to him in English and had them overnighted to him. I never got a reply, in any language, and later found out that he had recruited the personal services of the Academy's rabbi to work out these transliterations. I finally got it decoded by sending the notes to Dr. Leslie at Yale, who passed them on to some of her Yale Divinity School biblical-scholar colleagues. The upshot was Weida asking if, after all, we couldn't just get along."

In addition to such blatant pandering, the evasions, equivocations, and, most egregiously, the blame-shifting to cadets had kicked into high gear by the height of the sizzling southwestern summer. "There's an ongoing challenge of dealing with eighteen-to-twenty-two-year-olds and making sure they understand the values of our Air Force," Brady would tell reporters at the same press conference heralding the release of the report that bore his name, "most notably respect for the beliefs of others. . . . They come from very different backgrounds in terms of their experience with diversity. . . . Most of them know how to behave. Some of them need a little work. And sometimes behavior, in a pretty hot pressure-cooker environment of the Academy, results in some behavior that's not consistent with our Air Force. In those kinds of situations, you'll have the occasional religious slur, disparaging remark, and we jump all over that."

There was indeed a lot of jumping going on as the Air Force seemed to be hopping from one extreme to the other, alternately admitting a systemic problem that would take years to fix and then dismissing it as the overexuberance of a few excited cadets. Even aside from Brady's apparent confusion over whom the Air Force actually belonged to, in the end the report generated considerably more heat than light. In an interesting side note, Brady had had a long-standing connection to Weinstein's family within the small circle of ranking brass, with Mikey and Bonnie's brother-in-law (also an Academy graduate) working directly for the general in a prior Air Force assignment.

"It is not a whitewash, but it does resemble a milquetoast," opined New York representative Steve Israel on the subject of Brady's hemming and hawing. "There needs to be new leadership at the Air Force Academy." More and more elected officials had, in fact, begun elbowing their way into the center ring of the media circus.

For others, leadership at the Academy was just fine the way it was, thank you very much. Responding to Brady's reassurances that "there's nothing malicious going on, but that doesn't mean it's not inappropriate," Focus on the Family's ubiquitous Tom Minnery thundered, "They have taken the First Amendment . . . and beaten the Academy over the head with it." But it wasn't the Academy's fate that earned his most righteous indignation. That was reserved for the clear and present danger to his coreligionists. "It's now improper, illegal, and unethical to try and convert someone from one faith to another," Minnery agonized. "That goes to the heart of evangelism. We will never, never submit to that as Christians." Evoking the specter of sniveling soldiers and civilizational collapse, he went on to claim, "People who are in harm's way will quail before the rigors of battle if they do not have spiritual sustenance, and if we tell them that it's not appropriate to engage in spirituality, we're doomed."

Doomed as well, virtually from the moment it rolled off the presses, was the Brady report itself. At its core was a series of vague recommendations couched in vintage military bureaucratese, including "improve cross-flow of information," "reemphasize policy guidance," and "integrate the requirements for cultural awareness and respect across the learning continuum." The gist of all the double-talk seemed to be that the problem, having been kicked upstairs largely due to the brief forwarded to Defense Secretary Rumsfeld by Weinstein and Americans United, would promptly be kicked right back down by the Brady report, laying the blame primarily on cadets whose "overly aggressive expressions of their faith . . . created an impression of insensitivity regarding the beliefs of others."

Meanwhile, the comprehensive military command structure—specifically the Pentagon's Department of Defense, Air Force HQ, and the Academy itself—had, according to the report, "provided appropriate policy regarding the importance of non-discrimination and a climate of respect." "Inherent in military service is the very real potential that individuals may be asked to forfeit their lives in defense of the nation," wrote Brady in a stirring peroration that curiously echoed Tom Minnery's doomsday scenario. ". . . The ability to withstand the privations of military service and face the prospect of death in the performance of their duties requires strength of character that is founded upon their religious faith. It is their source of strength in times of trial."

"They say there's no atheists in foxholes," Weinstein counters. "Maybe that's true, but what if there were? Is it the assumption of Brady and others that such an individual wouldn't make a good solider because of what he believes or doesn't believe? Would he cut and run without a higher power stiffening his backbone? If that's the case, and if that's really the conviction of those who send our young men and women off to fight and die, than I guess the next step in building a better warrior is mandatory religious conversion." He pauses. "It all sounds a little too eerily familiar. Suicide bombers. Jihadists. A martyr's death. The promise of paradise. Isn't that the language of our enemy?"

☆ 13 ☆

"WE RESERVE THE RIGHT
TO EVANGELIZE THE UNCHURCHED"

By June of 2005, events surrounding the Academy's religious turmoil had reached critical mass. On the seventeenth of the month, two weeks after Rosa's speech to the Anti-Defamation League, a group of nine Muslim cadets came forward with their own allegations of rampant discrimination, centered around the school's intense curriculum, affording no time for Friday-night prayers at Colorado Springs' only mosque.

Four days later, the long-awaited inspector general's investigation released a preliminary finding that all but fully exonerated General Weida. Based upon unstated "applicable standards," the inquiry found that "the evidence does not indicate wrongdoing or misconduct" on the part of the Academy's unofficial inquisitor.

On June 23, an editorial appeared in *The New York Times* under the heading "Obfuscating Intolerance," charging the Brady report with "going on for page and page describing obvious and overt religious bias. But it tosses all these off as 'perceived bias,' as if the blame lies with the victims and not the offenders, and throws up a fog of implausible excuses, like 'a lack of awareness of what is impermissible behavior by military officers.'"

Five days later, the House Armed Services Committee held a hearing ostensibly to look into the religious climate at the Academy. Presided over by New York Republican John McHugh, chairman of the Military Personnel Subcommittee and known in his district as the "Champion of Dairy Farmers," the summer-afternoon session was a desultory fishing expedition that epitomized the glazed eyes and glacial response of much of the legislative branch to the issue. Pontificating politicians on both sides of the aisle lined up to hold their fingers firmly to the wind. Representative Lois Capps, a California Democrat, had, for example, forthrightly demanded an investigation into General Weida's misdeeds, signing, along with forty-six other congressional members, a letter demanding "quick action," and then releasing it to the Associated Press, all in a single news cycle. Wisconsin's David Obey, ranking Democrat on the House Appropriations Committee, trumped Capps with an amendment stipulating a thorough report in two months' time on "inappropriate proselytizing" at the Academy and, for good measure, requiring the Air Force to explain the peremptory dismissal of MeLinda Morton while they were at it.

Obey was later involved in a testy exchange with Indiana Republican John Hostettler, a staunch Baptist who also sat in on the hearings, after Obey lambasted the Academy on the floor of the House for "coercive and abusive religious proselytizing." "Like moths to a flame," Hostettler bellowed back, "Democrats can't help themselves when it comes to denigrating and demonizing Christians." He later retracted the remarks, while Obey's amendment went down to defeat—both outcomes a dazzling victory for political business as usual.

Meanwhile, Texas Republican Kay Granger fretted in a letter to colleagues about "the long-term impact this excessively negative publicity will have on those bright, energetic young people from all over America who are dedicating themselves to the service of our nation." Just getting warmed up, she went on to defend the Academy against any and all perfidious slanderers. "Let me state this clearly—," she wrote, poking a metaphoric finger in their chests, "I have never seen an institution face its problems more courageously, examine itself more carefully and set goals to achieve change more clearly that the USAFA. . . . The Academy is a national jewel. . . . It deserves our support and praise; not our criticism."

In what was likewise steadily gaining credence through sheer repetition, Colorado Republican Joel Hefley, whose Fifth Congressional District included the Academy, took up Minnery's mantra of the need for a spiritually fortified military with his complaint that the Air Force was, after all, "trying to build characters in young Americans here." Religious faith, he maintained, "is the kind of thing that drives people many times to make sacrifices you wouldn't make otherwise. You jump on a live grenade so it won't kill your buddy."

It was clear enough that no elected official was prepared to fall on a grenade to save the hallowed principles of the First Amendment. "I gave up on both parties pretty early," Weinstein sighs. "I realized that, with Republicans, it was always about man exploiting man, and with the Democrats, it's just the other way around." As a half-serious jest it underlines his impatience with bureaucracies of any stripe. "It was simply more trouble than it was worth trying to make something actually happen in Washington."

The subcommittee similarly expired on a gust of humid June air. A mildly absurdist aura pervaded Room 2118 of the Rayburn Office Building where the committee had gathered a paltry collection of expert witnesses, including Dr. Kristen Leslie, General Roger Brady, and retired colonel Jack D. Williamson, a chaplain from the Evangelical Friends Church. Williamson had conducted yet another investigation at the Academy earlier in the month, this time at the behest of the National Conference on Ministry to the Armed Forces, which had its musty antecedents in the War Department's 1901 decision to require ecclesiastical endorsement for its clergy.

Williamson had spent all of a day and a half with his team at the school and was at the hearing to reassure the committee that "well-reasoned and balanced solutions will require continued insightful leadership, openness, and respect by all who live and work at this premier institution."

"The three of us had been chosen because we had all written reports," Dr. Leslie remembers. "I was the academic, Brady was the spin doctor, and Williamson was the yes-man."

The sonorous drone continued through the long afternoon, with Brady trotting out the now familiar party line that religious disrespect was "a problem among the cadets" and reassuring representatives that, while sectarian prayers were not against current Academy rules, neither were they necessarily "appropriate." Dr. Leslie briefly kicked the proceedings into gear by asserting her concern with chaplains who didn't appear to know the distinction between evangelism and "good spiritual care" and suggesting the need for guidelines to spell out the difference. This prompted Texas Republican Michael Conaway to protest that such guidelines might end up being "anti-Christian." "I'm a Christian and Jesus Christ is my personal savior," he announced to no one's particular surprise. The blustering Hostettler piled on with his own profession of faith. "I'm a believer in Jesus Christ," he informed Dr. Leslie, adding with withering scorn, "I'm sorry if that offends you."

"What offended me was the fact that we were supposed to be contributing anything substantive to the debate in this forum," the Yale professor recounts. "Neither MeLinda Morton nor Mikey Weinstein had been called to testify, and those of us who had been were allowed a five-minute opening statement, followed by five minutes from the committee members. Even at that, we had to break halfway through for a vote. The whole thing was a travesty."

In an unexpected twist to the committee's rigorous rubber-stamping of the Academy's official version, Colonel Williamson surprisingly stepped out of line to assert the opinion of his team that "efforts to remedy the sexual assault scandal may have contributed to the current issue." When asked to explain himself forthwith, the soft-spoken chaplain cited findings that "some faculty and staff had expressed the opinion that student behavioral problems were viewed as moral deficiencies that could be corrected only with religious—primarily evangelical Christian—moral values."

The implications of this unexpectedly incisive observation passed unremarked as the hearing mercifully concluded on a call by the committee for Academy leaders to "further define appropriate religious behaviors tolerant of all denominations." With that, the mighty ship of state was docked for the duration.

What politicians were unable or unwilling to address was, on the other hand, tackled with alacrity by the national press. The story, in journalistic jargon, had legs, and those legs carried it to the front page of *The New York Times,* which followed up its editorial dressing-down of June 23 with an in-depth story on July 12 by national-desk reporter Laurie Goodstein. Headlined "Evangelicals Are a Growing Force in the Military Chaplain Corps," the piece would, like Rosa's admission, become yet another key pivot in the unfolding drama.

The piece opened with a vivid description of a four-day Spiritual Fitness Conference held at the Colorado Springs Hilton, organized and underwritten by the Air Force to the tune of $300,000. Attended by virtually the entire chaplaincy and their families, the event featured contemporary Christian praise music, workshops on megachurch pastor Rick Warren's megasuccessful *Purpose Driven Life* program, and a lobby full of merchandise booths from Focus on the Family and other fundamentalist heavy hitters. It was, wrote Goodstein, "just one indication of the extent to which evangelical Christians have become a growing force in the Air Force chaplaincy corps."

It was hardly news to Weinstein, but he nonetheless recognized the official *New York Times* imprimatur as a major step forward for his cause. Yet there was more to the story than simply an overdue stamp of legitimization. There, among a welter of facts and figures delineating the explosive growth of evangelical chaplains, was an stunning one-sentence declaration of intractable intent from Brigadier General Cecil R. Richardson, the Air Force deputy chief of chaplains. With the tight smile and wire-rim spectacles of a Midwestern insurance adjuster, Richardson had earned a degree in biblical studies at Evangel University in Springfield, Missouri, and his master's at Trinity Evangelical Divinity School in Deerfield, Illinois, before joining the Air Force and becoming the Protestant chaplain at Little Rock Air Force Base in Arkansas. Throughout the eighties, the chaplaincy corps shuttled him from Alaska to Washington, D.C., to the Iráklion Air Station in Greece, all the while moving him steadily up the promotion ladder. By the early nineties he had assumed the post of chief of the Education and Professional Development Division of the Air Mobility Command chaplaincy and, on making brigadier general in the summer of 2004, was charged with assisting the chief of the Chaplain Service in training and equipping more than two-thousand active-duty, guard, and reserve chaplains.

A member of the Assemblies of God denomination, Richardson garnered attention in the aftermath of the 9/11 attack on the Pentagon when he observed, "The most common part of our job is answering the question that many of these people are asking. They want to know 'Why?' . . . What we are trying to help people understand is that God created people with free will, and what we are seeing now are the results of the abuse of that free will. God is good, He loves them, and He wants to bring peace to them."

It was that sense of supreme confidence, of knowing and being able to articulate God's will even in the midst of an unfathomable national trauma, that undergirded his position of extraordinary influence at the very hub of the Air Force chaplaincy. And with that same unclouded assurance in the face of the roiling controversy that had engulfed the Academy, Richardson declaimed on the right of the Air Force's spiritual comptrollers to fulfill their divine mission in any was they saw fit. "We will not proselytize," he told Goodstein in an interview, "but we reserve the right to evangelize the unchurched."

"It was an absolutely astonishing statement on the face of it," Weinstein contends. "It said nothing and everything at the same time. To distinguish proselytizing from evangelizing is of course to create the ultimate distinction without a difference. Richardson went on to say that proselytizing is trying to convert someone in an aggressive way, while evangelizing is more gently sharing the Gospel. That is patently absurd. Both explicitly express the same active intent to convert, aggressively, gently, or to any other degree in between. According to the dictionary, to *proselytize* is to 'convert or attempt to convert.' One of the synonyms for *convert* is *proselytize*. And around and around we go. Then there's the ominous implication of the term *unchurched*. Which church is he seeking to unconnect its members from? Are Catholics 'unchurched?' Are Orthodox Christians 'unchurched'? After all, ever since the Reformation, every branch of Christianity has been at war with every other branch over which is the One True Church. Is an individual who doesn't speak in tongues, hasn't been slain in the spirit, or doesn't believe that God created the heavens and earth in seven days and nights by definition 'unchurched'?"

A few paragraphs earlier in the *Times* piece, Weinstein goes on to point out, a former Marine is quoted as saying that half of the eight chaplains he came in contact with during his military career told him his Mormon faith was "wicked" or "satanic." "Do Mormons qualify as 'unchurched'?" Weinstein asked. "And, of course, the status of Jews, Muslims, Buddhists, and Hindus is only too ominously clear, despite whatever prior attachment they might have to their faith tradition."

Weinstein's parsing of the declaration extended even to the word *we,* designating without naming those who reserve the right to evangelize. "Who are these mysterious *we?*" he wonders. "Given the level of authority from which Richardson speaks, it's only reasonable to assume that it applies to all members of the Air Force. Maybe that's just a paranoid supposition on my part, but if so, its given a lot of added weight by the fact that no one in the Air Force, or, for that matter, the Department of Defense, ever stepped forward to refute even the most tacit nuance of the general's boldly defiant claim."

The plain fact was that Richardson, with his statement in a front-page story in the nation's "newspaper of record," had drawn a defiant line in the sand, negating once and for all any pretext that evangelicals within the military were going to give up without a tenacious fight to retain and expand their turf. His statement quickly became the money quote of the story, widely republished in the days that followed and representing for Weinstein a challenge that simply couldn't be ignored. As July rolled into August, he launched a rubble-bouncing attack through his extensive network of TV, radio, and print media contacts, firing off steady rounds of releases, editorials, and letters, all pitched in the most passionate and provocative key, making full use of his gift for vivid image and lurid metaphor. "To make this astonishingly shameful statement," he wrote in a press release calling for President Bush to summarily fire Defense Secretary Rumsfeld, "constitutes a despicable, blood libel of our nation's revered Constitutional Bill of Rights." In a commentary headlined "Religious Freedom Has Gone AWOL in the Air Force," he compared the military to "the proverbial canary in the mine shaft" when it came to the right of religious freedom. "Sadly, the Air Force continues to allow this canary to asphyxiate in the toxic air of religious intolerance." Elsewhere he would liken "a military chaplain's role" to "a universal blood donor. That means the chaplain is there to serve the religious and humanitarian needs of all those in uniform and their families regardless of their belief systems."

Weinstein says, "Look, I know I'm perceived as a loose cannon by the religious right. Maybe I *am* a loose cannon. I see what's going on and I get angry, really angry, and I give expression to that anger in the most colorful and immediate terms at my disposal. That's who I am, take it or leave it, and, believe me, I've been told many times by many people that, for the good of my cause, I should step aside and let someone more measured and tactful and dignified take charge. Maybe I should, but first they will have to prove to me that what we're engaged in is a polite exchange of views instead of a bloody battle that only ends with the last person standing. We've long since forfeited the right to civil disagreement. Someone's going to win and someone's going to lose, and I don't want to be on the losing side knowing that I didn't use every last diatribe and embellishment and wild-eyed, hair-on-fire, foaming-at-the-mouth harangue to get my point across. There's too much at stake. As Gore Vidal says, 'Perhaps we should rename this country the United States of Amnesia.' We've seen this train leave the station innumerable times before, whenever radicalized religion has engaged the military. And it always goes in the same direction: Slaughterville. We do not get little ponds or puddles of blood. We get oceans of it. Pee-Wee Herman can't fight this constitutional battle. What's required now is Attila the Hun."

Weinstein smiles. "Besides, I've always loved a good fight."

✴ 14 ✴

AWKWARD, UNEASY, ALIENATED

With almost daily national and even international news coverage, the storm engulfing the armed forces and Weinstein had become a lightning rod for an increasingly vitriolic debate. "Let's rock," he would taunt Ted Haggard during the Christmas e-mail flap, and the religious right took up the challenge with a vengeance. "There was a lot a hate mail," Weinstein reveals, "and even anonymous phone-call death threats late at night. We had our tires slashed in our driveway and other 'colorful' displays of hatred and threats I'm not going to elaborate on. When it would get really bad we would notify the U.S. attorney for New Mexico. We were obviously touching a raw nerve."

"This country's founding fathers created this country with Christianity in mind!" read one typically outraged letter from "A Proud Christian and American," addressed to Pam Zubeck at *The Colorado Springs Gazette*. "If you chose to fight for America and get paid by America then you must accept her founding fathers beliefs . . . If you don't respect the USA, her founding fathers and its Christian beliefs you are free to leave the USA anytime . . . the door is open!"

"What was incredible to me was the simple ignorance," Weinstein comments. "Thomas Jefferson wrote a version of the gospel with all the miraculous events stripped from Jesus' life. Benjamin Franklin occasionally attended meetings of an occultic brotherhood called the Hellfire Club. But it was more than just a reductive historical memory that was at work here. It was the equating of Christianity with Americanism, as if the two were inextricably bound in some kind of divine millennial master plan. And then, of course, there was the constant implication that if you didn't like the country's prevailing religious consensus, or if it didn't like you, you were invited to leave. Where have I heard that before?"

Yet behind all the rhetorical excess ignited by the controversy, real people were confronting the real consequences of the Academy's high-handed policies, benign neglect, and, in its own military jargon, "slowrolling."

"As time passed I was increasingly contacted by people who wanted me to help them, lead them, or, more often than not, just listen to them," says Weinstein. "What I quickly came to see was that what, to many, was a constitutional abstraction, or just a fine point of religious doctrine, was a cause of real anguish and anger to those who had confronted it directly."

One of those who had experienced the coercive consequences of evangelical pressure tactics within a military command structure was Weinstein's own daughter-in-law, his oldest son Casey's new wife and a high-achieving 2004 Academy graduate (and classmate of Casey's) in her own right. Born Amanda Baranek in San Diego, she had moved with her family to Colorado Springs at age ten and, eight years later, after completing a sterling high school scholastic and athletic career, received a hard-earned U.S. senatorial appointment from Colorado, which, as the home of the Academy, is by far the most competitive state awarding the coveted slots. Amanda's tenure at the Academy was marked by conspicuous attainment. In her senior year, she was a cadet lieutenant colonel, outranking Casey, and was on the second group staff as an honor officer, overseeing adjudication of the honor code for a quarter of the entire cadet wing.

"When I was in the seventh grade I got really interested in math and science," recounts the forthright and vivacious twenty-four-year-old. "I also wanted to fly, and a friend of the family who was a liaison officer at the Academy encouraged me to apply. I think at the time what I really wanted was just to do something different, something exciting, and later on, even after I took an incentive ride as a cadet in an F-16 and found out I actually hated flying, I was still drawn to the Academy and the Air Force."

In the late summer of 2003, the beginning of her first-class (senior) year, Amanda met Casey in the Academy gym when he attempted to fix a broken television she had been watching while exercising in the work-out room. "It ended up kind of falling on him," Amanda remembers with a laugh, "but he was very gallant about it and ended up asking me for my instant-message screen name." The two would go on their first date shortly thereafter, with a visit to a Saturday-night service at New Life Church.

"My parents were kind of hippies," Amanda continues, "and they had experienced a spiritual encounter and were born-again before they had me. I don't know if I ever truly understood what their experience had been, and when they talked about having a personal relationship with Jesus I always felt a bit leery about the terminology, the way it was de- scribed. I couldn't exactly make the connection, but I've always thought of faith as a kind of pyramid that can be viewed from many different an- gles, and Christianity is the view I had been taught and accepted." As much as for the social interaction and a chance to get off base as for any conscious spiritual benefit, Amanda had regularly attended the youth- oriented Saturday services at New Life over the previous six months. "I enjoyed it," she explains. "It was very casual, with a lot of music and a relaxed atmosphere. At the time, I didn't perceive an attempt to push re- ligion, and a lot of cadets came there just to unwind. I thought it might be a good way to help Casey to get to know me, to introduce him to an important part of who I was and where I'd come from."

As the two young cadets continued their courtship, their conversa- tions would often turn to matters of faith. "We talked hypothetically about how we'd bring our kids up," Amanda continues, "and we made a point of learning as much as we could about each other's religion. I at- tended Jewish holiday services with him and he'd come with me to a church in Colorado Springs that I'd also been attending. I can't say we ever intended for one or the other of us to change. It was all about respecting each other for who we were, not for what we might become."

The couple would also attend occasional Monday night SPIRE classes together. The venerable Special Programs in Religious Education (SPIRE)—in place since the early eighties, coinciding with the arrival of many evangelical organizations in Colorado Springs—sponsored forums by churches and other religious outreaches, including Fellowship of Christian Athletes, Baptist Student Union, Navigators, Youth with a Mission, and Officer's Christian Fellowship, along with the Hillel Jewish organization, Latter-day Saints, Buddhist Studies, and others. "We went to some Bible studies," Amanda remembers. "Casey mostly just listened and I really appreciated him making the effort."

But the learning curve went both ways. Amanda says, "When *The Passion* came out, we went to see it together and Casey got very offended by various aspects of the movie." Objecting especially to Gibson's allegorical depictions of children as gleeful demons relishing the crucifixion and the crowd scenes of angry Hebrews, the film, says Amanda, "opened my eyes for the first time to how a Jewish person might perceive things differently from what I was used to. I would never have guessed it was anti-Semitic, it just didn't occur to me; but Casey took the time to show me how it looked from his perspective and, in the end, I could totally understand his point of view. I think that was a turning point for me, a moment when I saw the world as someone else might see it."

As Easter 2004 approached, the campus was inundated with promotions for an upcoming holiday extravaganza mounted by New Life. "It was called *The Thorn*," Amanda recounts, "and it was a big production, like a Christian Cirque de Soleil or something, with angels and devils swinging on trapezes. My SPIRE leaders had gotten free tickets and given me a pair, so I invited Casey."

In the meantime, Amanda was scheduled for a regular monthly meeting with the Academy commandant of cadets, General Weida. "It was part of my duties as a cadet group honor officer," she explains. "We got together to brief the commandant on upcoming honor cases." Arriving early for the appointment, she took a seat in the conference room and opened an inspirational Christian book she had been reading. "I don't re-member the name," she says, "but when General Weida came in he com-mented that he had read the same book and gotten a lot out of it."

It would have been only natural for any cadet to feel pleased to have made such a connection, however slight, with a senior Academy officer, a general no less. Amanda was no different. "It's hard to overstate how much authority and respect someone like the commandant had in our eyes," she says. "You could really live or die by a kind or critical word from him. There was always that striving to meet with approval, to get noticed and make an impression."

After a moment exchanging pleasantries, the general and Amanda were joined by Weida's executive officer, and talk turned immediately to the upcoming production of *The Thorn,* in which the executive officer was to play an Apostle.

"General Weida asked me if I was going to the program," Amanda continues, "and I told him that I was. They both seemed very pleased, and then the general told me to be sure and invite as many non-Christian cadets as possible."

A long silence ensued. "I felt weird," Amanda relates. "It was like the air suddenly got sucked out of the room. I kind of thought to myself what business was it of theirs *whom* I invited or why, and at the same time I couldn't help but wonder if this wasn't some kind of test. If I did invite every nonbeliever I knew, would I be getting extra credit from the general? And what if I didn't? Would he be disappointed? Or angry? It wasn't just awkward; it was confusing. The fact that I had, in fact, in-vited Casey suddenly seemed kind of hypocritical. By bringing him to church and Bible studies, the only thing I'd ever wanted was for him to know more about me and about what I believed. Suddenly, it seemed as if maybe I had some—or should have had some—ulterior motive, that sharing my life was really just a tool to convert him. I remember leaving that meeting doubting General Weida and, even worse, doubt-ing myself."

Too self-assured to entertain doubts about her motivations for long, Amanda would eventually accept Casey's proposal of marriage, even as she fought off her own mother's biblically derived objections to being "unequally yoked." "Sometimes," Amanda muses, "religion seems like nothing more than a way to drive a wedge between people. I'm not saying that I can't help Casey to grow spiritually and vice versa. But what happened that day in General Weida's office was like being part of some surreptitious scheme to rope my fiancé into believing what I believed. I wasn't even sure that what I believed was the same thing the general did. After that, we decided once and for all that, no matter what our differences, we would make up our own minds and follow our own path, regardless of who was trying to push us to make a life-changing decision."

The young couple's resolution reflected, as much as anything, a palpable distance that had emerged among a new generation of cadets between the military-career prospects offered by the Academy and its status as a top-drawer educational institution. "Neither one of us was looking to necessarily spend our lives in the Air Force," Casey maintains. "We were happy and honored to be able to serve our country, but there was a lot we wanted to do that we could never accomplish solely as careerists in the armed services. For us, it was a great opportunity, but we didn't feel like we had to buy into everything they were trying to sell. Whether or not we ever finally met with the approval of our commanding officers was less important than the tremendous value of a diploma from the Academy and of the years we would spend on active duty. That's just how we felt about it."

IT WASN'T A FEELING SHARED BY MANY OF THOSE WHO HAD PRECEDED them through the rigors and rewards of an Academy education, such as retired Colonel David Antoon, a 1970 graduate who would spend twenty-nine years as an Air Force pilot, doing two tours of duty in Vietnam and eventually overseeing test-flight programs at Wright-Patterson in Dayton, Ohio, where he and his wife, Linda, raised a daughter and three sons. Easygoing, bushy-browed, and of no particular religious persuasion, Antoon was typical of the sixties cadet caste who saw in the Academy and the Air Force a life's fulfillment. "It felt like you had been selected for a special destiny," he recounts. "We were an elite. We knew because they told us we were every day. It created a bond, to the Academy and to each other, a shared experience that set us apart and gave us an expectation of great things to come. Just the fact that you were a pilot, flying a C-130, gave you an enormous sense of accomplishment. The fact that they would entrust you with this incredibly sophisticated and expensive piece of equipment, not to mention the lives of your crew, was a responsibility that you rarely found in civilian life. We were proud of who we were and what we were asked to do."

Sharing that sense of pride and purpose was Antoon's eldest son, Ryan. "It was his dream to be an Air Force pilot from the time he saw his dad come home in a flight suit," Antoon asserts. "I took him flying for the first time when he was fourteen, and he soloed on his sixteenth birthday and had his pilot's license before he had his driver's license."

With a proud Air Force birthright, Ryan naturally gravitated to the Academy, which he visited frequently during his high school years. "They have a sports camp, which is a great recruiting tool," Antoon explains. "Ryan went every summer for five straight years. At six feet four with these long arms and a strong competitive streak, he's a natural athlete. Aside from playing hockey, basketball, and tennis, he's a technical rock climber and has had over two hundred skydiving jumps. He also attended the school's science camp, which is also very tough to get into. When it came time to go to college, he didn't try to get in anywhere else. It was only through the haranguing of his mother and me that he finally applied to Ohio State as a backup."

Receiving a coveted appointment in March of 2004, Ryan Antoon was invited back to the Academy for an initial orientation session about two months prior to beginning the harrowing rigors of Beast. "He'd already been so many times, I really didn't see the point," his father continues. "But he insisted, so we went out together."

The introduction to incoming cadets was conducted by General Weida, and at the end of a ninety-minute briefing, Antoon, whose life, in most important ways, had taken shape and direction at the Academy, knew there was something terribly wrong at his alma mater. "The whole thing set my teeth on edge," he recalls. "Weida must have used the term *warrior* dozens of times. It was a message very different from the one we had received as cadets. Back then, the emphasis was on leadership and the mission was clearly to train leaders. The intent wasn't just to produce good officers for the Air Force. The implication, based on the history of so many of its graduates, was that, when you went to the Academy, you were being equipped with the skills to be a leader in whatever field you might eventually choose. We weren't there just to learn the art of war. We were there to learn the arts of motivating and guiding and inspiring. That, in itself, was inspirational, and here that cherished idea was being replaced with all this saber-rattling rhetoric about the fierce determination and single-minded devotion and square-jawed, hard-assed swagger of some archetypal conqueror."

It's a page that could well have been lifted from Bobby Welch's play-book, *You the Warrior Leader,* where the distinction between both roles was radically conflated. "Victories in war are not won by parlor games in board rooms," Welch proclaims. "They are not won by those who remain well-dressed and manicured. This is blood-and-guts, dirt-and-mud warfare—low-crawling from trench to trench, house-to-house, person-to-person—all for the purpose of rescuing the perishing and caring for the dying. If Christians refuse to equip and train to be victorious war fighters, their friends, family members, and the world around them will continue to be dragged off to hell by the enemy."

The metaphorical flourishes aside, Welch's warrior leader was very much in the mold Weida had cast for the cadets from the first day of their introduction to the Academy and its stated goals. "It made my skin crawl," Antoon admits. "It would be hard to exaggerate just how diametrically opposed his language and attitude were to the values that had been instilled in us thirty-odd years ago. Sure, we understood that we were soldiers and that we would be trained to fight and, if necessary, even kill in the line of duty. But we were also taught to accept that responsibility soberly and with humility. It was something we accepted, not exalted. There was a civilizing aspect to what we had undertaken to accomplish at the Academy. Even at the height of Vietnam, with all its moral uncertainty, we could be proud of the peaceful intent, as individuals, we believed was the real purpose behind our preparedness. Somehow that had all been transformed into a kind of holy bloodlust."

While the bloodlust came though loud and clear in Weida's welcome, the holiness would come later, during a follow-up session in the Cadet Chapel. "Listen," Antoon continues, "I remember what it was like. When I went to the Academy there were five hundred more of us in the cadet wing than there are now: we were the so-called Vietnam hump. Back then, there were two Catholic priests, two Protestant ministers, and a rabbi for the whole cadet wing. For the most part, these were gray-haired pastoral types, right out of central casting. Now, suddenly, there were twelve strapping young evangelical chaplains, along with a lone Lutheran, one Catholic, and a rabbi."

In the event, the nonevangelical contingent of the chaplaincy corps had not been called on to attend the Cadet Chapel orientation segment. "Later, when I got to know Air Force Academy chaplain MeLinda Morton," Antoon relates, "I asked her where she had been that day. She said she was up in the balcony, watching, because she hadn't been asked to participate."

Instead, the incoming cadets and their families were greeted by a phalanx of enthusiastic pastors, standing shoulder to shoulder at the altar, as Chaplain Watties took his position at the pulpit. "It was monolithic," says Antoon, "and a little fascistic. Watties was talking about how there were Bible studies every Monday night at the Academy, half the cadet wing attended, and that they were working hard to get the other half as well. I later found out that the studies were being taught by members of the New Life Church and Focus on the Family who were bused in weekly. Everything Watties said was punctuated by hallelujahs and amens from the front line. I started putting it together with all the talk I'd heard about the warrior ethos that morning, and it finally dawned on me that the whole school had somehow become a giant Trojan horse for evangelicals to get inside the military. The whole thing was an exercise in brainwashing, and I literally shuddered to think what would happen to my son in this environment, especially given the high hopes and expectations he was bringing with him."

"It was a tent revival" is MeLinda Morton's terse description of the event. "And I guess I was a little surprised at David's strong reaction when we finally talked about it. I had gotten so used to these strident displays I was a bit numbed to it all. At the time I was much more upset about a baccalaureate ceremony I had attended in which Colonel Sill, then the chief of chaplains, had seen fit to preach a sermon against the ACLU for filing suit in some homosexual-discrimination case. That was the kind of thing that it took to get through to me anymore."

In between the morning session and the Cadet Chapel's lunchtime congregation, Antoon had been given other reasons to feel uneasy about the state of Academy affairs. "We were treated to a PowerPoint presentation by Colonel Deborah Gray," he recalls. "It was very extensive, even though it covered only a single subject: exactly how they were determined to prosecute to the fullest extent any suggestion of sexual harassment. What shocked me about it was the presumption of guilt rested entirely on the male cadets. I totally understood the need to create an environment that would allow young women to step forward if they had been compromised in any way. But this was total overkill, and, in point of fact, at the same time a nineteen-year-old cadet named Doug was actually facing a possible life sentence for what was widely acknowledged to be consensual sex with a female cadet. He lived under that shadow for a full year before he cut a deal and was allowed to leave the Air Force. It all seemed like so much overkill, and I couldn't help but wonder that, if they had gone such an extreme in this situation, what else was out of whack?" It was Weinstein's thirteenth-stroke theory all over again.

What was now completely out of whack was Ryan's confident expectation that the Academy would fulfill his lofty expectations. "We had been put into separate groups during the day," Antoon recounts, "and when we got back together again, we talked about what had happened. He had attended another orientation lecture from Weida with some cadets in attendance. They were standing in formation with their hands at their sides, but he noticed them counting off something on their fingers, and when he asked them later what'd they'd been doing, they told him they were toting up the number of times the general said the word *warrior.* He thought it was kind of funny. I don't think the whole evangelical thing bothered him nearly as much as the heavy emphasis they put on sexual harassment, but either way I could tell that things hadn't turned out exactly as he expected."

Antoon now faced what he calls "the most difficult decision I ever had to make as a parent. . . . I knew he relied on me, and the last thing I wanted to do was influence whatever choice he would make because of this feeling of dread I had. But the truth was, the Air Force Academy wasn't the same place it was when I had gone there. I felt obligated to tell him that, if he wanted my opinion based solely on what I had seen and experienced in that one day, it would be not to go. It may seem strange, considering how much the Academy had meant in my own life, and I have to admit that one of my foremost considerations would be the anxiety that I would go through knowing my son was being subjected to that kind of indoctrination. I felt guilty about that, but I didn't see any other option. In the end I told him that I would support him no matter what decision he made, but I knew that he was shaken by my response."

Seeking clarity on the sea change at the Academy, Antoon next contacted the Association of Graduates. "They told me that they don't get involved in policy issues," he says. "Right around that time, the first articles from Pam Zubeck started coming out in *The Colorado Springs Gazette*. When I read about what had happened with Watties's antics at Basic Cadet Training, I felt a little better about my honesty with my son. He would have been one of those who were singled out for 'burning in the fires of hell' if he didn't get right with Jesus."

As the time drew near for Ryan to inform the Academy of his decision to attend, Antoon could see that his son was struggling with the overwhelming consequences of his choice. "His mother and I spent a lot of time talking with him about his future," Antoon remembers. "It wasn't just the four years in college. It was everything after that. I tried to express to him the idea that while people who graduate from the Academy often go on to do great things, the qualities of character and ambition have to be there to begin with. He was going to accomplish what he set out to do, regardless. But I'm not sure he believed me."

The night before the acceptance deadline, Antoon looked out his kitchen window to see his son lying in the driveway, the family dog at his side, staring up into the starry sky. "I can't say I slept very well that night," he confides. "The next day I called the Academy and asked for a week's delay. And at the end of that time, Ryan decided not to go and started at Ohio State that fall. I hope and I believe that he owns that decision, but to this day I sometimes wonder if he doesn't regret it, and if somehow I let my anger and disappointment and concern for my son interfere with his life."

At the same time, Antoon remains utterly convinced that at the Academy, "something is broken." He says, "When this scandal broke wide-open, the cadets were reading the same newspapers and watching the same TV shows that everyone else was. They knew the administration was lying about what was going on there. How does that stack up with the honor code that demands, 'We will not lie, steal, or cheat, nor tolerate among us anyone who does?' I think there's been a lot of toleration in the military and the chickens are coming home to roost. I read about Abu Ghraib and Gitmo and all the 'renditions' and it makes me want to cry. There's a direct line between what's happening at the Academy and a man like General Jerry Boykin, who can be promoted to a high Pentagon post at the same time he's saying like 'Our enemy is a guy named Satan' and 'We in the army of God, in the house of God, kingdom of God, have been raised for such a time as this.' The last time I looked, I wasn't a citizen of the kingdom of God. I was a citizen of the United States of America, and the army was sworn to protect me and my family and my neighbors and not some belief that they'd secretly pledged allegiance to."

STRUGGLE FOR A DAUGHTER'S SOUL

Ryan Antoon's decision not to pursue his lifelong goal of attending the Academy may well have been influenced by his father's profound misgivings. Yet even that influence would pale when set against the distorting reality that had set in at the Academy and demanded agonizing choices.

"He that loveth his father or mother more than me is not worthy of me: and he that loveth a son or daughter more than me is not worthy of me." As one of the New Testament's more provocative statements, this warning by Jesus in Matthew 10:37 may have been merely a rhetorical flourish, reflecting the messiah's demands for total commitment, but at the Academy, in the full flush of its evangelical fervor, it took on an ominous import; all the more so given the school's proficiency in creating what amounted to an alternative family structure for its arriving cadets, with the same loyalties, accountabilities, and hierarchical rankings as any home environment. "Life will not be easy for parents," promised *The Air Force Academy Candidate Book,* "especially when the full impact of what has happened begins to sink in. 'You are losing your child forever,' said a mother from Mississippi. 'The next time you see him he will be a different person. That's when it will hit you. You realize that his childhood is gone forever.'"

Given the heavy evangelical emphasis on family values, it may seem incongruous that the influence of the Academy might conceivably be at odds with the emotional bonds to parents and siblings left behind. Yet the rigorous demands of duty, discipline, and devotion could, and often did, drive a wedge between the two. And those who succumbed to evangelical blandishments in that hothouse environment were, of necessity, forced to make even more wrenching choices.

Such was the case with Alicia Peasley, the eldest of three daughters of Alan and Cecilia Peasley and a cherished member of a devout Lutheran family from the rich farmlands of northern Michigan, outside the small town of Alpena, where the Peasleys had laid down deep and enduring roots.

"We were very active in our community and our church," says Cecilia, whose broad North Country accent and farmwife locutions disguise a keen intelligence and flashing wit. "My girls were in the youth group and the choir, and if we couldn't make it to services on Sunday, we felt there was something missing from the week. We weren't zealots or saints by any means. We knew how to relax and have fun together, and we were certainly capable of getting a little rowdy. But what we believed, we believed with all our hearts, and when we prayed, it was also from the heart."

The Peasleys owned a lush, four-hundred-acre spread where they raised cattle until forced by financial pressures to take outside jobs, Allen as a real estate broker and Cecilia as a nurse practitioner, a course in which she also taught at the local community college in her spare time. But they managed to hang on to the farm, growing hay and keeping horses, and in that idyllic setting Alicia came of age.

"She was a very stubborn child," Cecilia remembers, "very independent and a real tomboy. She loved sports, especially basketball, and had a large circle of friends. I hesitate to say that she was happy and well-adjusted because that's what every parent says when something goes wrong with their child. But the fact is, she was, and I attribute a lot of that to our care and love and the sacrifices we made as parents to make sure she had what she needed to realize her full potential."

That potential had yet to find an outlet by the time Alicia graduated from high school. "She really didn't know what she wanted to do," Cecilia remembers. "She was a top student and a natural athlete, and a former teacher of hers suggested that she might want to give the Academy a try. I wasn't so sure. We're not a military family, and I guess the fact that my first baby was going so far away had something to do with my mixed feelings. I also got a look at the application process and it seemed so daunting, what with the congressional recommendations and all, but I encouraged her to give it try because the school had such an excellent reputation."

Receiving a congressional appointment as a member of the class of '07, Alicia arrived at the Academy in June of 2003. "She wrote us a lot and seemed very excited about where she was and the people she was meeting," her mother continues. "The ambivalence had disappeared, and it sounded like she was thriving. Despite missing her so much, I was happy that she was beginning a new chapter of her life and was proud that she had made the grade at such a prestigious school."

At the same time, Cecilia was alert to any potential problems in the wake of the much publicized sexual harassment scandal. "Of course I was concerned," she confesses. "Alicia was a small-town girl, a long way from home. She was naïve, as any kid would be at eighteen, and I was very sensitive to changes in her mood when she wrote or called or came home for vacations."

During the Christmas holiday of her first year, Cecilia picked up the initial troubling signs of a change in her daughter. "She'd never had a boyfriend," she says, "and she told us that she'd met a guy at the Academy, another cadet named Craig, who was a strong evangelical Christian. But that's not what bothered me. It was her demeanor. She was distant and removed, not at all like the lively and gregarious girl we'd sent off that summer. I chalked it off to her being involved in a relationship for the first time, but when I asked her about it, it didn't sound like any budding romance I'd ever heard of. She said they spent a lot of time talking over his faith, very serious talks about the purpose of their lives and God's calling; things that I never knew she'd ever really thought about before. At the same time, I couldn't help but wonder why these two young people couldn't just go on a date, out to a movie, hiking in the mountains, or something that was just fun, plain and simple. Instead, it was like they were preparing for eternity or something. It was a little unsettling, all this religious preoccupation." In another twist of irony, Alicia's putative boyfriend was, in fact, the son of one of Mikey Weinstein's classmates, one he had known quite well—still another indication of how "small-world" the Academy's alumni really was.

After the winter break, the Peasleys next saw their daughter over the Labor Day Parents' Weekend nine months later. "In the interim we'd get occasional letters from her," Cecilia explains. "She'd also forward us e-mail, mostly things that, from the look of them, had been circulated around the campus and were biblical or inspirational in nature. I tried to tell myself that I was happy she'd found something to be passionate about, that she and Craig were praying and studying the Bible instead of drinking and smoking and having sex, but I couldn't really convince myself."

Convincing herself became even more difficult during the visit. Cecilia says, "She took us up to a beautiful home in the mountains where she attended a Bible study taught by an older couple. They seemed nice and I remember being very impressed by a whole gallery of pictures they had of cadets who had attended these studies over the years, literally hundreds of kids, and it was clear that Alicia was quite taken by these people. This couple let the cadets use their house and sometimes even their cars and would often drive down the mountain to pick them up at the Academy and take them back for the studies. I sat down with the woman for a chat, in the course of which she told me, in a sweet and caring way, that Alicia was a little bit too much of a tomboy and that her goal was to get her to wear a dress for the next social occasion. I remember thinking that it was great that my daughter had found someone who could be a substitute mother while she was away from home, but deep down inside I was asking myself, 'Who is this person? What's the link between her and Alicia, and why does it make me so uncomfortable?' Maybe it was just maternal jealousy, but I couldn't shake the feeling."

Cecilia would later hear that Alicia's new spiritual guides were acolytes of the doctrinaire fundamentalist Shepherding Movement, which placed a premium on more experienced members "shepherding" and directing every aspect of a newcomer's life, occasionally even dictating marriage partners. Founded in Fort Lauderdale, Florida, in the early seventies, the movement, led by a charismatic preacher named Bob Mumford, taught discipleship through "delegated authorities" who communicated God's messages directly and became the young believer's "covering," or protection.

"To all outward appearances they were a strong extended family," Cecilia asserts. "I think that sense of security is what drew Alicia in. As far as I'm concerned, they hooked her in with kindness and caring and then stole her soul."

On a subsequent school break, Alicia went to visit her devout boyfriend's Texas home instead of returning to Alpena. "When I saw her again," recalls Cecilia, "all she could talk about was how wonderful and perfect his parents were and how his mother had stayed home and raised children and kept everything spotless and clean. Here I was, a typical harried working mom, whose house wasn't always neat as a pin, and I was hurt by the comparison. Later we had an argument when she saw me and my husband have a glass of wine. She accused of us being drunk and threw some Bible verses at us. I was furious, but I also realized for the first time that she was actually embarrassed by her parents. I'm not really a very rigid person, not controlling, but she acted as if I was immoral and permissive. We weren't living up to some set of standards that she was now applying to everyone around her. And it seemed as if none of us really measured up."

Among those excluded from Alicia's ever-tightening circle were her oldest and dearest friends. "There were so many people she had been close to growing up, childhood friends who used to come to the farm and camp out under the stars with Alicia and her sisters. And now, when she was home, she never wanted to see them. They would call and she'd refuse to answer the phone. I remember distinctly when there was a party in town and she'd been invited. She turned it down, complaining that all her friends drank. I'm sure they did; a beer or two, like most kids these days do. Maybe I *was* too lenient, but I remember what it was like when I was growing up and trying to find my way in the world. Alicia seemed to have stopped asking questions, stopped being curious, as if everything was already settled and she had all the answers and couldn't tolerate anyone who didn't."

Early in 2004, the Peasleys returned to Colorado Springs, this time to be on hand to celebrate Alicia's nineteenth birthday. "I picked up on a lot of signs," continues Cecilia. "Whereas before she had stuck up snapshots in her mirror of her friends back home, now they were all gone, replaced by a picture of Jesus. I'd given her vitamins because she seemed pale and thin, and when I saw no improvement, I asked her if she was still taking them. She said she'd thrown them away because God would provide her with what she needed. One Sunday she took us to New Life Church. It was very impressive, I must admit, nothing at all like our little Lutheran congregation in Alpena, and the people were very warm and welcoming. But on the way back from the service, riding in the car with Craig, Alicia suddenly announced that she was going to be baptized. I was thunderstruck, and I guess in my shock I may have blamed him. 'She's already baptized, Craig,' I told him, 'and she's a died-in-the-wool Lutheran to boot.' They both minimized the whole thing, saying the baptism was just a way of recommitting to their beliefs, but by that time alarm bells were going off in my mind."

Those bells grew more clamorous in the aftermath of the Peasleys' visit to their increasingly estranged daughter. "It was March Madness," Cecilia remembers, "and Michigan State had made the finals. We were all thrilled and I called up Alicia, who had been a basketball fan forever, to share the excitement. It wasn't the fact that she didn't even know the play-offs were happening that frightened me the most: it was the flat, emotionless way she talked. I honestly didn't know what to say to her; it was as if I wasn't even talking to my own daughter, and I was just about to hang up when she told me she had something she needed to tell me. I braced myself, but nothing could really have prepared me for when she said that she was going to drop out of the Academy and become a missionary. My heart sank and there was a long silence on the line. I remember desperately thinking it must just be a phase she was going through. I didn't tell my husband what she was planning to do. It seemed as if my sharing it with him would make it more real. I was hoping against hope that it would all just pass."

It didn't. Cecilia subsequently discovered that her daughter had quit the Academy rugby team, and when she confronted her daughter about the peremptory move, she was informed that Alicia didn't want to be "unequally yoked" to her teammates, a reference to 2 Corinthians 6:14, in which Paul exhorts Christians, "Be ye not unequally yoked together with unbelievers: for what fellowship hath righteousness with unrighteousness? And what communion hath light with darkness?"

"I told her that maybe the team was the right place to be," Cecilia continues, "that maybe she could lead by the example of her life. That's when she told me that this older woman, who taught the Bible study class, had said that rough sports like rugby weren't part of God's plan for her life. At that point I was wondering just who the hell this woman thought she was, but I swallowed my tongue and instead reminded Alicia of what we called the Peasley Rule. Because we're not rich people, we couldn't afford to support our daughters' every whim. What they chose to pursue, they had to be serious about, whether it was in sports, education, or a career. Once they'd made up their minds, we were behind them a hundred percent. But they had to stick with it."

For Alicia, the Peasley Rule had clearly been superseded, and her mother began to entertain dark suspicions about what had replaced it. "Her rugby coach was Jewish," she reveals, "and they had been so close that, when his wife died of cancer, he had asked Alicia to be a pallbearer. I didn't have any evidence to back it up, but the thought kept sneaking in that maybe Alicia had quit the team because the coach didn't have the right faith."

In the ensuing weeks, a grim struggle ensued between mother and daughter over the cost and consequences of Alicia's newfound faith. "Sometimes she'd just break down on the phone and start crying," recounts Cecilia. "She talked about what a failure she was and how she couldn't live up to her ideals. I ask her if they really were her ideals to begin with, and whether or not Craig was pressuring her to become somebody she wasn't. I'd urge her to tell her boyfriend that she needed some space, and at one point she actually approached him about it. He told her that it was all or nothing, and that instead of questioning whether they should be together, she should be asking herself if she really belonged at the Academy. When I heard that, I started wondering whether women were really welcomed there or not. Maybe there was another message being sent, about knowing your place and being submissive and obedient and demure, like the Bible study woman and

Craig's mother. I was sick at heart and angry and scared, so I called her commanding officer."

Her conversation with her daughter's air officer commanding (AOC) did nothing to quell her misgivings and, in fact, ushered in a host of new concerns. "Despite the fact that I was obviously at my wit's end, he didn't seem especially surprised to be hearing from me," says Cecilia. "It was as if he had been expecting the call. I told him what was going on and that she'd announced she was considering leaving the Academy, and even that didn't rattle him much. I got a little carried away, demanding to know how such an intelligent and lively young woman could suddenly just decide to give up a first-rate education and become a missionary. 'She says she wants to carry the cross of Christ,' I told him, and he said to me, 'Well, Mrs. Peasley, maybe you just have to accept the fact that some people are called by God to carry the cross of Christ.' That didn't sit very well with me considering that this was a man in charge of the well-being of my daughter, and I told him so. I wanted to know why he wasn't doing more to keep Alicia from making a huge mistake with her future and, while he was at it, explain to me how they could allow outside influences to have free access to cadets. This was before I heard that half a dozen girls had already dropped out of the Academy at the urging of this couple and the Shepherding Movement."

It was also before she discovered that—at the same time as her anguished phone call to Alicia's AOC—an active investigation into evangelical influence at the school was in full swing. "He knew that," she insists. "He must have. Yet, he never once suggested that the problem was anything other than in my imagination. Believe me, there were times when I thought it *was* just me, that I was going crazy, but when I found out that I wasn't the only one who wanted answers, it just made me madder that they would have kept that from someone who had trusted her most precious possession to their care."

Cecilia's tenuous link to her oldest child continued to deteriorate throughout the fall of 2005. "She'd been awarded a twenty-five-hundred-dollar grant from the State of Michigan to help with her expenses," Cecilia remembers, "and we found out she had given it all away, along with some of money we'd been sending, to the missionary organization as a down payment on the eight-thousand-dollar training program—they required you to pay your own way through the program. It was right around then that I was talking to my own mother about everything that had happened, and she told me that I still had two daughters left, as if Alicia had died and it was time for me to write her off. Then a very close friend of mine actually did die, and as I was driving back from the funeral, I started crying out, saying that if she was in heaven and could hear me, then please send some help. A few days later I got a call from MeLinda Morton. If was as if my prayer had been answered."

Chaplain Morton, who had caught wind of the Michigan mother's anguish, confirmed many of the suspicions Cecilia had formed over the previous months. "Blanks were filled in," Cecilia says, "especially when it came to the Academy's attitude toward women. For all their talk, it seemed as if all they were really interested in was channeling as many bright young women as possible out of the system entirely. I don't know whether it was a reaction to the sexual harassment scandal they'd had, or some ingrained chauvinism, or just the way evangelicals saw the role of women, but the fact that they were simply willing to let Alicia go and become a missionary in some godforsaken place was all the proof I needed that they weren't interested in what she could contribute to the school or to the Air Force."

Under Morton's auspices, Cecilia eventually read the report prepared by Weinstein and Americans United for Separation of Church and State. "Bells started going off," she says. "Some of the same phrases, the same religious language, I'd heard from Alicia were repeated word for word, and I realized that my daughter could well have been present during some of the incidents that were reported. I remembered that she had said that when she was having trouble in basic training because of her asthma, she was told that, if she trusted in the Lord, He would pull her through. Now, I teach nursing, and if I ever told one of my students that, in an emergency, all that was necessary was to trust in God, they'd have my head on a platter and rightly so. But none of that seemed to make any difference to Alicia. Neither did all the anti-Semitic slurs and remarks about how unbelievers would burn in the fires of hell. She didn't deny any of it, and I had to remind her that that just wasn't how we had raised her. 'That's why you're not saved,' she said, and when I asked her if she really believed that all Jews were going to hell, even her rugby coach, all she could say was it was their problem, not hers."

Incensed by what she read in the AU report and encouraged by her fellow Lutheran MeLinda Morton, Cecilia's next call was to the Academy's superintendent, General Rosa. "He treated me like an overwrought mother, and I guess I was," she says. "But the fact was, he couldn't tell me what was happening at his school, right under his nose. He just kept saying to me that she was an adult and could make up her own mind. 'Is that what you tell the soldiers under your command?' I asked him. 'Do you tell them that they're adults and they can make up their own minds about following your orders?' I was one pissed-off mom and I was sick of hearing Alicia saying that God was telling her this, that, and the other thing. It was as if the Academy had allowed this one kind of Christianity to supersede every other value, as if someone was deciding whether we as parents were Christian enough, and, if not, then they had the right to take over our children."

A call to the Peasleys a short time later from General Brady, which Mikey had demanded he make, was prompted by Cecilia's threats to take her complaints to the press. Weinstein, meanwhile, had informed the press of Brady's born-again status, eliciting outraged protests from the general. "He screamed at me over my cell while I was at a baseball game," Weinstein recalls, "demanding to know how I could do such a thing, and I screamed right back excoriating him for having hidden something as relevant and potentially prejudicial."

Even then overseeing the report that would bear his name, Brady's attempt at appeasing Cecilia proved yet another infuriating exercise in condescension. "He dismissed it all by saying that sometimes parents feel powerless when their children don't turn out they way they want," she remembers. "'I beg your pardon, General,'" I said. "'We feel powerless when our children are seduced by religious cults with the consent of people like you, people whose salaries we pay. I sent my child to the Air Force Academy, for crying out loud, not the Branch Davidian compound! I've lost her. What are you going to do about it?'"

Despite the uproar that would follow the revelations of religious coercion at the Academy, Cecilia Peasley's struggle for the soul of her daughter would continue unaided by congressional hearings, front-page exposés, and equivocating reports. "The Academy left the door wide-open for this to happen," she says. "And they left me to pick up the pieces."

Those familial fragments are still scattered. "She came home at the end of her second year and spent the summer harvesting hay with her father, who she's always loved and respected and who represented the neutral figure that I couldn't be. All I could do was surround her with family and the things from her old life that might remind her of what she was leaving behind and hope for the best."

That hope has yet to be fulfilled. "We went out a few times to see her, but the tension was still there between us. She had started hanging out with the Navigators, who, to tell the truth, treated me like a pariah. I guess my reputation preceded me." She smiles, then allows with a sigh, "At least she decided to stay in school. She'll get an education. After that I guess I really will have to step away and let her life take its course. But it's sad. There is so much that's been lost between us, so much real communication that remains off-limits. I don't know if we'll ever be able to recover that."

Despite Cecilia Peasley's well-founded doubts there is, in fact, reason to hope that recovery and reconciliation are still possible. Her daughter Alicia was recently named to the high honor of Squadron Commander for the fall 2006 semester at the Academy, picking as one of her key support staff her classmate, Mikey Weinstein's son Curtis.

☆ 16 ☆

THE SILENCE OF THE BRASS

In the patchwork of American religious experience, the Peasley family drama is among the most common of threads. The child who rejects the faith of her fathers has been a cause of sorrow and estrangement from time immemorial, and in a country where the freedom of worship is a birthright, so, too, is the freedom of sons and daughters to break the hearts of mothers and fathers.

Yet, like Amanda Weinstein and the Antoons, Cecilia and Alicia Peasley played out their drama of faith and betrayal against a backdrop of precisely articulated limits, boundaries, and restrictions intended to rigorously demarcate the rights of citizenship from the cost of protecting those rights. From its inception, the Air Force was charged with safeguarding the enshrined liberties of the nation. To do so effectively, it necessarily had to curtail the liberties of its own members—isolating them from the jostling marketplace of belief and the right to promulgate and promote those beliefs—all in the overriding interest of maintaining the integrity of the mission. Nothing could be allowed to take precedence over that charge, nor to undermine the authority and obedience essential to preserving the focus and objective of its enforcers.

What offended the motherly instinct of Cecilia Peasley was not simply the loss of her daughter to a belief system alien to her own. It was the dereliction that aided and abetted that loss and the collusion of those in high places in the military who disdained the careful construction of church and state separation in the name of a higher calling; a calling that, to fulfill itself, required the premeditated usurpation of personal, political, and, in the final analysis, military power. In Cecilia Peasley's forthright formulation, "These people run the country. If they allowed this to happen at the Air Force Academy, what else was going on that we didn't know about?"

Mikey Weinstein's sense of mission was dramatically heightened by the stories told by the Peasleys and the Antoons and scores of others who looked to him to plead their case and, increasingly, exact retribution. "Of all the people I reached out to during this nightmare, Mikey helped me the most," asserts Cecilia Peasley. "He even personally traveled to see Alicia at the Academy and tried to talk with her. I don't know how much good it may have done but he earned my undying gratitude for at least trying to rescue my daughter."

"It was surreal," Weinstein remembers of his encounter with Alicia. "Trying to keep her from bolting to some backwater mission, I told her that of the billions of Americans who had been born since 1776, only fifteen thousand women had ever graduated from West Point, Annapolis, or the Academy. When that didn't work, I actually resorted to an appeal to her religious sensibilities. I suggested to her that an Academy ring on her finger would single her out as a paragon of virtue and achievement and give her more authority in her call to save souls for Christ. It was like I was doing the evangelicals' work for them!"

As the summer of 2005 wound down, Weinstein's multipronged media campaign increasingly converged on General Cecil Richardson's July 12 statement in *The New York Times*. "By reserving the right to evangelize the unchurched," he remarks, "Richardson had really shown the radical Christian hand. What might have looked like semantic hairsplitting to some was really a line in the sand, a point of no return in the efforts to influence and undermine. For me, it didn't come as much of a surprise.

By that time I fully understood that, in order to call themselves Christians, evangelicals had to proactively seek and win converts. It was in their DNA, irrespective of time, space, and the U.S. Constitution."

In the statement he issued calling for Defense Secretary Rumsfeld's firing, Weinstein went directly to the implications of Richardson's remark to the Bush administration's war on terror: "It is particularly egregious that the current leadership of the Pentagon fails miserably to see the myriad, inherent dangers of establishing a policy of evangelizing its 'unchurched' service members when we are in the midst of a bloody foreign war where our enemy falsely seeks to portray and exploit us, one-dimensionally, as invading Christian crusaders."

In point of fact, that single sentence on the front page of *The New York Times* had become the wedge that Weinstein relentlessly drove between the Pentagon's word-salad evasions and the hidden agenda he had become convinced was orchestrating the evangelical offensive.

"I was constantly asked by everyone whether I truly believed that Richardson was speaking for the Air Force, as a matter of policy, or if he wasn't rather just some kind of rogue operative, way off the reservation," Weinstein recalls. "I don't believe that for a second. The fact is, if he was the Pentagon's version of the village idiot, it would have taken them exactly a nanosecond to set the record straight, especially in light of the hammering they were getting from me in the media. But hours went by, then days, then weeks, then months, and there was still no retraction or clarification or even a statement of support. They just let it hang out there, boggling minds with the operational juxtaposition of the terms *evangelize* and *proselytize*. I know the Air Force and, more importantly, I know the system of accountability and liability on which the command structure lives and dies. Nobody makes a comment—for attribution by a general, especially on the front page of *The New York Times,* for crying out loud—without it being vetted upfront. Look what happened with Jerry Boykin."

Referring to the same deputy undersecretary of defense for intelligence, Lieutenant General William G. "Jerry" Boykin, who had incensed David Antoon and millions of others with his comments that he knew he could defeat a Muslim Somalian warlord because "My God was a real god and his was an idol," Weinstein insists that such incendiary remarks were implicitly sanctioned simply because they were not immediately and unequivocally censured.

According *The Los Angeles Times,* "The issue of officers expressing religious opinions publicly has been a sensitive problem for many years. 'What usually happens,'" a former head of the Army Judge Advocate General's office told the paper, "'is that somebody has a quiet chat with the person.'"

No one, apparently, was having that chat with Boykin. "The truth is," Weinstein asserts, "even after John Warner, the Republican head of the Senate Armed Services Committee, called for Boykin to step aside during a Pentagon 'investigation,' the general was eventually put up for a fourth star. However much of an embarrassment he might have proved to our national interest, not to mention a detriment to our relations with Islamic nations, he's obviously got powerful allies in high places who want his evangelical message comprehensively heard."

Weinstein's message was, however, also being heard, as witnessed during his return visit to the Academy's Graduate Leadership Conference in the last week of July 2005. "It was incredible to think back on everything that had happened in a year's time," he recounts. "I felt like the white elephant in the room, which didn't really bother me. In fact, I made sure to be noticed by wearing, backwards and 'gangsta' style, an NBC *Dateline* cap that Tom Brokaw's production crew had given me when he interviewed the family. I switched that off with one from the Yale Divinity School graciously given to me by Dr. Kristen Leslie. I figured if I was going to attract attention, I might as well make an impression. And I did. One of the attending grads asked me if I was trying to look like a rapper or something, which pleased me to no end."

For all the palpable tension surrounding the event, the deep-seated camaraderie of the graduates ultimately prevailed. "I really didn't want to cause a scene," Weinstein avers. "These were my brothers and sisters, and most of the time I just sat in the back of the room and listened." The amity prevailed, even after Weinstein discovered the inclusion of the letter by Texas Representative Kay Granger written in response to the House hearings that claimed that the charges of religious intolerance had been "blown completely out of proportion." "It was a real provocation," Weinstein insists, "but I let it go. By that time I had bigger

THE SILENCE OF THE BRASS   157

fish to fry, and I even managed to have a civil conversation with Johnny Weida, joking after our visit out to Jack's Valley that I hadn't seen enough overt proselytizing. It was somewhat awkwardly cordial, a time-out in the open warfare."

Battle lines were again joined in early August when Weinstein esca-lated his demand for heads to roll, adding Richardson and acting Air Force Secretary Michael Dominguez to the roster led by Rumsfeld. "We know now that the problem of religious triumphalism extends well be-yond the Academy," he wrote. "Change is needed at the Pentagon as well. Radical Islamists have twisted the purpose of America's Middle East mission by framing the war on terror as a 'cosmic battle' between Christianity and Islam." Three weeks later he launched another salvo, demanding to know why top Pentagon brass had "remained mute" on the controversy and asking, "Is it because they fear upsetting the na-tion's evangelical voters, a core constituency of the current administra-tion? Could it be because they share Richardson's sentiments?"

It was a fair question, considering a situation that had been simmer-ing at the U.S. Naval Academy at Annapolis since mid-2003. The flap began with a challenge by the ACLU over the constitutionality of prayers before midshipmen meals, following up on a decision by the Fourth Circuit Court of Appeals prohibiting a similar practice at the fa-bled Virginia Military Institute. The ACLU's Maryland chapter in-formed the Academy that "mandatory lunchtime prayer cannot pass constitutional muster," a claim the Navy rejected, inciting the usual round of right-wing bluster. If the ACLU isn't stopped, warned Repre-sentative Walter Jones, Republican of North Carolina, they will soon "try to control what prayer is said in the foxhole. I think it's time to fight."

The time, as it turned out, wasn't right for direct confrontation, and not until the glare of national exposure shone on the Air Force Academy did Navy brass, fearing the repercussions of their hard-line stance, re-lent and quietly issue new "instructions" to its chaplains, requiring strictly nonsectarian invocations at official events and drawing a sharp distinction between "divine services" and "command functions," with mandatory attendance being the primary designation of the latter. Even then, Navy Secretary Donald Winter left considerable wiggle room in the new regulations, suggesting, "In command functions, commanders shall determine whether a religious element is appropriate . . . with appropriate advice from a chaplain."

If the chaplain in question was one Lieutenant Gordon Klingenschmitt, the advice was a foregone conclusion. Klingenschmitt, ironically, if not tellingly, a graduate of the Air Force Academy who'd switched services to fill a Navy vacancy, had a long history of coming up hard against pluralistic policy, once claiming, "I don't wear the *P* of Pluralism on my collar, I wear the cross of Jesus Christ."

Front and center on a wave of fundamentalist fulminating following the new regulations, Klingenschmitt claimed that if Navy chaplains "talk about Jesus outside the chapel, we can be punished by our commanding officers with the full authority of the secretary of the navy." In late 2005 he held a press conference in front of the White House, demanding an executive order restoring the practice of prayer according to an individual chaplain's "faith tradition, as the law permits." While the legal precedent might have been fuzzy, Klingenschmitt was only too clear about his commitment to preach the gospel when and where he deemed "appropriate," announcing he would fast until the president responded, taking a slice of Communion bread as his final meal before the ordeal.

By the new year, the hunger strike was over, but the controversy raged on, fueled by dire pronouncements by such organizations as Faith in Focus, who ran a story on their Web site headline "Navy Comes out of the Closet, Decides to Hate the Name of Jesus Christ." John Whitehead, president of the Rutherford Institute, a conservative think tank, summed up the muddled reasoning surrounding the interface of religion and the military by declaring that the new Navy regulations "violate religious freedom and federal law, and there are several Supreme Court cases that have been pretty clear in affirming that, just because people are in the military, they don't give up their constitutional rights." Whitehead neglected to cite which cases made the issue "pretty clear."

In all likelihood the Navy had long since braced itself for evangelical ire after witnessing the fate of the Air Force's own interim set of religious guidelines, released on August 29, 2005. At first blush, the document, "Concerning Free Exercise of Religion in the Air Force," seemed to tackle the problem head-on. The proposed regulations addressed such key areas as "religious accommodation," "public prayer outside of voluntary worship settings," "individual sharing of religious faith in the military context," and even "e-mail and other communications"—a point-by-point response to many of the violations Weinstein had specifically brought to light. In a critical passage, the report's carefully crafted language made it clear that "in official circumstances, particularly situations where superior/subordinate relationships are involved, individuals need to be sensitive to the potential that personal expressions may appear to be official expressions," and that "the more senior the individual, the more likely that personal expressions may be perceived to be official statement."

"We were really encouraged," remembers Richard Katskee, assistant legal director of Americans United for Separation of Church and State. "They seemed to be on the right track and had even come to us for guidance and input. Our response was very favorable. We felt it was a sincere effort."

Evangelicals also thought the guidelines were a sincere effort—a sincere effort to undercut their prominence and power in the armed services. In the same week the guidelines were made public, Lieutenant General John Regni, a 1973 Academy graduate, was nominated to replace Rosa, who had taken a job as president of The Citadel, his alma mater. The Christian right—for no apparent reason, given Regni's sterling record and evident neutrality on the issue—greeted the newcomer to his precarious new posting with suspicion and outright derision. "What they need is someone that's real intolerant of Christianity to come in here" were the words put in Rosa's mouth by ham-fisted evangelical satirist Chris Davis. "And I think General Regni is the right man for the job."

Others saved their scorn for the Air Force's tortuous efforts to fashion a workable compromise to its embattled recommendations. "The Air Force seems to be fighting perceived religious intolerance with actual religious intolerance, ultimately telling the military chaplaincy how to pray," claimed Tony Perkins of the Family Research Council, with whom Weinstein had locked horns on MSNBC's *Hardball*. "Free expression of religion for all peoples is what the U.S. military has fought for since its inception; that concept should not be denied to those who have taken on the task of protecting our freedoms."

It was a theme tirelessly touted by outraged evangelicals. "We're in a time of war," was the dire counsel of retired Army colonel Bob Macginnis in a story for Focus on the Family's Web site Citizen Link, "and I think it's unfortunate that the Air Force has stomped on religious freedom and told commanders that they should chill any effort to express a faith in God, given that we have young men and women dying every day on the battlefields." Focus on the Family would immediately call on its huge constituency to flood the White House with protests over the guidelines, demanding President Bush "restore the right to religious expression" and evoking the most cherished icon of American patriotism. "To say that you can only have prayer in extraordinary circumstances," said Mat Staver, president of the Orlando-based Liberty Council, "I think is hypocritical and certainly not consistent with our founding fathers and George Washington—our first general and first president." Staver was referring to one of the more intriguing sections of the guidelines that, after insisting that "public prayer should not usually be included in official settings," went on to venture that "there may be extraordinary circumstances where the potential benefits for the welfare of the command outweigh the potential for causing discomfort. These circumstances might include mass casualties, preparation for imminent combat and natural disasters."

By that fall, the mobilization was complete. Led by the Christian Coalition, the protest campaign had deluged the White House with phone calls and e-mails while seventy House members signed a letter to President Bush asking for an executive order protecting "the constitutional right of military chaplains to pray according to their faith." It dismissed the guidelines' promotion of "non-sectarian prayers" as "merely a euphemism declaring that prayers will be acceptable only so long as they censor Christian beliefs." Chief of Air Force Chaplains (and Academy graduate) General Charles Baldwin meanwhile videotaped a message to all active-duty and reserve chaplains and their staff arguing his case that the guidelines needed to be changed. "This is America," he pleaded, "and for those of us who come from belief systems that require us to tell others of our faith and what we believe, this is so important that we feel free to do this."

For Weinstein, the guidelines had, from the beginning, bristled with equivocation. "'A brief, non-sectarian prayer may be included in non-routine military ceremonies,'" he quotes. "'Public prayer should not usually be included.' These are the kind of loopholes you could drive a truck through." Pronouncing the document "dead on arrival" and "only a meaningless set of nice words," Weinstein was relentless in his contrast of the guidelines to Richardson's unrepudiated *New York Times* statement. "It all started and stopped there," he asserts. "Anything that came afterwards can only be viewed in light of the Air Force's reserved right to evangelize the unchurched. You can't say you hate African-American people and then announce your distaste for racial discrimination. You can't say you love burgers and fries and then denounce fast food. There was a cognitive dissonance here and I wasn't going to let them get away with it."

Neither, apparently, were the evangelicals. In their own way as disgruntled as Weinstein by the import of the guidelines, they pushed to have the whole project sent back to the drawing board. In the fallout that followed, the Naval Academy announced that it would continue its tradition of lunchtime prayer in the cavernous Bancroft Hall midshipmen's facility, eschewing the proposal that a period of 'devotional thoughts' be substituted. The Maryland ACLU abandoned their plans to push the suit, with spokesman David Rocah observing that most midshipmen would be reluctant to "begin their career by suing the Navy."

By the time the Air Force returned with its "Revised Interim Guidelines Concerning Free Exercise of Religion in the Air Force," on February 9, 2006, it was clear that evangelicals both within and without the military hierarchy had won a resounding victory.

"It was a great disappointment," admits Richard Katskee of Americans United, "a huge step back. The new guidelines essentially gave a free pass to evangelical claims that proselytizing was a tenet of faith and could not be curtailed, even in the military and even in the face of the obvious damage inflicted on the command and control structure. I think it was clear in hindsight that the chief of air force chaplains, General

Baldwin, along with the certifying organizations of the Chaplaincy Corps as a whole, was pushing a very specific agenda throughout the process of creating the guidelines. They were tenacious."

That tenacity resulted in a terse document, telegraphing its intentions on a single sheet, whittled down from the original guideline's three, bullet-pointed pages. Announcing up front, "We will remain officially neutral regarding religious beliefs," eight brief paragraphs went on to define that neutrality in terms that barely disguised an obstreperous defense of the status quo. While acknowledging, "Leaders at every level bear a special responsibility to ensure their words and actions cannot be reasonably construed to be officially endorsing or disapproving any faith belief," the guidelines insisted that "subject to these sensitivities, superiors enjoy the same free exercise rights as all other airmen."

In a pivotal clause, the new guidelines stated, "Voluntary participation in worship, prayer, study and discussion" was "integral to the free exercise of religion. Nothing in this guidance," it went on with inexorable momentum, "should be understood to limit the substance of voluntary discussions of religion, or the exercise of free speech, where it is reasonably clear that the discussions are personal, not official, and they can be reasonably free of the potential for, or appearance of, coercion."

"Of course, it had already been well-established beyond a shadow of a doubt that what was going on at the Academy was in no way 'reasonable,'" maintains Weinstein. "That was the whole point. If the first set of guidelines was full of loopholes, this time around there were so many holes there was no room left for the loops. I thought if I read *reasonable* one more time, I was going to puke. There is no word in the English language more subjective in its interpretation and application, and it has suddenly become the standard by which all religious activity in the Air Force was to be measured. I hated to say I told you so, but I told you so."

WEINSTEIN FILES SUIT

The notion of filing suit against the Air Force for violation of constitutional rights had occurred to Weinstein the moment he opened the front page of *The New York Times* on July 12, 2005. "I had them dead to rights," he claims. "The legal side of my brain saw a slam dunk, but at the same time I wanted to be careful, to wait and see how events played out. By the time I went to the second Graduate Leadership Conference, the dimensions of the suit were taking shape, and at that point I mentioned the possibility to some of the alumni who were there. The one fact I had to make clear from the beginning was that I wasn't going after the Academy, at least not directly, as a named defendant. Ultimately the responsibility for all this rested with the Air Force, and that was my target. It's important to never forget that this is the most technologically lethal fighting force ever assembled by man, the cutting edge of our military might. These were the levers of power that were in jeopardy, and it made sense to go right to the source."

Deflecting his attack away from the Academy gave Weinstein some leeway with his fellow graduates. "I can't say they were all on my side after I let them know that I wasn't going after our beloved alma mater, but I did feel a lot of tension leaking out the air-conditioning ducts of Doolittle Hall. For many of us, there was a clear distinction between the Academy and all it had meant to our personal and professional lives, and the Air Force, which was a vast military bureaucracy like all the rest of them."

Convinced of his odds in court to comprehensively lay out a case that would determine the clear constitutionality of his cause and perhaps even establish a new and vital precedent in the ongoing intricacies of church and state separation, Weinstein nevertheless held back, determined to exhaust all avenues of direct appeal before launching an all-out legal assault.

"The first thing I did was try to contact the new air force secretary," Weinstein explains. Preston M. "Pete" Geren, a four-term Democratic representative from Forth Worth, who had been succeeded by none other than Kay Granger, had been named acting air force secretary by President Bush in late July, a few weeks after General Richardson's fateful *New York Times* remark. "I was gratified to actually get through to him, a concession I attribute entirely to my noise-making propensities in the press and the lobbying of some then sympathetic denizens of the Pentagon." Weinstein's request was simple and direct: "I told him to take it back. I wanted a retraction of Richardson's policy statement. It seemed like a litmus test to me. If they were willing to acknowledge that the Air Force did *not* reserve the right to evangelize the unchurched, then maybe there was the potential for more progress. Geren promised to look into it, and shortly afterward my legal counsel was put in touch with Mary Walker."

General counsel of the Air Force, blond, born-again, and with a penchant for red power suits, Walker first gained notoriety during the Academy's sex scandal when she insisted, "There was no systematic acceptance of sexual assault at the Academy." In other words, there *was* no scandal. A commission would later find that she had omitted the fact that Pentagon and Air Force brass were, in fact, well within the loop. Walker would later head the Department of Defense working group that issued the incendiary "Legal Arguments for Avoiding the Jurisdiction of the Geneva Conventions," which was widely considered to have laid the groundwork for the horrors of Abu Ghraib, declaring, "I am in the people-stretching business," a month before the abuses became public. Called "the most political general counsel I've ever seen" by an experienced Pentagon legal hand, Walker's name was removed from the Web site of The Professional Women's Fellowship, an offshoot of Campus Crusade for Christ and an organization she cofounded, once her involvement in government-sanctioned torture became widely known.

"She asked us to give her a week to respond," Weinstein remembers. "Seven days went by, then another seven. I had absolutely zero confidence that anything substantive would come of any of this, but I held back as long as I could."

Finally, on October 6, 2005, Weinstein directed his lead litigator, Sam Bregman, to file a Complaint for Violation of Constitutional Rights in the U.S. District Court for New Mexico in downtown Albuquerque, naming as defendants the United States Air Force and acting Secretary of the Air Force Pete Geren (see Appendix D). As plaintiff for the historic six-page suit, Weinstein alleged, "Over the course of the last decade, a pattern and practice has developed at the Academy where senior officers and cadets have attempted to impose evangelical Christianity into arenas that are clearly United States Air Force venues." These violations of the Establishment Clause, he went on, "are severe, systemic and pervasive and have fostered discrimination and harassment toward non-Evangelical Christians, non-Christians and non-religious cadets and Academy staff."

General Richardson was also writ large in the suit, along with Weinstein's repeated attempts to elicit repudiation of his comments from the Air Force. "Defendant Geren has refused to do so," the complaint alleged, "thereby ratifying this policy."

For injunctive relief, Weinstein sought that "no member of the USAF, including a chaplain, is permitted to evangelize, proselytize, or in any related way attempt to involuntarily convert, pressure, exhort or persuade a fellow member of the USAF to accept their own religious beliefs while on duty." Further: "The USAF is not permitted to establish or advance any one religion over another religion or one religion over no religion."

"That language came directly from an opinion by Supreme Court Justice David Souter in the Ten Commandments Kentucky courthouse-display controversy. I think that puts it pretty plainly. The guiding principle for our government is to ensure governmental neutrality between religion and religion and between religion and no religion. The United States Air Force is an arm of the government. You'd think that would be the end of the story. But, of course, displaying the Ten Commandments was found constitutional in Texas and unconstitutional in Kentucky in two decisions that came down on the very same day, under the very same test. We're obviously a very conflicted nation."

On the other hand, the conflict in Mary Walker's office over when and how to respond to Weinstein's ultimatum was resolved within seven hours of his filing. "Six and a half hours, to be exact," says Weinstein. "After months of waiting, that's how long it took them to get off their asses once I made my move."

Walker's long-delayed response added an extraordinary new dimension to the unfolding events. After claiming to Weinstein's counsel, Sam Bregman, that her reply had been delayed because "as sometimes happens in government, things don't get done," she went on to emphatically state, "There is no existing Air Force policy endorsing 'proselytizing' or 'evangelizing.' An earlier Chaplain Service document that might have been understood to represent such a policy statement has been withdrawn."

"It was incredible," asserts Weinstein. "Essentially, Walker had informed us that Richardson had actually referenced an existing written policy in his *Times* quote. I had to have that run by me a second time and then a third. What document? What statement? It was hard to keep from jumping up and down. For so long, I'd been fighting the impression that Richardson had been speaking off-the-cuff and for himself. Now, all of a sudden, the fucking general counsel of the Air Force was confirming that evangelizing the unchurched *was,* in fact, a policy and had been explicit all along!"

The smoking gun, which Weinstein quickly unearthed with the assistance of MeLinda Morton, was to be found in the handbook for the 2002 edition of the Basic Chaplain Course, produced under the auspices of the USAF Chaplain Service Institute and including "The Covenant and Code of Ethics for the Chaplains of the Armed Forces" (see Appendix E), written for the course by the National Conference on Ministry to the Armed Forces, and circulated widely within the Chaplaincy Corps. There, among such all-purpose pledges as "I will show personal love for God" and "I will never violate the personhood of another human being," was the single-line declaration "I will not proselytize from other religious bodies, but I retain the right to evangelize those who are non-affiliated."

"The basic drift of that part of the code," MeLinda Morton would later explain, "was that you were not supposed to engage in 'sheep stealing.' If you could somehow identify that these people were not branded sheep, then you could go after them. But if they were, you were to keep your mitts off."

"I was floored," admits Weinstein. "Retaining the right to evangelize was, word for word, what Richardson had said, and it turned out he was quoting chapter and verse from approved Air Force instructions. Of course, what I wanted to know right away was what other documents and regulations were squirreled away in Air Force files waiting to detonate like land mines?"

Potentially incriminating evidence stashed in the back offices of the Pentagon labyrinth wasn't the only thing threatening to blow up. The effects of Weinstein's suit were immediate and ferocious, escalating into midnight death threats, anonymous Jew-baiting e-mails and cell phone calls, slashed tires, and a vituperative press campaign. "We already had two attack-trained German shepherds," he says, "but we ended up getting guns just to be on the safe side. I was called Satan's Pet, the Devil's Lawyer, the Antichrist, the Field General of the Godless Armies of Satan, and the Most Dangerous Man in America, which was great billing for the speaking engagements."

"Mikey Weinstein . . . has outdone himself, even by his own standards of distaste for actively religious people," opined Focus on the Family's Tom Minnery. "He despises evangelism—that is, the practice of one person telling another about his faith." Although Weinstein might not like it, Minnery wrote elsewhere, "it is the job of an evangelical Christian chaplain to evangelize."

"I guess it wouldn't do any good to say that some of my best friends are born-again Christians," counters Weinstein. "But it's true. You can't have had a career in the Air Force, lived in proximity to Colorado Springs, or even been a citizen of this country without forming close relationships with Christians, and I include my daughter-in-law and, for that matter, all my in-laws in that category. But maybe Minnery's right about despising evangelism, not as the innocent interpersonal exchange that he describes, but the aggressive pursuit of converts, the kind that preys on human fragility and weakness and need. I've seen evangelical teaching tools that identify the most likely candidates to be saved: those who have had a death in the family or are in the middle of a divorce or who have lost their job. I wonder how they might feel if they knew their personal tragedies and sorrows were being charted on a graph of prospective inductees? Whatever happened to compassion for sake of compassion and not as a tool to score spiritual scalps?"

Not surprisingly, considering the high media profile Weinstein had assiduously cultivated as a battle necessity, others saw his lawsuit as naked self-aggrandizement. "Fifteen minutes of fame evidently isn't enough for Mikey Weinstein," read an editorial in *The Colorado Springs Gazette* the day after the complaint was filed. "Weinstein brought a lawsuit that will probably amount to nothing but a waste of taxpayers' money." It went on to reference one of Weinstein's more colorful caveats, evoking the "imperious, fascistic contagion that is sweeping throughout this country through evangelical Christians trying to infuse their parochial biblical worldview into the machinery of the state." "It seems," concluded *The Gazette,* "religious intolerance isn't a problem confined to the Academy."

"Guilty as charged," Weinstein cheerfully admits. "I *am* intolerant of religions that push a political agenda under the guise of sanctity and in direct contravention of the U.S. Constitution. Evangelicals are among the nicest people I know. But they should be ashamed of what they've allowed to happen in the name of their faith."

The requirements of that faith were drawn in the starkest terms in a newsletter published by the Navigators on October 11 in response to Weinstein's lawsuit. "We respectfully request that you not share this letter publicly," cautioned its authors, Darren and Gina Lindblom, from the Navigators' Colorado Springs staff. "Due to the law suit recently filed, the contents of this letter are confidential." It was easy to understand why. "Thank you for your prayers as we minister among cadets at the Air Force Academy," read the secret missive. "We feel our calling has been confirmed that the Lord has led us here for this time in history at the USAFA. Due to the climate of 'religious intolerance' and the recent law suit filed against the Air Force, we are vitally aware that we are on the front lines of a spiritual battle." Elsewhere, in what was called the "Lindblom Ministry Prayer Card" the couple praised God "that we have been allowed access by the Academy into the cadet area to minister among the cadets. We have recently been given an unused classroom to meet with cadets at any time during the day. This is a true answer to prayer." Describing an encounter with one particularly fervent cadet, Darren Lindblom asked, "What are you trusting the Lord for right now?" The answer was to "use me to impact the lives of 200 men with the Gospel by the time I graduate from the Academy."

"If I were Darren and Gina, I wouldn't want my newsletter to get around either," Weinstein observes drily. "This piece of evangelical propaganda was written in October of 2005. That's after the Yale report; after the Brady report; after the congressional hearings and after the interim guidelines and all the rest of the tap dancing that went on for almost two years. At one point, the Lindbloms boast of training and developing cadets to 'have a personal ministry among their peers at the Academy.' Nothing's changed and nothing will until we force it to."

It was a challenge that would not go unanswered by the full legal resources of the Air Force and its self-appointed evangelical allies. "We don't want to do anything that could keep someone from living their faith," fretted Representative Joel Hefley, speaking for a lion's share of his Colorado Springs constituency and joining fifty-eight of his fellow congressmen in drafting yet another alert to President Bush that "Christian military chaplains are under direct attack and their right to pray according to their faith is in jeopardy."

"What would America do if someone reserved the right to 'Islamize the unmosqued' or 'Judaize the unsynagogued?'" was Weinstein's pointed response, calling his evangelical opponents "bullies." But by late October he had more to do than trade rhetorical barbs. Anticipating the Air Force's contention that he lacked requisite "legal standing," he amended his complaint within two weeks of its initial filing to include four additional plaintiffs, including his son Casey and three of Casey's 2004 Air Force Academy graduate classmates, including Patrick Kucera, a twenty-four-year-old civil engineering major from Binghamton in upstate New York.

"Before I joined Mr. Weinstein's suit, I had filed a complaint of my own," says Kucera, who was raised Roman Catholic before becoming an avowed atheist. "Through a process called direct reporting agency, I bypassed my chain of command and submitted my report directly to the Pentagon. I had three major grievances: First was the general atmosphere at the Academy. As an atheist, I think I was more attuned to it than others might have been, especially the systematic ostracizing that went on. Secondly, I made charges against the inspector general for not taking my complaints seriously, as well as a military equal-opportunity officer who, I kid you not, actually tried to convert me when I expressed my concerns about attempts to convert me at the Academy."

Subsequently hearing of Weinstein's pending suit, he agreed to join without, he insists, considering the consequences to his Air Force career. "The first thing they teach us at the Academy is about maintaining our integrity," says Kucera. "I couldn't do that and keep silent about what was happening around me."

Another plaintiff who found it difficult to remain silent was Jason Spindler, a mechanical engineering major from Rome, New York, who had been raised in a conservative Jewish household. "Throughout my time at the Academy here were constant reminders that, no matter how I might have excelled as a cadet, I was still considered an outsider by many," says Spindler. "When I first arrived, I joined the marching band, the drum and bugle corps, playing trumpet as I had in high school. I got along well with my band mates, and it was a lot of fun until our performing schedule clashed with observances of the Jewish high holy days. I had been working hard with the rabbi to be able to recite the prayers as a lay leader and, given my background, it was very important to me that I participated. The policy at the Academy was that, if you were going to miss an event, you had to give written notice two weeks in advance. So I wrote a letter and, just to make sure, also e-mailed my request up the chain of command a full month before the services. It was only a week before the event that I found out my request had somehow gotten lost, and when I informed my band director, he flatly refused to let me go. He told me he didn't care what the religious observance was. I had to make a choice." It took a huddle of fifteen officers in conference with the Academy's rabbi to finally resolve the issue, but by that time, Spindler had soured on his drum and bugle corps experience. "I was getting e-mails from other members questioning why I had chosen my religious obligation over my duties to the band," he continues. "I quit at the end of the semester. For me, the whole incident pointed up a serious disconnect between Christians at the Academy and the rest of us. Everyone, for example, got Sunday off, but for Jews Friday night was the time set aside for worship and that was when physical training was scheduled. You could go to services if you chose, but that would exclude you from the team spirit that was so much a part of our training and open yourself up to accusations that you were wimping out."

The general insensitivity to religious expression outside evangelical strictures would, in time, take on a blatantly offensive tenor. "In my sophomore year," the articulate Spindler continues, "I was walking down the hall behind some senior staff cadet when I heard one of them tell a joke to the effect that Jews were the best magicians because they could come in a door of a building and go out the chimney. Despite the significant difference in our rank, I turned around and asked him if he would please not make remarks like that, and I think he was genuinely surprised that I would take exception to it. There was just simply no awareness, and when I later brought it up to my human relations officer I essentially got the same reaction. To me this was symptomatic of a broken system and the complete lack of a comprehensive institutionalized methodology. We had been thoroughly trained in proper sexual conduct and told not to lie, cheat, steal, or tolerate anyone who does. But where were the guidelines for religious respect? There is simply no direction from the top on how to endorse and embrace different religious views and, as a result, for someone like me whose beliefs shape who they are, there's a pervasive sense of exclusion."

Even in the face of administrative indifference, Spindler and a handful of other cadets would take on the educational process by themselves. "When I was named squadron commander, it was a great responsibility and I took it very seriously. At the time, there was a controversy at the school regarding putting biblical quotes and other religious material on official e-mail. After some of us protested, a decision was handed down forbidding the practice, but there were cadets in my squadron who couldn't get with the program. I remember one young woman in particular who was outraged at what she perceived as a denial of her right to free religious expression, and I spent a long time trying to explain to her how, in a military environment such as the Academy, it was important not to show favoritism in any way, shape, or form. The point of it all, for me, was that the administration had failed to create an atmosphere that allowed for maximum freedom of expression without causing offense to others."

That offense could often take indirect forms. For Bryce Batchman, another 2004 Academy graduate, evangelization was a persistent nuisance. "I was raised in a Christian family," Batchman recounts, "but I always had my doubts. I guess as part of my search for answers, I accepted an invitation to a meeting of the Officers' Christian Fellowship during my freshman year." Batchman immediately realized that the organization's "in-your-face faith" wasn't for him. "They were friendly but way zealous," he recounts. "They were always telling me that I had to talk to my bunkmates and invite all my unsaved friends to their events. After a couple of months I quit. But there was one guy, a senior cadet, who really stayed on my case, writing me e-mails constantly and telling me he was praying for my salvation. Eventually, whenever I'd see a message from him I'd just delete it and hope I never ran into the guy in the hall." Now identifying himself as an atheist, Batchman attributes OCF's "offputting version of Christianity" as "one of a series of events that helped me decide that there was no God."

By the spring of 2006, Weinstein had added yet another plaintiff—along with his son, Patrick Kucera, Jason Spindler, and another Jewish cadet, Ari Kayne—to the complaint; a vociferous master sergeant from Alamogordo, New Mexico, named Phillip Burleigh. A twenty-four-year veteran of the Air Force, Bureligh maintained that as a recruiter for the reserve, stationed at Holloman Air Force Base, he had been "subjected to regular and persistent proselytizing by his superior officers." The new twelve-page filing referenced Air Force recruiter meetings with guest speakers who exhorted the gatherings "to use faith in Jesus Christ while recruiting."

Despite Jason Spindler's contention that the Academy is a "strange piece of real estate" that breeds "an immature culture," it is clear from accounts of graduates who have taken up active duty posts that evangelical influence is ever-present within the Air Force as a whole. Bryce

Batchman, stationed at Bolling AFB in Washington, D.C., cites a first sergeant who constantly evokes Jesus' name in squadron staff meetings and "expresses frustration that prayer has been curtailed at the base." Casey Weinstein's wife, Amanda, recounts attending a mandatory event at her current stationing at Wright-Patterson AFB for the retirement of a lieutenant colonel who felt no compunction in exhorting the gathering to "seek Jesus in their personal and professional lives."

But perhaps the most egregious recent example of the wider reach of evangelicals in the upper echelons of the Air Force is that of Major General Jack J. Catton Jr., currently on active duty at Langley Air Force Base in Virginia, who in the late spring of 2006 sent a fundraising appeal on his official e-mail account to more than two hundred fellow Academy graduates from the class of 1976, many of whom are still on active duty. The pitch, urging his fellow alumni to make contributions to the campaign of Bentley Rayburn, a recently retired Air Force general (Academy class of 1975) running for Republican nomination to the House from the district surrounding Colorado Springs, asserts that "We are certainly in need of Christian men with integrity and military experience in Congress."

Catton's missive included a message from Rayburn referring to "the lack of any Air Force presence within the Congress." Rayburn proposed that "for those of us who are Christians, there is that whole other side of the coin that recognizes that we need more Christian influence in Congress."

"This should hardly come as a surprise to anyone," Weinstein remarks. "Connect the dots. Evangelicals have used the Academy as a wedge to insert their people in place within the entire command structure of the armed forces. It was only a matter of time before their agenda became activated, and the attempt to use their influence within the military to effect political change has been part of the strategy from the beginning. It's going to take some courageous individuals to stand up to them, such as those who put their careers at considerable risk by stepping forward in our suit. Yes, of course, it takes guts, but at the same time, the choice is clear and compelling. I think many of us have already arrived at the painful conclusion that the Air Force was not what it pretends to be, a place where honor and integrity and honesty were guiding principles."

Weinstein's suit was, in fact, becoming increasingly crowded with new participants weighing in on both sides of the battle. Within days of the original filing, the Alliance Defense Fund, the legal stalking horse for Focus on the Family and the Coral Ridge Ministries, claimed its right to be heard on behalf of F-16 fighter pilot Captain Karl Palmberg and Academy chaplain James Glass, who had done so much to obfuscate the development of RSVP over eight months in 2004–5. The First Amendment, insisted Joel Oster, ADF's senior legal counsel, "applies to everyone, including America's fighting men and women who are on duty twenty-four/seven." Their motion to intervene hammered home the specter of spiritually deprived warriors: "Their ability to share their faith and to candidly discuss religion as they put their lives on the line for this country will be in jeopardy." For his part, Palmberg would go so far as to equate the right to evangelize with the value of the deadly ordnance he carried over his five hundred hours of flying time: "I consider my constitutional right to discuss my faith without censorship or fear of retribution as valuable to the military and the future of our nation as the aircraft, bombs, and bullets I am trained to employ."

"I felt as if I'd made my point," Weinstein recounts. "The lawsuit had attracted a lot of attention and turned the heat up under the right asses. So I decided to see if I could cut a deal, just to test the waters." To that end, on October 14, just eight days after the initial filing, he had his litigators present the defendants with a settlement offer, sending a letter to Mary Walker. It requested that the Air Force "enter into a Stipulated Order with the United States District Court that no member of the USAF, including a chaplain, is permitted to evangelize, proselytize, or in any way attempt to involuntarily convert, pressure, exert or persuade a fellow member of the USAF to accept their own religious beliefs while on duty."

"I was feeling charitable," Weinstein remembers, "and had carefully crafted that language to reflect what I considered to be the bottom line of any negotiation. If they went for it, I could pack up my tent, declare victory, and go home for the rapidly approaching holidays."

They didn't. Rejecting the settlement, the Air Force, two days before Christmas, filed a motion to dismiss, larding it, in precise language of their own, with a thirty-page "Memorandum of Points and Authorities" that laid out their stubborn refusal to accommodate Weinstein or alter the evangelical status quo. At its heart was the contention that "any sermon or religious messages delivered by Air Force chaplains cannot be attributed to the Air Force as government speech."

"Who's paying their salary?" Weinstein countered. "What emblems are they wearing on their epaulets? Who are they appealing to when they make religious pronouncements? Look, I'm not suggesting that chaplains should not be allowed to do their job, but let's at least agree on a definition of that job. The same Basic Chaplain Course that reserved the right to evangelize the 'nonaffiliated' also says, 'I will respect the beliefs and traditions of my colleagues and those to whom I minister. When conducting services of worship that include persons of other than my religious body, I will draw upon those beliefs, principles, and practices that we have in common.' What more important principles and practices are held in common by all Americans than the freedom to choose, to not be coerced, to make up our own minds and follow our own hearts? When you deliberately foster an atmosphere where authority is exploited to promote a specific confession of faith, where career choices are dependent on conformity to that confession, and where peer pressure is encouraged to accomplish the job of conversion, you have turned a sermon or a message into government speech and blatantly violated the Constitution."

"Plaintiffs claims are also precluded by prudential standing requirement," the Air Force's motion to dismiss continued, asserting that Weinstein had insufficiently demonstrated "a direct and personal stake in this cause" or that "an injury in fact that is 'certainly impending.'"

"What was 'certainly impending' was a military coup by a cadre of zealots whose religious agenda overrode their sworn duty to protect the Constitution," Weinstein says. "My standing requirement was that of a former Air Force officer, a graduate of the Academy, and an American citizen. What began for me as a sense of personal betrayal by institutions to which I had dedicated my life, and graduated to the outrage of a parent whose children had been discriminated against because of their faith, had now become a clear and present danger to the principles for which so many had already fought and died. It had also become a pressing matter of national security. I had asked the question many times before: What does believing in Jesus Christ have to do with being a loyal American? I'm still waiting for an answer."

☆ 18 ☆

SINGLED OUT

The legal jockeying between Weinstein and the Air Force continued into the early months of 2006. In early January, responding to the defendant's motion to dismiss, the plaintiffs, specifically the four young second lieutenant graduates, asserted that they spent "every day as a member of the Air Force subjected to Christian rituals and prayers." There was no mere speculation that "they might be subjected to First Amendment violations some day. They are subject to these violations today."

Three weeks later, in their own response, the defendants' lawyers contended that the Air Force was "aggressively engaged in dealing with issues of religious expression," citing the diluted headquarters review-group findings of the previous summer at the Academy as proof. To drive home the point that the military brass was out in front of the problem, the Air Force, through its Justice Department lawyers, on February 13, further gave the courts notice of the revised interim guidelines, reaffirming a commitment "to protecting the free exercise of religion, prohibiting governmental establishment of religion and defending the

Nation." The plaintiffs' claims, they contended, "continue to suffer from a lack of ripeness for the additional reason that the guideline process remains ongoing."

"Something was ripe, that was for sure," quipped Weinstein. "The revised interim guidelines stunk to high heaven, and we immediately filed another motion to amend our complaint based on their blatant unconstitutionality both on their face and as applied."

And so it went, the thrust and parry rendering in dry legalese Weinstein's rage, Cecilia Peasley's agony, David Antoon's sorrow, and the welter of roiling emotions experienced by all those who had directly and indirectly been embroiled in the controversy over the previous two years. And there it might well have rested, the passions of both sides exhausted by the exigencies of justice until, in the ripeness of time, the appropriate parsing wrought compromise and accommodation and an approximation of truth.

Except that it didn't work out that way. Not for Mikey Weinstein. Always greater than the sum of its legal and ethical components, his struggle against religious hegemony in the military had a potent inner dimension. From the very beginning he was deeply invested in its outcome, and constitutional niceties notwithstanding, he had something urgently to prove, not just to his evangelical enemies, but also to himself. It was the tremendous motive energy behind his battle, the animating principle that took no prisoners and allowed no retreat, a stance that, in time, his adversaries and even his allies would come to greet with apprehension—volatile, intemperate, impolitic, and, some would caution him, perhaps counterproductive. It was no wonder he had earned the nickname Hurricane Mikey.

But Weinstein, in the heat of combat, was never disposed to questioning himself or speculating on his motives and methods. What might have seemed arrogant and inflexible to those he engaged was to him simply a measure of the conflict's ferocity, the utter duplicity of his foes, and, finally, his own hardened resolve. Simply put, Weinstein had, from day one, taken it personally.

He himself would not fully understand how personal until just before Memorial Day, 2005, when he emerged from taping an interview with CNN and found a call waiting for him from Pam Zubeck, *The Col-*

orado Springs Gazette reporter who had done so much to break the story in its earliest iteration. "Mikey," she said, her voice strained and hesitant, "our paper has just received a letter and we need to get a comment on it from you."

The letter, addressed to Zubeck, then Superintendent of the Academy General Rosa, and Jim Shaw, head of the Academy's Association of Graduates, was dated May 21 and referred to a front-page article appearing that same day with Zubeck's byline; detailing criticism of the Brady report for failing to take crucial testimony, including Weinstein's. "I have some information about one of your 'key critics' that you might find interesting," the letter read. "Michael Weinstein was a freshman cadet, Cadet Squadron Thirty Six, in the fall of 1973 when I was the Cadet Squadron Commander."

In his doolie year, according to the letter, Weinstein had found several "hateful" and "primitive" anti-Semitic notes taped onto the door of his room. These notes always seemed to appear just after lunch, when the hallway was crammed with cadets heading for afternoon classes. "I arranged," the letter continued, "for a cadet to sit in an adjoining room with the door ajar where he could see Michael's door by looking in a special mirror. The culprit was soon caught putting the hate-filled note on the door. It was Michael Weinstein." The letter-writer then went on to claim that Weinstein confessed to being responsible for all the anti-Semitic notes—and faced a possible court-martial. "But his bizarre conduct seemed to be a plea for attention and he was sent to counseling for behavior problems."

"Michael Weinstein deserves our sympathy," the letter concluded, "but not our credibility. To have Michael Weinstein serve as a spokesman for alleged religious bias at the Academy is supreme irony." It was signed by a "Retired Air Force Colonel, Class of 1974."

"My blood ran cold," Weinstein remembers. "In that one moment I realized just how far the other side was willing go in this struggle to discredit and smear me. At the same time, a flood of memories overwhelmed me, memories I'd done my best to forget for thirty-two years. I guess I must have lost track of time for a moment, of where I was and what I was doing, because the next thing I remember was hearing Pam Zubeck trying to get my attention on the phone.

"'This is huge story, Mikey,' she was saying. 'I mean, either way, it's a huge story. You're their fiercest critic and you're being accused of faking a hate crime. If you did it, then it totally discredits you, and if you didn't, then you're being slammed by the religious right.'

"I said, 'Pam, if you run with this, you do so at your own risk. Let me try and figure out what's going on here. Hold off until I can get some answers. If I can't, then you'll have to do what you'll have to do. But until then, do me this one favor.'"

As Zubeck considered the ramifications of his request, Weinstein stood with the phone to his ear, his mind reeling. "I was trying to figure out what to do," he recounts, "some way to deal with this, and at the same time fighting the feeling of being swept back to a moment in time I'd done everything in my power to put behind me. The only person alive who knew the whole story in its wretched entirety of what had happened to me that first year at the Academy was my wife, Bonnie. My sons and daughter-in-law didn't know. My oldest friends didn't know. The rest of my family didn't know. It was a secret and one that I had kept carefully hidden ever since. Now, suddenly, it all threatened to come spilling out in front of the whole world."

The events Weinstein was wrestling with, along with the consequences of their seemingly now-inevitable exposure, had begun in the fall of 1973, during his first semester at the Academy. "I was shell-shocked, like all of my other classmates," he remembers. "Every morning I woke up thinking, 'God, what am I doing here?' The academics were a real bitch, which I half-expected, but I'd fooled myself into thinking things would go a little easier for me since I'd come in as an intercollegiate athlete and was officially recruited for NCAA tennis. I figured I'd have a few special privileges and my coaches and teammates to watch my back, but that wasn't the way it worked. The intercollegiate tennis program didn't start in earnest until the second semester, so there was no difference between me and every other miserable, homesick doolie there.

"It was so cold," Weinstein continues. "It got dark early. Fall was descending into winter. It was like being caught in the long shadows of a continuing nightmare. I had to take boxing as part of the physical education program that first semester and received a low blow in one of my fights. It hurt like hell and I started taking aspirin to dull the pain. A lot of aspirin. After a day or two, I started shitting blood, and one morning I was standing at attention with the rest of my classmates at the breakfast table in Mitchell Hall and fainted right into the orange-juice dispenser. They took me to the hospital, and ten days later I'd gone through massive amounts of blood transfusions. It turned out I was allergic to aspirin."

In those ten days, during which Weinstein dropped over thirty pounds, he vaguely remembers his parents coming out from Vandenberg Air Force Base in California, where his father was stationed, to sit by his bedside. "I found out later that the cadet wing really saved my life," he recounts. "They put the word out that a fellow cadet was in serious trouble and needed A-positive blood because I had already completely exhausted their stock. If it hadn't been for them, I don't know if I'd be here today. It's amazing to me, but even in those first days of the first semester of our first year, there had been a loyalty instilled that would stay with us for the rest of our lives."

The ordeal, according to Weinstein, was "the closest thing to a religious experience I'd ever had. Maybe it was coming so close to death. Maybe it was the second chance it represented, not just to keep on living but also to live a whole different life. I remember lying in bed at night looking out the window at the moon and stars and thinking I wasn't going to make it at the Academy, that I'd lost two weeks' worth of classes and that I'd never catch up. And, you know, it didn't seem so bad. There was a part of me that was glad to have an excuse not to go on."

His hemorrhaging, meanwhile, continued unabated. "The blood would go right through me, literally, every forty-five minutes. It was cold when they put it in, and it hurt like hell until they hooked up a blood warmer, and they were talking about cutting me open in a series of exploratory surgeries to see if they could find the leak. This was in the days before arthroscopy, and I kept imagining them pulling out my intestines like a bicycle tire. I was scared to death and I prayed like a motherfucker, probably for the first time in my life, saying, 'God, if there's anything you can do, please help me.' And the next day it suddenly stopped. My doctors were totally incredulous. Is that cause and effect? I don't know."

The crisis past, Weinstein was still too weak to attend classes. "I would faint if I stood up," he continues, "so some of my Academy instructors came to my hospital room with books and a chalkboard and I did my regular lessons there." During his convalescence, the small cadre of Jewish cadets in his class also visited Weinstein. "It was during the Yom Kippur War of 1973," he recounts. "They'd come in at the end of each day and draw diagrams for me of the Israeli and Arab front lines. We shared a real sense of camaraderie, a feeling of pride with each battle won."

After two additional weeks, Weinstein was finally released. "I still really didn't want to go back," he confesses. "Now that I knew what was really going to be required of me, I just didn't want to face it. I dreaded trying to reacclimate myself to all the demanding rigors, like getting up for a rifle run at four in the morning, terrified to be rudely awakened from a sound sleep and screamed at by upperclassmen. But I had no choice. I was good to go."

Struggling to catch up with his studies, Weinstein also managed to keep one eye on the historical developments in the Middle East in the fall of 1973. "I decided that I wanted to take some of my cadet pay and donate it to the United Jewish Appeal," he says. "It wasn't much to begin with, but I sent a letter up the chain of command requesting that eighteen dollars be sent to them from my monthly cadet paycheck. Eighteen, of course, is a very significant number for Jews, symbolizing life, and we often contribute money or give monetary gifts in multiples of eighteen. I had this vague idea that I wanted to help show my support for the war, and I couldn't think of how else to do it. I'd never written a check in my life, so I just asked payroll to earmark the money."

The decision, according to Weinstein, "must have pissed somebody off." Shortly after he made his salary deferment request and not more than a week out of the hospital, he was studying in his quarters with his two doolie roommates. "They put us in three-man rooms at first while the weeding-out process was under way. Eventually, after those who couldn't cut it had dropped out, you'd get transferred to a two-man billet.

"I don't know who noticed it first," Weinstein continues. "We were really absorbed in our work, but one of us saw a folded piece of paper, torn from a notebook, that been slipped under the door. That was kind of unusual. Normally, in those days before cell phones and e-mail, if they wanted to get in touch with you, they'd post a notice on the bulletin board outside your room. This was something different. I went over and picked it up, and the first thing I saw was a swastika crudely drawn on the top two-thirds of the sheet. Underneath it, in this strange wispy writing, were the words 'You can run, Jew, but you can't hide.'"

The three young cadets stood silently staring at the toxic message and each other. "There was no question who it was intended for," says Weinstein. "Burnie Peters was an African-American Protestant guy, and Ron Kennedy a caucasian, was also a Protestant. I was the only Jew in the room. We had no idea what was going on. We were constantly being tested by the upperclassmen, harassed and taunted in all kinds of ways, but this seemed way over the line, even for that kind of sanctioned hazing."

Was the message a response to his naïve but well-meaning attempt to support Israel in her struggle for existence? "I don't know," Weinstein admits. "At the time that never occurred to me. I was so freaked out. It was terrifying on a lot of levels, not the least being that I was eighteen years old, a long way from home, with absolutely no one to turn to in the Academy hierarchy, and trying desperately to fit myself into an adversarial, ritualistic environment that I just barely understood. To be singled out like that, and for that reason, seemed then like the ultimate exclusion. In a Spartan place where the loss of individual identity and integration into the system was hammered into you day and night, being branded as a 'Jew,' as someone fundamentally different, took on a whole new utterly terrifying connotation. I was suddenly an outsider in a world where there was no room for outsiders."

Over the next twenty-four hours three more notes were slipped beneath the door, each bearing the outsize swastika that had become the trademark of Weinstein's tormentor or tormentors. "I was going home for Thanksgiving," he continues, "and when you left the Academy, you had to let the administration know way in advance, even to the point of providing your flight number if you'd made a plane reservation. It was like Delta or Frontier or something and I had to make a change at LAX to get a connection to Santa Maria, California, which was the closest airport to Vandenberg. But whatever it was, one of the notes had all the information and, in the same weird, barely legible handwriting, threatened to blow up the jet I was on."

Frantic and bewildered, Weinstein was unsure whether even to inform his superiors of the hate mail. "Maybe it was a test, I thought. Maybe it was a sick joke. I couldn't imagine that this was happening without someone high up knowing about it. The Academy was such a buttoned-down militaristic place. You couldn't take a dump without having to report it. It seemed impossible that this was going on unnoticed. All I could do was hang on and hope that it stopped sooner or later."

It didn't. "After that first day I was on my way to chemistry class in Fairchild Hall in the morning, this huge, six-floor academic building, and I was in a big hurry because I was really late and I knew I was probably going to get in trouble—demerits or something—and that was the main thing on my mind. I was wearing my parka; I remember that, because it was freezing cold, and when I got to the landing heading toward the second-floor classroom, I heard someone behind me. I didn't think much of it, the place was always crowded, but then I felt a sharp pain at the back of my head and lost consciousness. I don't know how long I was out, but when I came to, there was a colonel bent over me and I was lying facedown in a pool of my own blood."

19

IN A ZONE BEYOND FEAR

"I must have been lying there for a while because the blood had turned sticky and I ached all over. I had had the shit kicked out me, but after that first blow I blacked out, and from then on out I was just a punching bag. They ended up throwing me down the stairs, to the first-floor landing, which is where the colonel found me. I wish I could say that I fought back, that I gave as good as I got, but it just wasn't so. I was a victim, and having to admit that, even now, fucking pisses me off and makes me feel ashamed."

It is that sense of dishonor, an abiding humiliation that rubs against Weinstein's lifetime of self-sufficiency and scrupulous autonomy, that would keep him from revealing all the salient aspects of the harrowing ordeal to anyone except his wife for over three decades. "I had promised myself even as a kid that I would never let myself become a Jewish victim," he asserts, "like all those who lined up passively for their turn in the gas chambers. I'm an American, goddammit, and I know what the law says about my liberty and my equality and my right to hold my head up and take my place in a free society. No one can take that away from me, but how do you fight an enemy who hides in the shadows and coldcocks you from behind? It was frustrating, but more than that, it was hideously degrading, and my people have been degraded enough over the course of our history."

To a remarkable degree, Weinstein's guiding principles had already largely been formed by age eighteen. The torment he was to suffer at the Academy, where he had hoped to prove his exceptional qualities to himself and to the world, would shake but not shatter that resolve. But it also created a strange discord that echoed through his life up until the moment he received Pam Zubeck's fateful phone call. "There's a real part of me that has always felt like a failure," he reveals. "I've wondered so often if I couldn't have done more, stood up for myself in some way, made them pay, whoever *they* were. At the same time, I hated myself for letting it happen and always felt, all rational arguments aside, that it was somehow my fault. It was the thing I hated most: the surreal concept of Jewish guilt, of somehow being responsible for what happens to us, of deserving what we get. I've fought against that my whole life, but I guess I was also fighting against an irrational shame buried deep inside of me."

This emotion struggled to surface at what would turn out to be a critical juncture in Weinstein's life. "I didn't see it coming," he confesses, on the subject of the trauma of his first son Casey's departure for the Academy in 2000. "For those first eight days, when he was in the initial part of Beast, we had absolutely no communication with him, and every night I had horrible, vivid nightmares that the same thing that had been visited on me my doolie year was going to come down on him. They were incredibly real and detailed. I could see it played out over and over again, except instead of happening to me, it was happening to Casey. It got so bad, Bonnie started insisting that I at least consider getting some counseling, but then the first letter came from Casey. He wrote that he loved being at the Academy, that he knew for sure that he was in the right place, and just like that, the nightmares stopped. But somewhere back there, the fear must have still been festering."

Following the assault on Weinstein in Fairchild Hall, the swastika-scrawled messages kept coming, each with an escalating message of hate, and each inexplicably slipped under the noses of the Academy and the Air Force's Office of Special Investigations (OSI), summoned to get to the bottom of the still unfolding case. "I'm not sure exactly, but there

were probably ten to twelve notes over a two-week period," Weinstein recounts. "I lost track after a while. To tell you the truth, I think I was in a
state of shock after getting beaten up. They sent me back to the hospital
to check me out for two days. I think my father came out again from Vandenberg Air Force Base in California and I couldn't believe I was back to
square one. My world was falling apart. I had such high expectations for
myself and for the Academy, and it was all turning to shit."

The OSI had, meanwhile, put in place an operation that smacked of
an overwrought spy novel. "They got some 1973 graduates (brand-new
second lieutenants) and dressed them up as current cadets to follow me
around, which was really stupid since practically everyone must have
known that they'd just gotten out of the Academy. They actually con-
cocted a plan where they put another OSI. agent in my closet to wait for
the next note to be dropped. I think it even happened once, but by the
time the guy rushed out the door, the hall was empty. It was really Key-
stone Kops stuff, and it all seemed so half-assed. But I was eighteen and
this was the fucking OSI. What was I going to say?" The OSI also interviewed Weinstein's roommates. "They were told to keep an eye on me,"
he relates, "and were under strict instructions not to tell anyone that
they had been officially ordered to follow my whereabouts. In some very
real and visceral ways it was as traumatic for them as for me."

Along with the constant anxiety of the ongoing harassment, Weinstein was acutely aware that his future hung in the balance. "Half of me
wanted to just pack up and leave," he continues, "but the other half was
determined to stick it out, and I knew that if I fell too much further behind in my studies, I wasn't going to be able to ever catch up anyway.
There was also the question of my physical condition. I'd been really
sick and then gotten badly beaten, and even if you're boxing and get
knocked out, it can screw up your pilot qualification. At that time, of
course, everyone's ultimate ambition was to fly a fighter jet, and I was
no different. I was hanging on by a mere thread, I couldn't concentrate;
I was jumping at the slightest sound, not really eating or sleeping. And I
was more alone than I'd ever been in my life. I felt utterly and completely isolated from the entire human race."

Compounding the sense of isolation was that, among the some forty
Jewish cadets—about 1 percent of the student population—Weinstein

alone had been singled out. "Nobody else was going through this," he explains. "In fact, I'd never gone through it before myself. This was my first encounter with virulent anti-Semitism, and I just wasn't prepared for the psychic damage it caused."

The OSI's plan was to try to isolate Weinstein in various locales around the Academy, watching and waiting for the assailant to strike again. "They put me in the library, in the rec rooms, moving me here and there, like a piece of live bait. I definitely started wondering how hard this could really be, to find this motherfucker, when they decided to station me up in a fifth-floor bathroom at Fairchild Hall. They stuck me in a stall and told me to wait there, which I did for the whole afternoon, missing more classes. I was also under direct orders not to tell any of my fellow cadets, including Burnie and Ron, my roommates, what was happening and why I was out of action so much. It was torture."

The ruse failed to snag the culprit, and Weinstein returned to his room to find another note slid under the door. "This was going on for over a week now, and the OSI. was getting a little desperate, but it was nothing compared to how I felt. For lack of a better plan they took me back up the next day to the Fairchild Hall bathroom and put me in that stall again. By that time I wasn't sure what was worse: the harassment or being a pawn in this stupid charade. I sat down on the toilet and waited. Nothing happened and nothing happened, and then something happened."

Weinstein heard the echoing sound of footsteps on the polished tile. "'Lieutenant?' I said, thinking it was the one of the recent Academy graduates who were supposed to be shadowing me." He saw a pair of polished black military-issue shoes appear outside the stall. "Then, suddenly, the door comes crashing open, slamming me backwards and knocking me out. Again. Only this time it was worse. Whoever it was really did a number on me: ribs, face, the works. The OSI agent later maintained that he'd lost track of me in the crowd on the Terrazzo on the way to Fairchild, but by that time I didn't know what to believe or who was on my side anymore. I was in a zone beyond fear."

Weinstein was again rushed to the Academy hospital. "They patched me up as best they could," he continues, "and sent me back to my room, again with specific orders to tell no one what had happened. I prepared a roughly fifteen-page single-spaced handwritten statement detailing everything that had happened to me, and a few days later I was ordered to the main administrative offices to meet with the OSI. They told me I might need to agree to take a 'routine' polygraph test. I agreed, but by that time I had totally lost all trust and confidence in them. They escorted me to this tiny, windowless room where a man who had previously identified himself as an OSI officer, wearing civilian clothes, was waiting. I remember a young airman guarding the door and being instantly wary, as if I was stepping into a trap. The OSI officer told me to sit down, and the first thing I noticed when I took the chair was this syringe lying on the blotter. It was the most threatening thing I'd ever seen, much more terrifying than if he'd had a loaded gun. While I was staring at it, he opened a file in front of him, flipped through the pages for what seemed like an eternity, and then looked at me with a disingenuous smile and spoke in a calm, measured tone with just the slightest tinge of . . . what . . . condescension? Arrogance? Whatever it was, it set my teeth on edge.

"He said that, after a thorough investigation, the OSI had come to the official conclusion that I was the one who had been writing the notes. To myself. 'Isn't that true, Cadet Weinstein?' he asked me, but I could barely hear him over the roaring in my ears. The fragments of a million thoughts were surging through my head and I was trying frantically to make sense out of what I'd just heard. 'How could you possibly think that?' I wanted to shout, but the words wouldn't come. 'Haven't you talked to my roommates? They were there, they saw it happen over and over again. What do you think, that I beat myself up? Twice? That I put myself in the hospital? Are you insane? Am *I* insane?' I opened my mouth, but still nothing came out. The room was spinning and somehow that syringe was still the only thing that I could really focus on. It was huge, an absurd prop, like a turkey baster or something. Were they going to drug me? Were they going to beat it out of me?"

Then the OSI officer slid a sheet of paper across the desk to Weinstein. "He had that same sick smile on his face," Weinstein continues in a low voice. "He said that all I had to do was sign this confession, that I'd done all this to myself, and that if I did, they'd just make me march a bit around the 'tour pad' on the Terrazzo for punishment and then painlessly disenroll me. He made it sound so simple, so effortless: the easiest thing in the world. Just go along with it and the nightmare would be over. I could go home. I'd be free. Then he picked up the syringe. He said if I didn't sign, he could 'always get to the bottom of this' by injecting me with truth serum—sodium Pentothal—and then interrogating me in lieu of the polygraph I'd previously agreed to take. At that moment, I couldn't imagine anything worse ever happening in my life. Was this the end of everything for me?

"I wish I could say I was a big, brave hero," Weinstein continues, returning again to the recurrent theme of shame inextricably bound up with the horrific incidents he was reliving. "But that wasn't the way it was. I started to cry. I stood up, sobbing inconsolably. He stood up. And I hit him as hard as I could. It felt like I'd slammed my fist into a brick wall. He went down, like a tree, and my fist throbbed in tremendous pain. I turned to the airman, who was armed but absolutely petrified. A look passed between us, as if we were both trying to comprehend what had just happened. Then I bolted, out the door and down the stairs, crying like a baby. I don't remember how, but I made it back to my squadron dorm room. I was still crying, almost hysterical. I don't even remember if Burnie or Ron were in the room. I crawled into bed in a fetal position, and after that the lights just went out. I was paralyzed. All I could think of was that I'd hit an officer. And I had absolutely no one in the world to confide in as to why I had done it." Throughout this entire OSI investigation, I'd never once been advised of my Constitutional rights nor offered the assistance of a military or civilian attorney.

Of all the surreal aspects of his ordeal, it was this—the striking of an officer—that would subsequently cause Weinstein the most anguish. "It's impossible to explain if you've never been in the military," he insists. "It's not just that physical violence against a superior officer is a court-martial offense. It's not even that you've dishonored the rules and regulations in the most egregious way. It's that you've struck out against the whole system that you've been trained to unquestioningly obey. Military authority may be abused, as it was by evangelicals at the Academy, but it is in no way arbitrary. You're taught from day one that following the chain of command is the most essential element to shaping character, to fulfilling your duty, to keeping faith with your fellow airmen, sailors, soldiers, and Marines. Civilians will never understand that. For them, authority is there to be questioned and tested, in elections, on the job, in parent-child relations. The fundamental premise of military life is that authority has already been tested, on the battlefield, where life and death hangs on your ability to follow orders. Power is vested by rank, and the status of rank is sacrosanct. By hitting an officer, even in a situation as crazy, threatening, and outrageous as the one I was in—I was denying my place in a society that had given me a reason for living. That wasn't a response I'd learned after merely a few months at the Academy. It had been instilled in me from the moment of birth, as the son of a fighting man and a member in good standing of a military family in the most extended and exalted sense of that term."

In the depths of his despair, Weinstein now turned to his immediate family. "My father is not normally a boat rocker," he maintains. "That's another aspect of military authority, the ingrained belief that your superiors have your interests at heart. But there was obviously something going on here that violated that belief and even he couldn't deny it. After I phoned home and told him what was going on, he got in touch with a cousin of mine who was an attorney in Las Vegas." Weinstein pauses, struggling with a new range of feelings. "The guy was an 'immigration lawyer'—I don't know how else to put this—who basically handled cases between Sicily and Las Vegas. I think you get the idea. That's all there is to it. I never really wanted to know what happened, what strings he pulled, but within twenty-four hours I got a phone call at the squadron CQ desk with cryptic instructions to go up to the Flatiron in the dead of night where someone who could help would be waiting for me."

The Flatiron is a stone-slab formation approximately half a mile from the Academy grounds up the first steep eastern incline of the Rocky Mountains serving as the western border of the huge Academy reservation. There, before big football games, cadets traditionally painted school-spirit signs visible from virtually the whole Academy below. "I got up there about two in the morning," Weinstein recalls. "It was freezing cold and a full moon was out, and there was this guy from the Anti-Defamation League who told me that we had to meet there because the Academy had refused him access to me. He had a small tape recorder and he took down my story. And after about two hours, when I was finally done, and shaking uncontrollably from the cold and the profound impact of the realization of these events, he told me they were going to send a letter to the Academy, warning them not to touch a hair on my head and to let me stay in school without punishment or any mark on my record, and if they didn't, he'd go straight to *The New York Times* and be ready to coordinate a whole exposé with Senator Barry Goldwater, who was about to come out to the Academy as head of the Board of Visitors, and a bunch of other shit that I couldn't believe I was hearing. I was numb, literally and figuratively. It was like being trapped in some endless loop of intrigue and deceit, and every twist and turn took me further from the life I'd known and the dreams I had."

He pauses again, casting back to the eighteen-year-old he was, helplessly ensnared by sinister forces using him for purposes he couldn't begin to fathom. "I think the worst of it was," he finally says, "after that, when it just abruptly stopped: the notes, the harassments, the threats of expulsion . . . everything. It's like it never happened, and no matter how hard I tried, later in my life, to get to the truth by talking to my old roommates, speaking with Academy graduates of that era, and filing comprehensive Freedom of Information Act requests to establish a detectable paper trail—anything at all to prove that it all actually happened—it just . . . went away. And all I was left with . . . was this wretched, dead feeling."

Words again fail Weinstein, as he tries to make sense of these traumatic events and their aftermath. "Getting off the hook, so to speak, didn't really help at all," he reveals. "The way it happened, this kind of underhanded, dark-of-night skulduggery, was ultimately just humiliating. In the years that followed I've sometimes wondered what it might have been like if I'd stood up and fought back and said, 'Fuck all of you. I never did what you accused me of. How *dare* you? I'm going to make you pay for what you put me through.' But I didn't. Instead I let a lawyer from central casting 'fix it' for me, and there I was, meeting a stranger with a tape recorder in the middle of a freezing night who wanted to blackmail the U.S. Air Force if they didn't leave me alone, as if I couldn't take care of myself, as if no Jew could ever take care himself by just standing up for what's right. That was the last thing I ever wanted, to have it 'handled' by some guy in a back office with connections. I've fought against that smear on my people all my life, and maybe I did it because I was ashamed of what I had allowed to happen in my name.

"Look," he continues, his characteristic intensity flaring again, "I know what people will think when they know the whole story: that everything I did to stop radical Christians from taking over the Academy was my way of getting back at those who made me suffer so cruelly and feel endlessly guilty and ashamed. And maybe it's even partially true. Maybe I do have a personal stake in winning this war. One thing really stuck out to me when I read the Navigator's newsletter after I filed the lawsuit. They said that their God had led them here, to the Academy, for this time in history. I can really relate to that. Maybe I was led here, through my experiences, to this time in history, too. Maybe that's the only way one person can find the raw passion and commitment and sheer stubbornness to keep fighting—when it matters personally. I always considered what I had done—hitting that officer—to be a cowardly act. But maybe it's the catalyst for everything that has happened since. And if so, then, just maybe, it was worth it.

"It doesn't do any good for me to say that some of my best friends are Christians," Weinstein acknowledges. "Or that I married one and so did my son. The fact is, I'm upfront about it, I don't *like* what a lot of evangelicals say and do in the name of Jesus. I don't *have* to like it. I don't like their smugness. I don't like their self-righteousness and their absolute certitude about everything in this and the next life. I don't like that they think they know what's best for me and will stop at nothing to impose it, to enforce their answers to the deep questions of life, the questions each one of us has the basic human right to answer or not answer for ourselves. And maybe all that, in some obscure way, comes from what happened to me when I arrived at the Academy, so full of high ideals. Whoever it was who put me through all that hideous pain hated me for one reason: because I was a Jew. I don't know what the distinction is between that hatred and a faith that says Anne Frank and Jack Benny and Dr. Seuss will be lit up eternally like Fourth of July Roman candles in hell simply because they refuse to believe the 'inerrant' biblical worldview of fundamentalist Christianity. But, to me, it's a distinction without a difference."

* 20 *

A DARK SECRET BROUGHT TO LIGHT

It took one of Weinstein's lawyers approximately sixteen hours to track down the perpetrator of the letter to Pam Zubeck, the Academy superintendent, and the executive director of the Academy Association of Graduates accusing Weinstein of writing a string of anti-Semitic notes to himself and being sent to intensive counseling by the Academy for his "behavior problems."

"They met in a Starbucks, I think it was, in Colorado Springs," Weinstein recounts. "It was over Memorial Day weekend 2005, and in about ten minutes after carefully explaining the lunacy of that letter's accusations, my legal counsel got a full written retraction. I can't say he didn't twist his arm but, if he did, it was in a courteous and professional way. In fact, what he told him was something like if he persisted with these absurd allegations, Mr. Weinstein would pursue vigorous and immediate litigation in which the perpetrator would lose everything he owned, everything his children might come to own, and everything any of them ever hoped to own. He pointed out in no uncertain terms that the accusations in the letter constituted a defamation and that I would never

ever rest until my name was completely cleared, which implied, very directly I think, utterly destroying this guy in the process."

But Weinstein's counterattack depended on more than intimidation. There was the simple matter of his sterling Academy record. "I was on the Superintendent's List—which is the Academy equivalent of, among other things, a college dean's list—for seven of the eight semesters of my education. This isn't just an academic honor. It also consists of ratings from officers and cadets on your leadership potential and military bearing. The only reason it wasn't eight out of eight is because no cadet is eligible during his or her first semester as an incoming doolie. I was a two-time summer squadron commander who graduated as an Honor Graduate, which was the equivalent of a magna cum laude at a civilian college. I competed in intercollegiate tennis, and there is simply no way any of this could have occurred if I had been guilty of the claims made in that letter, starting with a court-martial or honor code violation, not to mention serious behavioral counseling like I was some kind of a mental case. The Superintendent's List was reserved for the best of the best, and I'm proud to say to this day that I was among that elite every single semester that I was eligible during my four years as a cadet.

"It's also true," he adds quickly, "that my record at the Academy would have been impossible to accomplish if it had ever been known that I struck an officer. Obviously, the cover-up was incredibly thorough."

In a direct communication with all those who had been sent the initial letter, Weinstein's attorney took pains to point out, "It is illogical to assume that an investigation as sensitive as notes with swastikas and death threats pushed under the door of a Jewish cadet would be 'handled' in any manner by the cadet chain of command. It would have been an OSI matter, then and now." Weinstein expands on the point: "To anyone with even a passing knowledge of military law, it's ridiculous on the face of it to assume that by sending me to a shrink, the matter would have been in any way resolved. This was criminal activity, and if they'd really believed that I'd done it, they would be obliged to prosecute me."

"All these arguments made sense" to the accuser, wrote Weinstein's lawyer in a laconic turn of phrase. "He told me that he had no firsthand knowledge of the investigation's final result. And he assumed that the results had occurred as he indicated in his letter. However, with the information I presented to him, he fully agreed to retract his allegations. That retraction is attached."

"I recently sent a letter to you regarding Mr. Mikey Weinstein, US Air Force Cadet Class of 1977," read the retraction. "The purpose of this letter is to retract my remarks in that letter. I did not have all of the information I needed to arrive at the conclusions stated in my letter. I apologize for my hasty communication and I retract everything I said in the letter."

Weinstein says, "I got the news driving with Bonnie out to Dyess Air Force Base in Abilene, Texas, to visit a close family friend and fellow Academy graduate who's a B-1 bomber pilot out there. I called Pam Zubeck, who agreed to kill the story on the basis of the retraction. My first reaction was one of enormous relief. But then I realized immediately that I'd have to tell my kids the whole story. Somebody was obviously out to smear me, and if it had gone this far, who knows to what lengths they might go the next time? I didn't want Casey and Amanda and Curtis reading about this in the newspaper or seeing it on TV or wondering if the innuendos were true or whether everything I was doing was just a vendetta against the Academy. As painful as it was, they had to know what had happened to their old man. That decision was one of the most painful I'd ever had to make, and I felt vivid anger about being forced to make this choice."

But as time wore on, Mikey's rage turn to a grudging acknowledgment that he had perhaps, after all, kept his dark secret too long. "Telling the kids was a kind of liberation," he recounts. "It wasn't just that they took it in stride. I think that it helped them to understand a little better who I was and where I was coming from. What I thought might discredit my fight in their eyes, in the end strengthened it. The fact that someone would want to bring me down that badly made what I was doing seem even more compelling. I think they still share a genuine love of the Academy with me, a respect for what it can offer anyone with the guts and the brains to get there in the first place. I still have feelings of pride and fear and innocence lost when I drive through those gates, a kind of awe that's completely untouched by what happened to me there and the fact that, after all these years, I've never gotten an apology, or even an acknowledgment that it even happened at all. At the same time, no one's under any illusions. The Academy didn't descend from the sky on angels' wings. It's a human institution, and as such, it needs to be protected . . . sometimes from itself. The truth is, I was embarrassed by what happened to me at the Academy, and I didn't want my kids ever to feel that same unrelenting sense of shame."

Yet coming to terms with one of the darkest chapters in his life would, in time, trigger a new and deeply ambivalent reassessment of Weinstein's own Academy career. "Immediately after the whole episode was finally over in the late autumn of 1973—but with no sense of closure or justice—all I wanted to do was get out. Fuck this place. Fuck it to death. I remember running across the Terrazzo on the marble strip, in the midst of all those cadets scurrying like ants below the snowcapped mountains, and thinking that there was somebody watching me even then; someone who hated me because I was a Jew and even more so because I was still there. I was pissing them off just by being here in circulation, and it was that spite that kept me going one a day at a time for a while. I'd tell myself, one more day, then I'm fucking out of here and good riddance. Then, pretty soon, it was time to go home for Thanksgiving, and then winter break, and I'd come back each time saying to myself, just one more day, and each day turned into another day, and I started doing well, better and better in every aspect of the Academy program. I made the Superintendent's List and got to wear a star and a wreath on my uniform, and then it was NCAA tennis season and I was a pretty decent player, and pretty soon I wasn't living day to day anymore and eventually I was an honors graduate of the United States Air Force Academy commanding all the prestige that entails. And I was proud of what I'd accomplished, except for that part deep down inside that was always afraid that someone would find out: that I'd been accused of writing hate mail to myself, that I'd struck an officer; that someone had once hated me enough to try and destroy me at the age of eighteen."

And there was also, in the toxic repercussions of those dark winter days, an even more profound ambivalence waiting to be found. "The more I thought about it," he reveals," the more I realized those two hellish weeks had really colored my whole Air Force career. In a very real sense I had let them get away with what they did to me. I let myself be seduced by the Academy mystique all over again. I bought into a lie, even knowing it was a lie. I saw myself as an accommodationist, a collaborator. I'd turned a blind eye to something rotten at the core of that place, something that should never have been countenanced or ignored, all for the sake of what it could do for me. I'd never fully comprehended it before, but I *had* taken on the guilt of that crime—a crime against an innocent eighteen-year-old—day by day, one day at a time, hiding behind all the honor and the glory and the prestige and never coming to terms with what I had lost in the bargain. It's a kind of innocence that you never get back again, a kind of idealism that's essential to believing in the mission and in the knowledge that you might be called upon to die for it. And I told myself that I had it, that I really did believe in that motto on the wall, about not lying, stealing, or cheating, nor tolerating among us anyone who does. But I *had* tolerated it, and by doing so, I'd been lying to myself. For years."

It's a unique revelation for Weinstein, a reflective interlude and a perspective on himself that, for now, doesn't revert to the old hard-nosed verities. "Maybe it was the best thing that could have happened to me," he muses, "having my darkest secret brought to light. For a long time I worried that it would undermine what I was trying to do to save constitutional freedoms at the Academy, and, by extension, the whole military. The religious right could point at me and crow that I'd just been trying to get even for years and finally got my chance. But I know now that these parts of my life are really two sides of the same thing. Those who accept some religious consensus because it's advantageous to them and to their careers have as much to answer for as those who are pushing that consensus. Sometimes silence is a crime. Maybe if I'd stood up back then—never mind that I was eighteen and wet behind the ears and scared shitless—if I'd stood up anyway, maybe I could have changed something, made it more difficult for those who had no respect or understanding of Academy tradition to try and enforce their will. Yeah, sure, it was a grudge match. Maybe I thought I was taking up the cause for every Jew who ever felt like an outsider, for every one of my people who was forced to make the choice between converting and dying. I don't believe Anne Frank is burning eternally in hell, and I'm deeply offended by anyone who does. I'm not willing, just because we wear the same uniform and pledge the same allegiance, to look the other way. Been there. Done that. Never again."

From the deeply conflicted elements of his Academy experience, Weinstein would go on to construct his diverse and high-profile career and both the skill set he acquired from his West Wing years and the extraordinary connections he would cultivate there proved of enormous value in his impending face-off with Academy, Air Force, and Department of Defense evangelicals. "I was ready for this fight," he avows. "In some ways, it seemed like I had been preparing for it my whole life. During my time in Washington I received a very nuanced education in the methods of moving government, finessing the press and navigating the bureaucracy, all of which I had occasion to use more than once."

At the same time, he admits, "There was always this lurking fear that maybe, one day, someone would walk into my office and accuse me of writing hate mail to myself and striking an officer. That feeling never went away, even after the exhaustive background security clearance I went through for the White House job. If anything, that should have convinced me that whoever had buried the evidence had buried it deep, but I never quite got there. In my worst moments, I expected to be exposed for cowardice and insubordination. It was like the rattling chains of a ghost that never quite faded away."

In the meantime, life went on. In 1998, Bonnie Weinstein was first diagnosed with multiple sclerosis, and the couple's life took a sharp turn. "Suddenly," Weinstein explains, "money didn't seem so important. I was no longer interested in amassing assets so that one day when we were seventy we could go on our first cruise together. From that point it was very much about living for today, for Bonnie, and deriving as much enjoyment as possible out of friends and family and the simple pleasures of life. It was about being, as much as possible, in the moment and not waiting for some gilded payoff in the rosy future when you're too old and tired to appreciate it."

The flow of Weinstein's words winds down for a moment as he weighs the implications of his tumultuous life and times. "Of course," he says at last, "it's not about the future. It's never been about the future. I've always been able to handle what tomorrow brings. It's the past that can sometimes weigh you down: coming to terms with who you were and what you thought your life would become. That can be a bitch. But if you'd asked me back then if I could've imagined myself doing what I'm doing today, fighting this fight, I'm not so sure it would've seemed all that unlikely. Sometimes I think that everything I've ever done, who I am and what's important to me, has led up to this moment. I'm in this for every American. I'm in it to win it; for the Constitution, for my children and for Cecilia Peasley and her daughter. But I'm also in it for myself. As much as I found at the Academy—a life of painfully revealed purpose and confidence and the well-honed ability to realize that purpose—I also lost something there. I know I can never get it back. But maybe I can help other people from losing it."

⋆ 21 ⋆

LOOKING BACK AND LOOKING FORWARD

The battle raged on, its skirmishes, feints, and frontal assaults staged not only in the national and international media and in courtrooms from New Mexico to Washington, D.C., but in the personal and professional lives of those caught up in the knotty conflict.

"There are inevitable consequences to standing up and speaking out," asserts Casey Weinstein in a frank appraisal of the fallout from his father's fight. "I'd say, first of all, it has damaged my relationship with some of my classmates from the Academy, which I think is more painful than simply losing a friend, considering how closely knit we had all, out of necessity, become during our time together. Relationships you form in that period of your life are meant to last a lifetime, and when they don't, you feel the pain. I've had fellow cadets write to me questioning whether the things that I revealed—the events and situations that started the ball rolling in the first place—ever happened at all. And when we get together face-to-face, it's like the proverbial five-hundred-pound gorilla in the room. Some of my close friends have become wary and watchful. It's as if they don't know how touchy I'm going to be, like I might take offense if they said 'God bless you' after I sneezed. And it's not just friends. There are members of our extended family that claim to have been permanently alienated by what's been going on."

Yet, for the young airman, the cause is well worth the cost. "It didn't take me long to realize that the abuses I'd seen at the Academy had spread into the service as whole," he continues. Following graduation, the first assignment he received as an active duty officer was to Keesler Air Force Base in Biloxi, Mississippi. "I was training in combat communications," he recounts, "and was being briefed by Lieutenant General Harry Raduege, who at the time was the director of the Defense Information Systems Agency. He made a PowerPoint presentation and at the top of every slide, a big eye had been superimposed. As soon as I saw it, I had a sick feeling in my stomach, and I found myself getting angrier and angrier as his religious rhetoric ratcheted up. Sure enough, at the end of the lecture, he told us that the eye did indeed represent God watching over us, and that as officers in the United States Air Force we were constantly under divine surveillance. He encouraged us to read the Bible wherever we were deployed and that nothing was more important than being a good servant of God. He wrapped it by assuring us that the day anyone told him to stop giving such advice was the day he would turn in his resignation. I was floored and immediately brought a complaint up through my chain of command, which went exactly nowhere. But I did have the satisfaction of subsequently hearing from one of my classmates, who had attended the same or a similar lecture, when the general brought up the subject of some 'crazy lieutenant' who had the audacity to complain about his presentation. I guess I made an impression."

The impression Casey Weinstein made worked both ways. "On the one hand, people know who I am and know who my father is," he explains. "I think if there's even a hint of prejudicial action against me, they know my dad will be all over them in a heartbeat. On the other hand, it's foolish not to acknowledge that all this has probably been detrimental to my Air Force career. Like any branch of the service, the Air Force puts a premium on conformity and compliance. That's how we do our job. But when something is wrong and needs to be fixed, sometimes that takes a sole individual stepping up and letting his or her voice be heard. That sets you apart and singles you out and that can make it difficult in an organization that values uniformity in every sense of the word."

By late 2005, Mikey Weinstein had come to the realization that the military organization in question was hardly in a hurry to resolve the questions he had set before it. Characteristically impatient with the snail's-pace deliberations of the courts, he threw his personal energies and comsiderable funds into the creation of the Military Religious Freedom Foundation, launched in early 2006.

The immediate impact of the foundation's formation can be read in the frenzied response of Focus on the Family, which, through its CitizenLink Web site, blared the headline "Antagonist of Christians in the Military Steps It Up," going on to declare, "Mikey Weinstein creates a foundation to oppose sharing faith."

According to Kelly Shackelford, chief counsel of Focus on the Family's legal arm, "The problem with these groups is that they like to pretend they are for religious freedom. Actually, the position is to be restrictive of people's religion." Also piling on was Bruce Fister, executive director of the Officers' Christian Fellowship. "We're not beating people over the head with our beliefs," he insisted, "but we do feel like it's important to explain the hope that we have when somebody asks."

"At the Academy asking was never an option," Weinstein shoots back. "Coercion was the norm and the foundation was formed to stop exactly the sort of practices the Officers' Christian Fellowship has been given tacit permission to pursue by the administration and, more importantly, by the Air Force and other service branch command structure."

Weinstein would go on to recruit an impressive advisory board from across the spectrum of his comprehensive contacts. Along with such familiar names as MeLinda Morton, Dr. Kristen Leslie, and David Antoon, the foundation attracted a number of retired high-ranking officers for whom evangelical encroachment had become a clear and present danger to the armed services they had served with such distinction. Among them: Vice Admiral Bernard Marvin Kauderer, who, during a thirty-three-year naval career, commanded the submarine forces of the

U.S. Pacific and Atlantic fleets, the first time both theaters were ever under a single officer. He also commanded all NATO submarine forces. An Annapolis classmate of Weinstein's father, Kauderer's reasons for lending his name and prestige to the foundation were simple. "It's a basic principle," he says. "Young men and women in the military should be secure in their own beliefs, whatever they might be. They have the right not to be harassed or intimidated, especially when such actions impinge directly on the good order and discipline that is essential for any military organization to carry out its mission. This is simply good policy."

Richard Klass, a former Air Force colonel and Air Force Academy graduate from the class of 1962, agrees. Klass flew over two hundred missions as a forward air controller, including action during the Tet offensive and the battle of Khe Sanh, and his numerous honors include a Silver Star, Legion of Merit, Distinguished Flying Cross, and Purple Heart. A Rhodes Scholar and White House Fellow, Klass also served as assistant professor of political science and a flight training instructor at the Academy. "I hadn't really known the extent of the problem," Klass reveals, "before I went to a graduate leadership conference in the summer of 2005. It was there that I met Mikey Weinstein for the first time, after hearing him defend his position in a restaurant where we had all gone the evening the conference ended. I remember him asking someone if they believed that Catholics were Christians and the answer he got from that guy—that they weren't because they didn't have a 'personal relationship with Jesus Christ'—really shocked me. Later this same guy defined the difference between a gung ho born-again believer and a fervent Muslim. The first, he said, was compelled to go out and save people. The second was compelled to go out and kill people. Jesus Christ, I thought to myself, quite literally. What's going on here?"

Klass, a lifelong Catholic, stops short of labeling evangelical encroachment in the military as a conspiracy. "But it's clear," he acknowledges, "that this goes far beyond the Academy. It's hard not to find the correlation between the abuses Mikey has uncovered and the Bush administration's ongoing attempts to breach the wall of separation between church and state."

According to John J. Michels Jr., another outstanding member of the foundation's advisory board, that breach is more akin to a long, slow erosion. A retired Air Force lieutenant colonel, Michels is a classmate of Weinstein's from the Academy who later attended Duke Lake School and established himself as a respected attorney with a high national profile, thanks in part to the injunctive relief he won against the federal government over the military's anthrax vaccination program. "There has always been a significant religious presence at the Academy and, in a larger sense, in the armed services as a whole," Michels asserts. "These are people who, of necessity, deal with death and the taking of life. Many of them have seen all the stupid ways there are to die in combat and that, naturally, raises some big questions that religion without question helps to address. At the same time, we're drawing a large percentage of our military personnel from the southeastern region of the country, a place where a martial culture is recognized and rewarded. It also happens to be the Bible Belt, so it's hardly surprising that fundamental Christianity is so prevalent in the military. That's not an excuse for what happened at the Academy. It's a fact."

The fact, Michels continues, is the persistence of what he calls "institutional tolerance." "They should have gotten a handle on this a long time ago. The fact that they didn't and, to a significant degree, still haven't points to a basic and egregious misunderstanding of the role of religion in our national life.

"I don't believe in stamping out every expression of faith in the public square," Michels continues. "Belief in a higher power is, and always has been, a powerful moral tool. I think some entanglements of church and state are inevitable, for instance, in the area of churches providing social services. That is manifestly a good thing. By the same token, evangelicals can hardly be faulted for wanting to actively spread their message. That's an essential tenet of their religion, and the freedom to practice that religion is their inalienable right as Americans. But that stops at the gates of any military institution, and what we've seen over the course of the last decade is evangelical Christians inside the armed forces providing free access to their coreligionists. In my view that's what Mikey's foundation has been created to remedy."

The need for that remedy, according to Reza Aslan—one of a number of high-profile members of the foundation's advisory board from outside the military—reaches well beyond the confines of the Academy, the Pentagon's purview, or even the national interest. "This is being felt around the world," says the author of the internationally acclaimed book *No God But God: The Origins, Evolution, and Future of Islam.* Aslan should know. The first of a new generation of articulate young Muslim intellectuals and president of Harvard's chapter of the World Conference on Religion and Peace, he is a respected international expert on Islam and the Middle East, a frequent television and radio guest, a scholar, and a media consultant on issues of religion and politics who is both blunt and empathetic in his warnings. "This idea, promulgated among religious extremists on both sides, that we are in the midst of a cosmic battle between Islam and Christianity will become a self-fulfilling prophecy unless we move quickly and aggressively to counter it. This is not a clash of civilizations, and if we insist on framing it that way we will reap the whirlwind. What is most revealing about the whole concept of an apocalyptic civilizational clash is that both the evangelicals and the jihadists use it to justify their actions. What we are actually seeing is a titanic struggle for the heart and soul of Islam itself, and as long as we persist in casting every Muslim as the enemy we will be dragged further and further into that struggle.

"It's one thing," Aslan continues, "to employ this Manichean religious rhetoric in the name of political expedience. It's quite another to put boots on the ground and wings in the sky for the purposes of ushering in Armageddon. Using the military as an instrument of sectarian subjugation will be an unmitigated disaster for the West. By keeping religion out of the armed forces we can take the first step in stripping radical ideology from an enormously complex and volatile conflict. I can't think of a more important task."

The foundation's intriguing cross-section of scholars, political strategists, and public figures also includes Republican Party consultant Doug Turner; Richard Schlosberg, onetime CEO and publisher of both *The Los Angeles Times* and *The Denver Post*; ambassador Joseph Wilson, who in July 2003 alerted the media to the Bush administration's false claims regarding Iraq's nuclear program and paid with the outing of his wife, CIA agent Valerie Plame; and Robert T. Herres, a four-star general, former vice chairman of the Joint Chiefs of Staff, commander of NORAD, and head of the operation that captured Panamanian dictator

Manuel Noriega in 1989. Also at the forefront is Pedro Luis Irigone-garary, a Cuban-born Topeka attorney who gained national and international attention in his fight against a creationism curriculum installed by the Kansas Board of Education. "I have an immense respect for the military," says the voluble Irigonegarary, "but I'm also a strong critic of what I call the waste of military courage by those who send our young men and women off to the war. And I can't think of a bigger waste than telling those brave soldiers that they're fighting a holy crusade. Look," he adds after a thoughtful pause, "At D-Day, Eisenhower asked the blessing of God. Patton prayed for good weather. The notion that God is on our side has been entwined throughout our military history. It comes with the territory. But shouldn't each individual have the freedom to decide what God they are fighting for and praying to? It's that right to worship as we please that has been one of the abiding reasons we send our sons and daughters off to die. We need to preserve that right at all costs."

"It is incredibly heartening to see who's lining up behind this organization," says Weinstein. "For all the polarization of American life we've seen over the past several years, it turns out that the issue of church and state separation is a great unifier regardless of one's political party affiliation or personal religious faith."

Yet, despite the efforts of men and women of goodwill to maintain that unifying principle, the polarization of which Weinstein speak seems ever more starkly drawn as the country continues to fragment along social, political, and spiritual fault lines. Even in the midst of what might well be the deepest schism in the American body politic since the Civil War, Weinstein warns against demonizing the adversary with simplistic generalities.

"It's simply wrong to paint every evangelical with the same brush," he insists. "I'm firmly convinced that it's possible to have a strong, even a fervent, belief and still respect the constitutional rights of your fellow American citizens. From the first time I ever heard it, I was impressed by the Alcoholics Anonymous idea of drawing its members through attraction, not promotion. There's a potential model there, I think, for fundamentalists, at least in the workplace: lead by example, not by marketing and publicity and high-pressure sales tactics. What happened at the Academy, and what's still happening in the military at large, may go beyond the work of a handful of zealots, but, thank God, it's far from the consensus view of most mainline American Christians."

Indeed, that reality puts yet more urgency to Weinstein's work. "The fact that there is not one overriding view among Christians argues even more strongly that we need to keep the levers of power out of their hands, or those of any single religion. Look, even among evangelicals there are doctrinal and political divides. Traditional evangelicals, who comprise about twelve percent of all Americans, oppose evolution, believe the world will end in a battle between Jesus and the Antichrist, and that abortion should be highly restricted or never legal—all by a wide margin. Centrist evangelicals, about ten percent of the population, believe those same things in considerably fewer numbers, and so-called modern evangelicals, weighing in at about three percent of Americans, hardly believe them at all. I think it all begs the question: If Christians with an avowed evangelical agenda gain substantive control of the military, can we expect that their next move will be against the ideologically impure in their own ranks? Will we one day see a sectarian bloodbath like the one now occurring in Iraq between Sunnis and Shiites, who, after all, are just two branches of the same religion who happen to disagree on fundamental doctrine?"

For Weinstein, whatever might still be left to decide on the issue of church and state separation, the question of church and military separation has long ago been settled. "It's a no-brainer, historically speaking," he continues. "Anytime you put weapons in the hands of religiously motivated individuals, they will quickly find each other, organize themselves, and go looking for some heretics to kill. We profess to be baffled at the militant ideology of terrorists who are willing to sacrifice themselves to take out a few more infidels. But where do we draw the line between them and Bobby Welch's warrior leaders with his call to create a 'force multiplying army' intent on capturing the enemy's domain? I know the argument: militant imagery and language is only being used in a spiritual context, to describe the battle for souls. I don't buy it. We're now in the midst of a brutal war in the Middle East between two societies that both claim the special providence of God—there are some who even describe it as a 'clash of civilizations.' Is it really such a stretch to extrapolate spiritual warfare into the realm of actual bullets and bloodshed? Are we at risk of arming and equipping an army of our own fanatics single-mindedly focused on ushering in the kingdom of God by converting, or killing, every last unbeliever? This isn't my for- mulation. The evangelical credo is clear on this point: the gospel must be preached to all the world. Every knee will bow and every tongue con- fess. That's a mission of conquest, and America—where the right to worship freely is a bedrock principle, perhaps *the* most significant civic innovation of our founding fathers—has a responsibility to oppose that mission and vigorously deprive it of material and logistical support."

Acutely aware of the part his own heritage plays in the cause he es- pouses, Weinstein is insistent on emphasizing inclusiveness. "This is not a Jewish issue," he says. "That should be obvious, despite the fact that anti-Semitism was the face of religious intolerance that first pre- sented itself to me and to my sons and the one to which I was genetically predisposed to respond. It is naturally of great personal consequence that Curtis's and Casey's encounters with religious bigotry occurred at the Academy, which is where I first encountered it as well. Of course, from a historical perspective, Jews have always had the unfortunate role of scapegoat thrust upon them. But I'm under no illusions that what happened to my Jewish sons and my Christian daughter-in-law could not have happened to the son of a patriotic American Muslim or Bud- dhist or agnostic or atheist. I wouldn't be surprised if it already had. Perhaps what's significant about the Jewish dimension of this story is a certain acute awareness, inbred over centuries, of our status as peren- nial victims of suffering. Every Jew differs in how he or she responds to that legacy. My response, even early, was a resolution to reject it com- pletely. To the degree that I've succeeded in that goal, I have tried to make myself into a formidable adversary to those doing the afflicting. Hell, I don't know, maybe it took a Jew to bring this to light . . . a Jew with an attitude of defiance and confrontation."

To be sure, Weinstein's famous "attitude" has been key to bringing this story to the front pages and keeping it there. His indefatigable de- termination and truculent disregard for the niceties of public discourse have earned him as many enemies as allies, which leaves him unde- terred. "This is my war," he says, "and I'll fight it the way I fucking want to. Of course, I need all the support I can get, and I welcome it all, but this, for me, is visceral. It touches on absolutely everything I love and hate, and if I step over the line in my passionate defense and obstinate attack, at least people know that, on this issue, I'm as serious as a heart attack. The battle cry of our foundation is that we are *out* of the business of merely comforting the afflicted and are now *in* the business of afflicting the comfortable."

Weinstein's seriousness can, in close proximity, seem overwhelming. His sprawling and gracious Albuquerque home takes on the aura of a beleaguered bunker as he wages his war by phone and fax and e-mail. His anger is never out of reach, foulmouthed explosions of bitterness are launched against the evangelical forces that sometimes seem to feed on the rancor he pours forth. Yet at the same time, Weinstein wears his heart on his sleeve, his eyes welling with tears as he speaks of his love for family and country and, in the most perplexing paradox of this complex and contradictory man, the Air Force and the Air Force Academy. In those special moments, a tenderness suffuses his expressive face, a kind of delicate helplessness before both the beauty and the ugliness of the world. "It was Dante," he concludes, "who said that the darkest places of hell are reserved for those who remain silent, particularly in times of moral crisis. I will not be silent." It was Sinclair Lewis who said, "When fascism comes to America, it will be wrapped in the flag, carrying a cross." And it is Mikey Weinstein who says that it is not too late to reclaim our birthright as Americans who are blessed with freedom regardless of race, color, or creed.

Fierce and unsparing in his love for his family, his heritage, and his country, he reserves a special place in a hell of his own devising for those he deems unworthy of citizenship in the great American experiment, an experiment worthy of his intense affections and boundless devotion.

APPENDIX A

Department of the Air Force
Headquarters United States Air Force Academy
USAF Academy Colorado

30 July 2004

MEMORANDUM FOR CH COL MICHAEL WHITTINGTON

FROM: CH CAPT MELINDA MORTON
       HQ USAFA/HCX
       1st GROUP CHAPLAIN

SUBJECT: After Action Report: BCT II Chaplain Practicum Training: Special Program in Pastoral Care, with the resources, supervision and selected students of Yale Divinity School.

1. 22 July–28 July Dr. Kristen Leslie and Graduate Students from the Yale Divinity School, along with USAFA active duty and reserve chaplains, participated in a BCT II, Specialized Practicum in Pastoral Care.
    1.1. The Yale team participated in all aspects of USAFA BCT Chaplain pastoral care exclusive of privileged communication.
    1.2. Yale team members lived in Jack's Valley with USAFA Chaplains, observing and actively participating in worship services, Basic Cadet and Cadre visitation, SPIRE, BCT training courses (LCR, Obstacle, Confidence, and Assault), Self-Aid Buddy Care and Honor instruction. In addition, practicum members observed and participated in Cadet Chapel services, and GE briefings, services and general pastoral care.
2. The Program Objectives for BCT II Chaplain Practicum Training: Special Program in Pastoral Care were as follows:
    2.1. Provide USAFA/HC chaplains rigorous assessment and advanced training in specialized pastoral care to victims of sexualized vio-

lence and practical methodologies for the prevention of sexual assault

2.2. Provide USAFA/HC chaplains this detailed assessment and specialized pastoral care training in the demanding practicum environment of Basic Cadet Training. Improve chaplain mission support (care to cadets) through real-time, practical and supervised application of enhanced chaplain counseling techniques, cadet-centered pastoral interaction and specifically directed ministry of presence.

2.3. Improve USAFA/HC chaplain crises and pastoral care response to cadets by addressing pastoral care issues in the training environment.

2.4. Provide a dynamic practicum environment where USAFA/HC chaplains may work with credentialed experts in the field of pastoral care to victims of sexualized violence.

2.5. Provide critical reflection on the USAFA/HC chaplain role in the Academy Response Team (ART) process.

2.6. Provide the USAFA/HC team well-developed feedback on pastoral care for victims of sexualized violence, cadet ministry and worship events, organization of ministry of presence, general and crisis pastoral counseling protocols and implementation of Agenda for Change items.

2.7. Provide USAFA/HC chaplains resources to extensively and critically examine cultural influences prevalent in the cadet population. Develop practical and pro-active chaplain ministry skill-sets to positively influence USAFA climate and culture changes.

3. Yale Practicum Team (YPT) members provided daily structured feedback and detailed observations to the USAFA Practicum coordinator, Chaplain Morton. Chaplain Morton passed all feedback to Chaplain Watties, the US-AFA chaplain in charge of all BCT and Summer Ministries.

4. On 28 July 2004, the Yale Practicum team provided the entire USAFA Chapel staff extensive verbal assessment. This feedback session occurred following a regularly scheduled staff meeting, held in the USAFA BCT Chapel tent, Jack's Valley.

5. YPT major assessments and suggestions for improvement of USAFA pastoral care are as follows:

5.1. Talent and enthusiasm of USAFA Chaplains. YPT noted the enthusiasm and individual talent of chaplains delivering consistent and intentional pastoral care. The staff was appropriately organized and scheduled to serve BCT cadets and cadre as well as cadets experiencing GE and other summer training and academic environments.

5.2. Credibility bolstered by chaplain presence. YPT indicated that an appropriate number of active duty and reserve chaplains were available for pastoral care and counseling. In addition, chaplain's ministry of presence at training courses, tent visitation and throughout the BCT program lent credibility to statements of care and concern.

5.3. Gender issues. On the assault course, YPT observed women cadre confronting women BCT cadet trainees. (Challenging verbal confrontation is appropriate to training in the Assault Course environment.) The YPT noted that these verbal critiques were focus on gender rather than on performance as a contribution to the team. This very public and gender-based interaction may contribute to a perpetuation of negative climate and culture. Women Cadre indicated that they were trying to make the trainees "strong and emotionally well-prepared for cadet life." Chaplains observing these interactions apparently did not recognize these exchanges as inappropriate training.

5.4. Challenges to pluralism. YPT observed consistent specific articulations of Evangelical Christian themes during general protestant services. (BCT and GE) Protestant Cadets were encouraged to chant the phrase, "This is our Chapel and the Lord is our God." Protestant Basic Cadets were encouraged to pray for the salvation of fellow BCT members who chose not to attend worship. During general protestant worship in Jack's Valley, attending Basic Cadets were encouraged to return to tents, proselytize fellow BCT members, and remind them of the consequences of apostasy. (Protestant Basic Cadets were reminded that those not "born again will burn in the fires of hell.") Protestant Basic Cadets were regularly encouraged to "witness" to fellow Basic Cadets. Protestant Basic Cadets were commonly told that Jesus had "called" them to the Academy and military life. Protestant Basic Cadets were informed that God's plan for their life included attending USAFA.

5.5. YPT clearly articulated a concern that such stridently Evangelical themes challenged the necessarily pluralistic environment of BCT. YPT expressed a concern that the overwhelmingly Evangelical tone of general protestant worship encouraged religious divisions rather than fostering spiritual understanding among Basic Cadets. YPT suggested that the USAFA Chaplain Service reconsider the worship dynamics and Chaplain/Basic Cadet interaction during BCT. YPT suggested focusing on aspects of ecumenical teamwork and developing an appreciation of spiritual diversity.

6. The YPT expresses great appreciation for the USAFA Practicum Experience. Active Duty and Reserve Chaplains gave graciously of their time and experience, creating a helpful learning environment and facilitating the assessment process.

Kristen J. Leslie
Assistant Professor in Pastoral Care and Counseling
Yale Divinity School
Director, BCT II Chaplain Practicum Training: Special Program in Pastoral Care

MeLinda S. Morton, Ch Capt
1st Group Chaplain
USAFA
Practicum Coordinator, BCT II Chaplain Practicum Training: Special Program in Pastoral Care

APPENDIX B

Report of Americans United for Separation of Church and State on Religious Coercion and Endorsement of Religion at the United States Air Force Academy

Americans United for Separation of Church and State has received numerous complaints from a variety of sources, representing diverse religious backgrounds, about extremely troubling religious policies and practices at the United States Air Force Academy. We have investigated those complaints and come to the conclusion that the policies and practices constitute egregious, systemic, and legally actionable violations of the Establishment Clause of the First Amendment to the United States Constitution.

Coerced Religious Practice

Americans United has received reports from former and current cadets—confirmed by members of the U.S. Air Force Academy's "Permanent Party"[1]—that Academy faculty, staff, members of the Chaplains' Office, and upper class cadets frequently pressure members of the Cadet Wing to attend chapel and undertake religious instruction.

1) We have been informed, for example, that, during a Basic Cadet Training session attended by a team of observers from the Yale Divinity School, one of the Academy chaplains—Major Warren "Chappy" Watties—led a Protestant worship service in which he encouraged the attending cadets to return to their tents and proselytize cadets who had not attended the service, with the declared penalty for failure to accept this proselytization being to "burn in the fires of hell." Although literally hundreds of witnesses can attest to the fact that Major Watties ran the service and encouraged attendees to proselytize their non-attending classmates, we are informed that the Academy has downplayed

---

1 The Permanent Party includes those permanently assigned to the Academy as faculty and staff.

the significance of the incident, reporting to the Air Staff at the Pentagon that the chaplain who conducted that service and encouraged proselytization of cadets was not a member of the Academy's Permanent Party but instead was merely a visiting Air Force reservist. That report is incorrect: Major Watties is a full-time chaplain at the Academy. Indeed, he enjoys the distinction of having been named as the U.S. Air Force's current Chaplain of the Year. What is more, the Air Staff has now expressly condoned Major Watties' actions—at the same time that the Academy is denying that Major Watties ever made the statements reported by the Yale Divinity School team and the other attendees at the service. See Pam Zubeck, Air Force deems chaplain's call appropriate, *Gazette* (Colo. Springs), Apr. 27, 2005.

More generally, the Yale Divinity School team reported, and our complainants have confirmed, that Academy chaplains regularly encourage cadets to "witness" other cadets—i.e., attempt to convert them to evangelical Christianity. We have also been informed that, when cadets declined to attend chapel after dinner during Basic Cadet Training, they were made to suffer humiliation by being placed by upper-class cadet staff into a "Heathen Flight" and marched back to their dormitories. Similarly, we have learned that, at a football practice just before an Easter Sunday, head football coach Fisher DeBerry informed the cadets on the team that he expected to see them in church for Easter services. All of these incidents—which are, we have been assured, merely a representative sampling of routine occurrences at the Academy— constitute forms of unlawful religious coercion or pressure by members of the Academy's Permanent Party and the Cadet Wing.

The United States Supreme Court has consistently held that, "at a minimum, the Constitution guarantees that government may not coerce anyone to support or participate in religion or its exercise, or otherwise act in a way which 'establishes a [state] religion or religious faith, or tends to do so.'" Lee v. Weisman, 505 U.S. 577, 587 (1992) (quoting Lynch v. Donnelly, 465 U.S. 668, 678 (1984) (alteration in original). To be sure, it is both constitutionally permissible and appropriate for the armed forces to provide military chaplains insofar as this is necessary to ensure that service-members can satisfy their spiritual needs. See Sch. Dist. v. Schempp, 374 U.S. 203, 226n.10 (1963); Katcoff v. Marsh, 755 F.2d 223, 237–38 (2d Cir. 1985). But neither chaplains, nor other members of the Academy's Permanent Party, nor even upper-class cadets— who are, of course, imbued by the Air Force with command authority over under-class cadets—may aggressively proselytize for any particular faith. See, e.g., Baz v. Walters, 782 F.2d 701, 709 (7th Cir. 1986) (finding that public-hospital chaplain cannot proselytize patients because, although government could lawfully provide hospital chaplains, it must "ensure that the existence of the chaplaincy does not create establishment clause problems," and "[u]nleashing a government-paid chaplain who sees his primary role as proselytizing upon a captive audience of patients could do exactly that").

2) We have also been informed of numerous instances in which prayer was a part of mandatory or otherwise official events at the Academy. For example, we have learned that each mandatory meeting of the cadet cadre during Basic Cadet Training has opened with a prayer, and that many other official events at the Academy—including mandatory meals in Mitchell Hall (the Academy's Cadet Dining Facility), mandatory awards ceremonies, and mandatory military-training-event dinners—have been opened with prayers. The federal courts have upheld certain forms of government-sponsored prayer in only two very narrow contexts: prayer at the opening of legislative sessions (see Marsh v. Chambers, 463 U.S. 783, 790–91 (1983)), and prayer at university graduation ceremonies (see Chaudhuri v. Tennessee, 130 F.3d 232 (6th Cir. 1997); Tanford v. Brand, 194 F.3d 982 (7th Cir. 1996)). But a central rationale for the decisions allowing prayer at university graduation ceremonies is that those events are "significant, once-in-a-lifetime event[s]," for which nonsectarian, non-proselytizing prayer may be appropriate as a means to solemnize the occasion. Doe v. Duncanville Indep. Sch. Dist., 70 F.3d 402, 406–07 (5th Cir. 1995); see also, e.g., Chaudhuri, 130 F.3d at 236. As for other school activities, which are "far less solemn and extraordinary" than graduation ceremonies, the courts have consistently held that officially sponsored prayer is impermissible. See, e.g., Doe v. Santa Fe Indep. Sch. Dist., 168 F.3d 806, 823 (5th Cir. 1999) (rationale for permitting nonsectarian student-initiated prayer at university graduation ceremony "hinged on the singular context and singularly serious nature of the graduation ceremony," and did not apply to school sporting events), aff'd on other grounds, 530 U.S. 290 (2000); Chaudhuri, 130 F.3d at 236; Ingebretsen v. Jackson Pub. Sch. Dist., 88 F.3d 274 (5th Cir. 1996) (striking down state statute permitting student-initiated prayer at school sporting events); Duncanville, 70 F.3d at 406–07; Jager v. Douglas County Sch. Dist., 862 F.2d 824 (11th Cir. 1989) (striking down regulation calling for holding of invocations at high-school sporting events).

Especially pertinent is the decision of the United States Court of Appeals for the Fourth Circuit in Mellen v. Bunting, 327 F.3d 355 (4th Cir. 2003), cert. denied, 541 U.S. 1019 (2004), in which the court held that the Establishment Clause strictly prohibited school-sponsored prayer during mealtimes at the Virginia Military Institute—even though cadets were not required either to attend meals or to participate in the prayers if they did. Id. at 371–72. Among the reasons for that holding was the court's conclusion that "the First Amendment prohibits [a publicly funded military academy] from requiring religious objectors to alienate themselves from the [academy] community in order to avoid a religious practice." Id. at 372 n.9 (citing Lee, 505 U.S. at 596).

And even in the very limited contexts where courts have approved government-sponsored prayer, they have made clear that only nonsectarian prayer is allowed and that prayers specific to any particular faith invariably violate the Establishment Clause. See, e.g., Wynne v. Town of Great Falls, 376 F.3d 292 (4th Cir. 2004) (town council violated Establishment Clause by opening sessions with prayers containing references to Jesus Christ), petition for cert. filed, 73 U.S.L.W. 3473 (U.S. Jan 28, 2005) (No. 04–1052); Bacus v. Palo Verde Unified Sch. Dist. Bd. of Educ., 52 Fed. Appx. 355, 356–57 (9th Cir. 2002) (school board's practice of ending prayers with phrase "in the Name of Jesus" "displays the government's allegiance to a particular sect or creed," namely Christianity, and therefore violates principle that "one religious denomination cannot be officially preferred over another"); Coles ex rel. Coles v. Cleveland Bd. of Educ., 171 F.3d 369, 371, 385 (6th Cir. 1999) (Board of Education's practice of opening meetings with prayer held unconstitutional in part because "the prayers in this case were clearly sectarian, with repeated references to Jesus and the Bible"); Rubin v. City of Burbank, 124 Cal. Rptr. 2d 867 (Cal. App. 2002) (references to "Jesus Christ" in prayers that opened city-council meetings held unconstitutional).

Meals, cadet cadre meetings during the course of Basic Cadet Training, and the like are all, of course, relatively routine occurrences at the Academy—and certainly not once-in-a-lifetime events. And hence, even nonsectarian, non-proselytizing prayer—much less the explicitly Christian prayer that apparently occurs with some frequency at such events at the Academy—cannot be squared with the strict mandates of the Establishment Clause. And although the constitutional violations here are made all the more egregious by virtue of the fact that attendance at these events is mandatory for cadets (see generally, e.g., Lee, 505 U.S. at 587), the Establishment Clause would prohibit prayer in these contexts even if the events were entirely optional, insofar as cadets were forced to choose between being subject to a prayer in order to attend and fully participate in an Academy event, on the one hand, and refraining from attending the event, on the other (see Mellen, 327 F.3d at 372 n.9; see also, e.g., Santa Fe, 530 U.S. at 312 ("'[i]t is a tenet of the First Amendment that the State cannot require one of its citizens to forfeit his or her rights and benefits as the price of resisting conformance to state-sponsored religious practice'" (quoting Lee, 505 U.S. at 596)); Thomas v. Review Bd., 450 U.S. 707, 716 (1981) ("A person may not be compelled to choose between the exercise of a First Amendment right and participation in an otherwise available public program.")). Nor does it make any difference to the constitutional analysis whether cadets at the events are required either to speak or otherwise to participate actively in prayers. For the Supreme Court has held that merely requiring objectors to maintain silence during a prayer constitutes coerced participation in that prayer. See Lee, 505 U.S. at 593. And the Fourth Circuit has held that, in light of the special nature of military-academy life, the mere presence of cadets at an official prayer is unconstitutional, even if there is no requirement that the cadets remain silent or stand at attention. See Mellen, 327 F.3d at 371–72.

3) In addition to receiving reports of coerced attendance at religious services and prayers at official events, we have also learned of a number of other methods by which members of the Permanent Party and upper-class cadet staff have encouraged or put pressure on classmates and under-class cadets to engage in religious practices generally, and most especially in evangelical Christian religious practices.

For example, we have been told that a number of faculty members have introduced themselves to their classes as born-again Christians and encouraged their students to become born-again during the course of the term. We have also been informed of at least one instance where a history instructor at the Academy ordered students to pray before they were permitted to begin their final examination for the course. In addition, we have received copies of a full-page "USAFA CLM 2003 Christmas Greeting" published in the Academy's newspaper, the *Academy Spirit*. The "Greeting" lists approximately 300 signatories—arranged by Academy department—who jointly declared their "belie[f] that Jesus Christ is the only real hope for the world;" announced that "[t]here is salvation in no one else;" and directed cadets to contact them in order to "discuss Jesus." Among the signatories are 16 heads or deputy heads of the Academy's academic departments, 9 permanent professors, the then-Dean of the Faculty, the current Dean of the Faculty, the then-Vice Dean of the Faculty, the Academy's Director of Athletics, and the Academy's head football coach, as well as spouses of these and other members of the Academy faculty and staff. And we have received copies of a sign placed on every plate in the Cadet Dining Hall and posted widely throughout the Academy announcing a Christian-themed program related to the movie *The Passion of the Christ*. The flyers announced that the program was sponsored by the Christian Leadership Ministries "in coordination with the Office of Cadet Chaplains," and stated that "This is an officially sponsored USAFA event—please do not take this flyer down"—a notation that does not generally appear on flyers announcing programs of a non-religious nature.

The Establishment Clause of the First Amendment to the U.S. Constitution forbids public officials from taking any action that "has the purpose or effect of 'endorsing' religion." County of Allegheny v. ACLU, 492 U.S. 573, 592 (1989). Impermissible governmental endorsement of religion occurs whenever a public official—such as a military officer or faculty member at a public educational institution—takes any action that "'convey[s] or attempt[s] to convey a message that religion or a particular religion is favored or preferred.'" Id. at 593 (quoting Wallace v. Jaffree, 472 U.S. 38, 70 (1985) (O'Connor, J., concurring in judgment)) (emphasis in original). Reduced to simplest terms, the Supreme Court has held that the Establishment Clause prohibits any official action that promotes religion generally or shows favoritism toward any particular faith. See, e.g., Bd. of Educ. v. Grumet, 512 U.S. 687, 703 (1994) ("a principle at the heart of the Establishment Clause [is] that government should not prefer one religion to another, or religion to irreligion"); Allegheny, 492 U.S. at 604 ("Whatever else the Establishment Clause may mean (and we have held it to mean no official preference even for religion over nonreligion), it certainly means at the very least that government may not demonstrate a preference for one particular sect or creed (including a preference for Christianity over other religions)."); Larson v. Valente, 456 U.S. 228, 244 (1982) ("The clearest command of the Establishment Clause is that one religious denomination cannot be officially preferred over another.").

When faculty members evangelize or proselytize in the classroom, the message is manifest: To please their instructors, cadets should embrace the instructors' faith. And when large portions of the Academy's Permanent Party issue a joint statement in the Academy's official newspaper espousing one particular creed and encouraging cadets to approach them about it as the path to "salvation," the message is equally clear: To curry favor with the officers who hold sway over their lives, cadets should seek religious instruction from those officers. In short, faculty members and other officers who use their official positions to communicate such messages—as so many members of the Academy's Permanent Party have—are sending a strong and unequivocal message of the Academy's and the United States Air Force's unconstitutional endorsement of religion.

4) What is more, we have received numerous reports about non-Christian cadets being subjected to proselytization or religious harassment by other, more senior or upper-class cadets, thus reinforcing the message of endorsement conveyed by the Permanent Party. Even setting aside the fact that these upper-class cadets apparently are not punished for their conduct (even when they attack

other cadets using religious epithets—a common occurrence at the Academy, we have discovered), upper-class cadets are, of course, given command authority over their subordinates; and hence, they act in an official capacity under the auspices of the United States Air Force. As one recent Academy graduate explained the situation to us, upper-class cadets have virtually total control over the lives of under-class cadets—and therefore often exercise far more direct influence than even the Academy's Permanent Party does. For that reason, not only does harassment by an upper-class cadet constitute official governmental conduct, but cadets who face proselytization or religious harassment from upper-class cadets will naturally conclude that mimicking their superiors' religious beliefs and practices is necessary to succeed at the Academy—or at least to avoid the wrath or ill-will of those with the power to punish. Harassment by upper-class cadets—especially when combined with proselytizing of cadets by the Permanent Party—thus creates a pervasively religious atmosphere that sends "a message to non-adherents that they are outsiders, not full members of the political community." Allegheny, 492 U.S. at 595. That divisive message, communicated by faculty, staff, and upper-class cadets, constitutes a clear violation of the Establishment Clause. See id. at 593–94 (government must refrain from conveying message that religion generally, or any religious belief in particular, is favored or preferred).

Pervasiveness of the Problem

Because of the nature of the military command structure, the Academy leadership is singularly well-positioned to stamp out official religious discrimination and favoritism by giving appropriate orders and enforcing them under the terms of the Uniform Code of Military Justice. By the same token, actions by senior Academy leadership in the officer ranks that undercut attempts to achieve those ends send a strong message to cadets about what conduct is permissible and even favored at the Academy—a clear and unequivocal endorsement of religion in violation of the First Amendment. And in that regard, complaints from multiple sources make clear that violations of the Establishment Clause are not merely aberrant acts by a few rogue individuals, but instead are reflections of *systematic and pervasive religious bias and intolerance at the highest levels of the Academy command structure.*

1) Notably, we have received a host of reports about incidents in which Brigadier General Johnny Weida, in his official capacity as Commandant of Cadets, has endorsed religion generally and his own faith (as an evangelical

Christian) in particular, in clear violation of the Establishment Clause. General Weida has, for example, officially endorsed "National Prayer Week" in a mass e-mail message to the Cadet Wing that can only be described as a prayer and a directive to pray. Among other things, General Weida's e-mail message instructed cadets to "[a]sk the Lord to give us the wisdom to discover the right, the courage to choose it, and the strength to make it endure"; and the message informed the cadets that "He has a plan for each and every one of us." Similarly, in an official "Commander's Guidance" document, General Weida instructed cadets that they "are accountable first to your God." Such official proselytization and prayer by a public official is, of course, the hallmark of unconstitutional conduct under the Establishment Clause. See Allegheny, 492 U.S. at 592 (government officials may not take action that "has the purpose or effect of 'endorsing' religion").

And if those incidents were not enough to demonstrate the severity of the problems at the Academy, it seems that General Weida has established a system of code words that he shares with evangelical Christian cadets in order to provide them with opportunities to proselytize others in the Cadet Wing. Specifically, at a Protestant chapel service during Basic Cadet Training, General Weida told the attendees the New Testament parable of the house built on rock—a metaphor for building faith on the firm foundation of Jesus. See Matthew 7:24–29; Luke 6:46–49. General Weida then instructed the cadets that, whenever he uses the phrase "Airpower!," they should respond with the phrase "Rock Sir!," thus invoking the parable from the New Testament. General Weida advised the cadets that, when asked by their classmates about the meaning of the call and response, the cadets should use the opportunity to discuss their Christian faith. And General Weida regularly invokes the "Airpower!" call in official statements in order to prompt the religiously based "Rock Sir!" response.

Indeed, General Weida has used his "Airpower!" call-and-response to undercut even the few attempts that have been made at the Academy to address particular incidents of religious intolerance and coercion—thus sending an especially strong message of favoritism toward Christianity and those who share General Weida's Christian faith. For example, after the Academy received complaints arising out of the placement on every cadet's plate at mealtime of advertisements for a screening of the movie The Passion of the Christ, Lieutenant General John Rosa apparently ordered General Weida to read to the fully assembled Cadet Wing an official "apology" (or, more accurately, a statement, drafted by the Chaplains' Office, of the Academy's policy regarding the posting and distribution of flyers). But General Weida opened his remarks with the "Airpower!" chant, thus sending the strong message that cadets should ignore his perfunctory reading of the statement. What is more, throughout General Weida's speech, a quotation from the New Testament Book of Ephesians was projected onto several large screens strategically positioned throughout Mitchell Hall (the huge Cadet Dining Facility where General Weida addressed the Cadet Wing at the mandatory noon meal), further reinforcing General Weida's message of official endorsement of Christianity and belying any apparent message of religious neutrality, inclusion, or toleration. Similarly, in a mass e-mail message sent to the Cadet Wing in the wake of the incident over the *Passion of the Christ* flyers, General Weida instructed cadets to "be very careful about forcing your faith into your professional realm"; yet he opened the message with the "Airpower!" invocation, thus unequivocally incorporating his own faith into his "professional realm."

General Weida's incitement of cadets to proselytize other cadets in his preferred form of Christianity, and his creation of the call-and-response system to facilitate their doing so, are particularly clear instances of official Academy endorsement of religion. And his undercutting of any message of religious toleration, mutual respect, or separation of church and state through his well-timed use of that mechanism only serves to underscore the message that the Academy command gives preference to evangelical Christianity over other faiths.

At a more basic level, we have been informed that General Weida has cultivated and reinforced an attitude—shared by many in the Academy Chaplains' Office and, increasingly, by other members of the Academy's Permanent Party—that the Academy, and the Air Force in general, would be better off if populated solely with Christians. A stronger message of official preference for one particular faith is hard to imagine. And because, as a number of senior Air Force career officers have now confirmed for us, Air Force Academy cadets and junior Air Force officers rapidly come to the conclusion that rewards go to those who think like their general officers, these young people learn that professional success comes with emulation of the practice of explicitly incorporating Christianity into the performance of their official duties. So when leaders such as General Weida support and contribute to a culture of religious intolerance and official favoritism, Establishment Clause violations become commonplace.

2) Thus, it should come as no surprise that other members of the Air Force Academy's Permanent Party are equally unrestrained in their egregious violations of the Establishment Clause. As we have already described such widespread practices as faculty members proselytizing in the classroom and directives from Academy chaplains to proselytize other cadets, we will

not belabor the point unduly by trying to recount all of the violations by Academy officials about which we have received complaints. But to underscore the open, notorious, and pervasive nature of the violations, we do wish to call special attention to the actions of one other member of the Academy staff—head football coach Fisher DeBerry—as his conduct in violation of the Establishment Clause is not only clear, but also longstanding and well-documented.

Last fall, Coach DeBerry placed a banner reading "I am a Christian first and last*** I am a member of Team Jesus Christ" in the locker room used by the Academy's football team. He posted the banner just two weeks after the Academy had initiated a program of religious sensitivity training—a topic to which we will return later—and one day after General Rosa had informed the Academy's Board of Visitors of his plans for addressing religious intolerance at the Academy. See Pam Zubeck, DeBerry gets sensitivity training, *Gazette* (Colo. Springs), Dec. 1, 2004. Although DeBerry supposedly received "counseling" from General Rosa concerning the banner (see id.), DeBerry's official favoritism towards Christianity has not wavered: He has since been quoted as saying that religion is "'what we're all about'" at the Academy (Todd Jacobson & Pam Zubeck, AFA coach says religion is paramount at school, *Gazette* (Colo. Springs), Feb. 26, 2005 (quoting Coach DeBerry)). He has also stated that he continues to "advise his players to attend church the day after games." Id. He has further stated that, after games, the team members and he "get on our hands and knees and we wrap our arms around each other and we thank God for the opportunity of having competed that particular day." Id. We have also been informed that DeBerry routinely gives speeches at official Academy and prep-school events, and that his speeches have overtly sectarian themes and are invariably laden with explicit references to Jesus. Indeed, DeBerry has consistently incorporated religion into his coaching and the performance of his other official duties throughout his many years at the Academy. See e.g., Jacobsen & Zubeck, supra (noting DeBerry's self-report that he has held team prayers during his entire 21-year coaching career at the Academy).

Yet aside from the one occasion of "counseling" by General Rosa over the "Team Jesus Christ" banner, it seems that no action has ever been taken to discipline Coach DeBerry for his behavior—and certainly none that was sufficient to cause DeBerry to change that behavior. On the contrary, the Colorado Springs *Gazette* recently reported that General Rosa has announced that it is permissible for DeBerry to lead the football team in prayers, as long as those prayers do not promote any particular religion. See Jacobsen & Zubeck, supra.

3) But General Rosa's statement of policy is wrong as a matter of law. The U.S. Supreme Court and all other courts to consider the question have held that officially sponsored prayer may not be held at athletic events at public educational institutions. See, e.g., Santa Fe Indep. Sch. Dist. v. Doe, 530 U.S. 290, 305–08 (2000) (striking down student-initiated, student-led prayer before football games); Ingebretsen v. Jackson Pub. Sch. Dist., 88 F.3d 274 (5th Cir. 1996) (striking down state statute permitting student-initiated prayer at sporting events); Jager v. Douglas County Sch. Dist., 862 F.2d 824 (11th Cir. 1989) (striking down regulation calling for holding of invocations at high-school sporting events). Indeed, the U.S. Court of Appeals for the Fifth Circuit has ruled that coaches or other school employees may neither participate in nor supervise prayer during practice or in the locker room before a game, even if the prayer is initiated and led by the students themselves. Doe v. Duncanville Indep. Sch. Dist., 70 F.3d 402 (5th Cir. 1995).

Among the many reasons that team prayer accompanying sporting events at public institutions has been held to be unconstitutional is the fact that attendance at games is not voluntary for members of the team; and, in any event, the courts have held that the Establishment Clause forbids even what are clearly designated as voluntary pre-game prayer sessions because the hierarchical nature of the coach-player relationship might make team members feel pressure to attend. See, e.g., Doe v. Duncanville Indep. Sch. Dist., 994 F.2d 160, 165 (5th Cir. 1993) (coach's involvement in religious activity with students would be "perceived by the students as inducing participation they might otherwise reject"). Thus, it is irrelevant as a legal matter as well as illusory as a practical matter that Coach DeBerry purports to allow non-Christians to opt out of post-game team prayer (see Jacobson & Zubeck, supra (relating not only DeBerry's description of supposed opt-out right for non-Christians, but also his report that no team members have ever exercised that right)).

Official Discrimination Against
Non-Christians and Non-Religious Cadets

We have also received multiple reports of unequal treatment of, and official discrimination against, non-Christian cadets who wish to attend religious services or study sessions.

1) It is our understanding that Christian cadets who wish to attend Christian religious services and religious study sessions (such as "Sunday school" or Bible study) on Sundays are eligible for "non-chargeable passes"—i.e., special passes to

leave the Academy grounds that do not count as regular leave. By contrast, cadets who celebrate the Sabbath on other days of the week—such as Jewish or Seventh-Day Adventist cadets, who celebrate the Sabbath on Saturday—are not able to obtain such non-chargeable passes to attend Saturday services off the Academy grounds. Indeed, we have been told that Saturday Sabbath observers frequently are denied any opportunity at all to attend religious services because mandatory events such as training, parades, and football games are routinely scheduled for Saturdays, and cadets are not permitted to miss those activities in order to attend religious services. Meanwhile, such mandatory events are not scheduled for Sundays, when they might otherwise conflict with the ability of cadets to attend Christian worship services.

The provision of special passes for attendance at Christian religious services and religious study sessions that are not available on equal terms to persons of other faiths is a straightforward instance of one faith being preferred over others, in violation of the Establishment Clause. See, e.g., Allegheny, 492 U.S. at 593–94, 604; Larson, 456 U.S. at 244. Simply put, the Air Force is constitutionally obligated to ensure a diversity of religious viewpoints in the religious programming that it provides; and granting special favors to Christians or special status to their preferred forms of religious observance is highly improper. See, e.g., Katcoff, 755 F.2d at 226–27 & n.1 (approving provision of military chaplaincy in part because Army "provid[ed] religious facilities for soldiers of some 86 different denominations" and did not favor any particular faith over others); Adair v. England, 183 F. Supp. 2d 31, 56–58 (D.D.C. 2002) (Navy's chaplaincy policy favoring liturgical over non-liturgical Christians held to be presumptively unconstitutional).

2) We have also been informed that Academy officials have discriminated against non-religious students by denying them other privileges that are routinely available to religious students. For example, General Weida has authorized cadets to hang crosses or other religious items in their dorm rooms, whereas Academy regulations prohibit cadets from displaying non-religious items in similar fashion. In addition, we have been informed that at least one cadet was denied a non-chargeable pass to attend a Freethinkers' meeting off base because the officers and the cadets in his chain of command regarded Freethinkers' meetings as not faith-based, and therefore not entitled to the same treatment given to Christian worship or study. And, based on that same official determination, the officers and cadets in the chain of command also denied this same cadet's request to form a Freethinkers' "SPIRE" group under the auspices of the Academy's Special Program in Religious Education.

When the cadet complained about these and other incidents to the Academy's MEO office (i.e., its equal-opportunity office), the officer in charge, Captain Joseph Bland, refused to recognize the complaint as one for religious discrimination because the cadet had identified himself as an atheist. Captain Bland then attempted to proselytize the cadet into Catholicism. We understand that Captain Bland was competitively selected as, and currently holds the title of, the U.S. Air Force's MEO Officer of the Year. In sum, the Air Force officer charged with investigating and resolving complaints of religious discrimination at the Academy, and recognized by the Air Force as being the outstanding MEO officer for that entire branch of the service, not only had a fundamental misunderstanding of the legal definition of religious discrimination (see generally, e.g., Wallace v. Jaffree, 472 U.S. 38, 53–54 (1985) ("the individual freedom of conscience protected by the First Amendment embraces the right to select any religious faith or none at all")), but also thought it entirely proper to commit a straightforward violation of the Establishment Clause in the course of performing the official duties of the MEO office.[2]

The Supreme Court has consistently held that the First Amendment prohibits government from preferring religion to non-religion just as much as it prohibits government from preferring one faith to any other. See, e.g., Grumet, 512 U.S. at 703 ("a principle at the heart of the Establishment Clause [is] that government should not prefer one religion to another, or religion to irreligion"); Texas Monthly, Inc. v. Bullock, 489 U.S. 1, 8–9 (1989) (plurality opinion) (it "is part of our settled jurisprudence" that First Amendment "'prohibits government from abandoning secular purpose in order to put an imprimatur on one

---

2 Additionally, serious Establishment Clause concerns are implicated by the composition of the Chaplains' Office and the SPIRE program. In this regard, we are informed that the Academy's Cadet Wing consists of approximately 30% Catholics, 30% non-evangelical Protestants, and 30% evangelical Protestants, with the remaining 10% including Jewish, Islamic, and other non-Christian cadets as well as cadets who elect not to declare any religious affiliation. Yet the Academy's chaplains' core is overwhelmingly composed of Protestant chaplains, virtually all of whom are evangelical Christians. The vast majority of the SPIRE groups are designated as "Protestant." And all of the "Protestant" SPIRE groups are evangelical. The United States District Court for the District of Columbia has held, however, that the Navy's chaplaincy program was presumptively unconstitutional because two-thirds of the Navy's chaplain slots were filled with liturgical Christian clergy, when liturgical Christians constituted only one-third of the Navy's religious personnel. See Adair, 183 F. Supp. 2d at 56–58. Under Adair, the dramatic mismatch between the overwhelming numbers of evangelical Protestant chaplains and SPIRE groups, on the one hand, and the actual percentage of evangelical Protestants in the Cadet Wing on the other, would be strong evidence of an unconstitutional preference for evangelical Christianity over other Christian and non-Christian religious denominations.

religion, or on religion as such, or to favor the adherents of any sect or religious organization'" (citation omitted)); Epperson v. Arkansas, 393 U.S. 97, 104 (1968) ("The First Amendment mandates governmental neutrality between religion and religion, and between religion and non-religion"); Torcaso v. Watkins, 367 U.S. 488, 495 (1961) (government cannot "constitutionally pass laws or impose requirements which aid all religions as against non-believers"); Everson v. Bd. of Educ., 330 U.S. 1, 18 (1947) (First Amendment "requires the state to be a neutral in its relations with groups of religious believers and non-believers").[3]

Providing non-chargeable passes to cadets for attendance at religious services and study sessions—and specifically Christian ones—without providing similar opportunities to attend non-religious alternatives clearly constitutes providing a special benefit to religious cadets not available to others. Additionally, it is our understanding that while a few of the Academy's SPIRE groups are run by Academy chaplains, the Academy also permits several outside Christian groups to host SPIRE groups, thus affording them special access to the Academy facilities and to the cadets, while denying the same privilege to an outside Freethinkers' group. Doing so is plainly the "unjustifiable assistance to religious organizations" that slights both non-believers and adherents to alter-

---

3 Thus, the Supreme Court held in Texas Monthly, for example, that a state violated the Establishment Clause by enacting a sales-tax exemption for religious periodicals without extending the exemption to non-religious periodicals. 489 U.S. 1. The plurality explained that when a law directs a benefit exclusively to religious organizations, the government "'provide[s] unjustifiable awards of assistance to religious organizations' and cannot but 'conve[y] a message of endorsement' to slighted members of the community." Id. at 15 (plurality opinion) (quoting Corp. of Presiding Bishop v. Amos, 483 U.S. 327, 348 (1987)). Similarly, in Estate of Thornton v. Caldor, Inc., 472 U.S. 703 (1985), the Supreme Court struck down as violative of the Establishment Clause a state statute that provided Sabbath observers with an absolute right not to work on their Sabbath (id.at 710–11), holding that the statute constituted unconstitutional governmental preference for Sabbath observers over "other employees who have strong and legitimate, but non-religious, reasons for wanting" a particular day off. Id.at 710 n.9. And the lower federal courts have similarly held governmental benefits to be unconstitutional when they are directed exclusively to religious organizations or persons. See, e.g., Finlator v. Powers, 902 F.2d 1158, 1162–63 (4th Cir. 1990) (statute exempting "Holy Bibles" from state's retail-sales and use taxes violated Establishment Clause); Haller v. Pa. Dep't of Revenue, 728 A.2d 351 (Pa. 1999) (sales-tax exemption for religious articles, Bibles, and other religious publications sold by religious organizations violated Establishment Clause); In re Springmoor, 498 S.E.2d 177 (N.C. 1998) (statute granting property-tax exemptions to nursing homes only if homes were owned, operated, and managed by religious or Masonic organizations violated Establishment Clause); Thayer v. S.C. Tax Comm'n, 413 S.E.2d 810 (S.C. 1992) (exemption from use tax for religious publications violated Establishment Clause); Port Wash. Union Free Sch. Dist. v. Port Wash. Teachers Ass'n, 702 N.Y. S.2d 605 (N.Y. App. Div. 2000) (religious-holidays provision of collective-bargaining agreement violated Establishment Clause by giving religiously observant teachers more leave than non-religious teachers).

native religions, in violation of the First Amendment.[4] Texas Monthly, 489 U.S. at 15 (quoting Amos at 348).

Inadequate Remedial Measures

We do not know what disciplinary actions, if any, senior Air Force Academy leadership has ever taken as a result of any complaints of religious intolerance or harassment. We are aware that the Academy has recently instituted a program known as "Respecting the Spiritual Values of All People." But firsthand, eyewitness reports confirm that this "RSVP" program is woefully inadequate to address the pervasive and systemic problems of official religious intolerance, discrimination, and coercion at the Academy.

First of all, we have been told that the RSVP program as currently constituted is not the program of religious sensitivity training originally developed by members of the Chaplains' Office and sanctioned by the team of outside experts from the Yale Divinity School. As it was described to us, the original proposal was to implement a program to expose attendees to forms of religious expression with which they are unfamiliar; to teach toleration and mutual respect in order to counteract the official culture of religious discrimination and coercion at the Academy; and to explain the importance of ensuring that official conduct is strictly neutral with respect to religion. But we have learned that the program was substantially modified after a visit from the Air Force's chief of chaplains— Major General Charles Baldwin—and that the resulting RSVP program does not adequately teach and promote the fundamental constitutional requirement of separation of church and state.

---

4 In that regard too, the determination that a Freethinkers' group is not religious, and the denial of non-chargeable passes and the denial of permission to form a SPIRE group on that basis, cannot be squared with the federal courts' recognition that legal protections for "religion" necessarily must extend not only to mainstream religions, but also to any other deeply held belief systems. "In considering a first amendment claim arising from a non-traditional 'religious' belief or practice, the courts have looked to the familiar religions as models in order to ascertain, by comparison, whether the new set of ideas or beliefs is confronting the same concerns, or serving the same purposes, as unquestioned and accepted 'religions.'" Africa v. Pennsylvania, 662 F.2d 1025, 1032 (3d Cir. 1981) (quotation marks, brackets, and citation omitted). As long as a sincerely held belief system "confront[s] the same concerns" (id.) as a traditional religion, in other words, government lacks the power to assess the validity of that belief system, and must afford it the same treatment as any recognized, mainstream religion. See, e.g., United States v. Seeger, 380 U.S. 163, 184 (1965). And hence, the Academy's official determination that Freethinkers' meetings are non-religious and unworthy of treatment as a religion may well constitute an unconstitutional preference for traditional religious sects and creeds over what as a matter of law must also be treated as a religion.

We have also learned that even the watered-down message of this current incarnation of the RSVP program is being implicitly undercut. Among other things, we have been told that senior Air Force Academy officials—including General Weida—have just within the past few days, and during their actual duty hours, attended a program (held by an evangelical Christian group and specifically endorsed by the Air Force Academy Office of Cadet Chaplains) that identified "secularism" and "pluralism" as specific threats to "the followers of Jesus." This program, which was attended by General Weida and other senior Air Force Academy officials, directly contradicted the message of mutual respect and toleration that the RSVP program purportedly conveys. Furthermore, the Office of Cadet Chaplains endorsed the program notwithstanding the fact that the Chaplains' Office is the entity charged with conducting the RSVP program—thus casting serious doubt on the sincerity of the Chaplains' Office's commitment to the stated goals of the RSVP program.

Effect of Religious Discrimination
at U.S. Air Force Academy

Finally, we are aware of at least two cases in which highly qualified individuals were dissuaded from attending the Academy and entering into the Air Force officer corps—despite longstanding and fervent desires to do so—after learning of the official culture of religious intolerance and hostility toward those who do not subscribe to and practice evangelical Christianity. When the Air Force is denied the service of the country's best and brightest young people because they feel excluded from the Academy by religious intolerance, the armed forces and the Nation as a whole are weakened. What is more, in light of the traditional role that military-officer training has played in cultivating local, state, and national leaders in both the public and private sectors, the effective exclusion from the Academy of highly qualified, highly motivated young men and women on the basis of their religion—or their unwillingness to conform to the religious practices of those in charge—is the very archetype of the "message to non-adherents that they are outsiders, not full members of the political community," that the Constitution forbids. Allegheny, 492 U.S. at 595. A public institution that conveys that message straightforwardly violates the Establishment Clause. See, e.g., id.

***

The investigation by Americans United for Separation of Church and State into the policies and practices of the United States Air Force Academy has revealed numerous flagrant and egregious violations of the Establishment Clause of the First Amendment to the U.S. Constitution, as well as a general climate of religious coercion and official hostility toward those who do not practice evangelical Christianity. *We have concluded that both the specific violations and the promotion of a culture of official religious intolerance are pervasive, systematic, and evident at the very highest levels of the Academy's command structure.*

This report was prepared by the Legal Department of Americans United for Separation of Church and State. For further information, contact:

Ayesha N. Khan, Legal Director
Richard B. Katskee, Assistant Legal Director.

APPENDIX C

Executive Summary of the Report of the Headquarters Review Group
Concerning the Religious Climate
at the U.S. Air Force Academy,
22 June 2005

On 2 May 2005, the Acting Secretary of the Air Force, Michael L. Dominguez, directed the Air Force Deputy Chief of Staff, Personnel, Lieutenant General Roger A. Brady, to form a cross-functional team to assess the religious climate at the United States Air Force Academy (USAFA) and their progress in integrating principles of respect in their character development program. Specifically, the team was directed to assess policy and guidance on the subject, appropriateness of relevant training for all personnel at USAFA, practices in the Academy community that would either enhance or detract from a climate that respects both the "free exercise of religion" and the "establishment" clauses of the First Amendment, effectiveness of USAFA mechanisms in addressing complaints on this subject, and relevance of the religious climate to the entire Air Force. The team was not tasked to investigate cases of specific misconduct, nor to determine individual accountability, but to refer specific cases to appropriate authorities, including the Air Force Inspector General. Two specific cases involving individuals who have been mentioned repeatedly in the press (Brigadier General John Weida and Captain Melinda Morton) are being reviewed by Inspector General channels; therefore, these cases are not resolved in this report. Seven other specific cases reported to the team were referred to the chain of command for follow-up.

The Deputy Chief of Staff, Personnel, assembled a team (with Headquarters representatives from Personnel, Judge Advocate General, General Counsel, Chaplain Service, Legislative Liaison, Public Affairs, Manpower & Reserve Affairs, Secretary of the Air Force and the Air Force Chief of Staff Command Staffs, as well as the Office of the Secretary of Defense and the United States Naval Academy) which reviewed policy and guidance documents, court cases, press reports and findings of previous groups that had reported on the issue of religious climate at the USAFA, and coordinated with the academy staff in preparation for the on-site visit. The team was informed on issues of concern by previous surveys, team reports and media coverage.

The HQ USAF team found a religious climate that does not involve overt religious discrimination, but a failure to fully accommodate all members' needs and a lack of awareness over where the line is drawn between permissible and impermissible expression of beliefs. The Academy is aggressively engaged in dealing with an issue that has been the subject of rigorous debate throughout the Nation's history. The Superintendent responded to some well-publicized events early in his tenure and, upon finding evidence of some concern about religious bias in anonymous surveys he conducted, began a much broader effort to incorporate the importance of religious respect in the Academy's character development program. This continuing effort to nurture a climate of respect for the diversity of beliefs at the Academy has received the support of the USAFA community, including many who have expressed concern. The team found that the events that have been reported in the media framed the discussions and were cited repeatedly by individuals expressing concern about the religious climate. The team also researched the background behind the widely reported "55 complaints," in reality a collection of observations and events reported by about thirteen people, and purported to have taken place over a four-year period. Throughout the assessment, the methodology used by the Review Group, using both individual interviews and focus groups, did not yield empirical data regarding specific events, but facilitated important discussions that aided the team in assessing the overall climate.

During the visit, the team was made aware of seven specific events of what appeared to be questionable behavior, and these events were referred to the chain of command for follow-up. The team identified nine findings regarding the overall climate and made nine recommendations that are detailed in the report.

The findings covered the following areas:

- Perception of religious intolerance.
- Inadequate guidance regarding religious expression.
- Training concerning religious diversity and respect.
- Occurrences of perceived bias.
- Accommodation of religious observances (to include flexibility in cadet scheduling process and dietary needs).
- USAFA access for affiliated chapel programs.

The recommendations include actions that are required of USAFA and of HAF in the following areas:

- Develop policy guidance for Air Force commanders and supervisors regarding religious expression.
- Reemphasize policy guidance for commanders and staff judge advocates regarding appropriate endorsement and advertising of unofficial or affiliated groups of which Air Force members may be a part and oversight of these groups that have access to Air Force personnel.
- Reemphasize the requirement for all commanders to address issues of religious accommodation up front, when planning, scheduling, and preparing operations.
- Develop guidance that integrates the requirements for cultural awareness and respect across the learning continuum, as they apply to Airmen operating in Air Force units at home as well as during operations abroad.
- Direct USAFA to develop an integrated plan, as part of its overall character development program, that promotes increased awareness of and respect for diverse cultures and beliefs in its military, academic, and athletic curriculum.
- Provide plan for ensuring a single focal point for cadets, as well as permanent party, to raise issues regarding the human relations climate.
- Continue robust use of internal controls to assess climate and implement corrective action. Additionally, coordination among the associated agencies should be reviewed to improve cross-flow of information to command.
- Provide continuing opportunities for all cadets to learn about, discuss, and debate issues of religion and spirituality in a developmental setting with peers and role models, as such discussion is essential to character development.

These findings and recommendations regarding the religious climate at USAFA can be summarized in three areas: institutional policy, cadet behavior and faculty and staff behavior.

The Department of Defense, HQ USAF and the USAFA leadership have provided appropriate policy regarding the importance of nondiscrimination and a climate of respect. However, there is a lack of operational instructions that commanders and supervisors can use as they make decisions regarding appropriate exercise of religion in the workplace.

The team found that failure to address the religious needs of cadets of minority religions, during the planning phase of academy schedule development, placed the burden for seeking religious accommodation on the cadets. This created the impression among some cadets that USAFA was insensitive to their religious beliefs and needs.

There were reports made to the team by cadets of religious slurs and disparaging remarks between cadets. Two particular incidents were referred to leadership by the HQ USAF team for follow-up. Both incidents have been resolved to the satisfaction of the complainants. The cadets, both individuals and in focus groups, reported that such events do occur occasionally but have become less frequent over the last two years, indicating an improving climate. The examples of religious slurs and disparaging remarks presented to the team are clearly unacceptable and cannot be tolerated. They also accentuate the importance of understanding that the USAFA is about the development of character in 18–22 year olds who are becoming adults, which includes interacting with others cadets of different belief systems and determining what they themselves believe. This growth process sometimes involves inappropriate behavior. USAFA leadership is dealing with that behavior appropriately.

There were also reports, usually framed in the context of events reported in the media, that some cadets had been overly aggressive in the expression of their faith, offending some and, in some cases, creating an impression of insensitivity regarding the beliefs of others. Likewise, some members of the faculty and staff also have strong religious beliefs that have, on occasion, been expressed in ways that others found offensive. While these expressions appear to be well intentioned, they reflect a lack of awareness that their position as instructors and government officials made these expressions inappropriate in a particular setting. USAFA leadership has identified some of these expressions of faith as inappropriate in the environment in which they were made, and has taken action to correct them.

While the team talked to individuals who were concerned or who had been offended by what they regarded as a climate of religious bias, a significant majority of individuals contacted, including cadets, faculty and staff, expressed the opinion that the overall climate had improved over the past two years. Many attribute this improvement to the efforts of the USAFA leadership in implementing the Agenda for Change (a map for cultural change at the Academy directed by SECAF and CSAF) and the recommendations of other review groups, as well as leadership placing special emphasis on the subject of respecting a diversity of views in the area of religion. Many individuals were not aware of the issue or had only been made aware through media reports.

Clearly, there are challenges of respect and accommodation that the USAFA leadership must continue to address very aggressively. The HQ USAF team found they are doing that. While overt discrimination and other clearly inappropriate behavior cannot and will not be tolerated, what exactly does or does not constitute "establishment" is not always as clear. The task of providing for free exercise of religion, while not appearing to establish a religion, is complex enough in any government setting. Arguably, it is even more complex in a military environment and yet again more challenging in a university, military setting.

In an effort to minimize the risk of discrimination or the perception of "establishment," some might suggest that religion and discussion of it be minimized, outside the statutory allowances specific to the chaplaincy. However, this would have at least two equally undesirable effects. First, it would ignore that clause of the First Amendment that protects the free exercise of religion. Second, and perhaps as important, it would deny the unique nature of military service.

The development of leaders of character is the mission of the USAFA. And, it is undeniable that for many individuals their character development is inseparable from their religious beliefs. Hence, it is incumbent upon the USAFA to afford the opportunity for cadets to develop their character in that context, while respecting the fact that cadets have differing religious beliefs or may have none at all. Put simply, the academy should provide appropriate development opportunities to meet the needs of all cadets. Unnecessary restriction of that opportunity would have a deleterious effect on the character development of cadets at a particularly formative time of their lives.

Similarly, inherent in military service is the very real potential that individuals may be asked to forfeit their lives in defense of the Nation. Again, for some individuals, the ability to withstand the privations of military service and face the prospect of death in the performance of their duties requires strength of character that is founded upon their religious faith. It is their source of strength in times of trial. Deliberately minimizing the ability of cadets and their role models to discuss these weighty issues in a developmental setting, including their foundational beliefs, would undermine the maturation and character development process we seek to foster.

While this challenge is daunting, it is not "Mission Impossible." The task is not simple, but the principle is. The USAFA, and the Air Force as a whole, must create and nurture a climate founded on respect, the very bedrock of our core values of Integrity first, Service before self, and Excellence in all we do.

Critical for all Airmen is that these principles become integrated into every aspect of our training and continuing education. Critical to commanders is that they be given a set of guidelines upon which to base decisions regarding how they recognize and build on the inherently spiritual nature of their people and create the conditions that demonstrate the value of and respect for the great diversity of belief systems within our Air Force.

ROGER A. BRADY
Lieutenant General, USAF
Deputy Chief of Staff,
Personnel

APPENDIX D

IN THE UNITED STATES DISTRICT COURT
FOR THE DISTRICT OF NEW MEXICO

MICHAEL L. WEINSTEIN,
        Plaintiff,

vs.

UNITED STATES AIR FORCE and
PETE GEREN, Acting Secretary of the
Air Force,

        Defendants.

COMPLAINT FOR VIOLATION OF CONSTITUTIONAL RIGHTS

COMES NOW the Plaintiff, by and through his attorneys of record, The Bregman Law Firm, P.C. (Sam Bregman and Eric Loman) and in support of his Complaint for Violation of Constitutional Rights, states the following:

Parties and Jurisdiction

1. Plaintiff Michael L. Weinstein ("Plaintiff") is a resident of Bernalillo County, New Mexico and a citizen and taxpayer of the United States of America.

2. Plaintiff is an honor graduate of the United States Air Force Academy ("Academy") and the parent of two active duty members of the United States Air Force ("USAF"), including one cadet currently at the Academy. Plaintiff is also the father and father-in-law of two recent Academy graduates, both of whom are currently on active duty with the USAF. As such, the actions and policies of the USAF affect Plaintiff in a direct and cognizable fashion.

3. Upon information and belief, the USAF is a branch of the United States Military and operates the Academy in Colorado Springs, Colorado.

4. Upon information and belief, Defendant Pete Geren is the Acting Secretary of the U.S. Air Force.

5. The USAF operates three bases in New Mexico, including Kirtland Air Force Base, which is located in Bernalillo County, New Mexico.

6. This action is based on violations of the United States Constitution and 42 U.S.C. § 1983, a federal statute.

7. Jurisdiction and venue are proper in this Court.

Factual Allegations

8. The staff and faculty of the Academy, in the interest of our future national security, molds our future leaders into outstanding young men and women into Air Force officers with knowledge, character, and discipline; motivated to lead the world's greatest aerospace force in service to the nation.

9. Over the course of at least the last decade, a pattern and practice has developed at the Academy where senior officers and cadets have attempted to impose evangelical Christianity into arenas that are clearly United States Air Force venues in violation of the Establishment Clause of the First Amendment to the United States Constitution.

10. During a Basic Cadet Training session attended by a team of observers from the Yale Divinity School, one of the Air Force Academy chaplains (Major Warren Watties) led a protestant worship service in which he encouraged cadets to return to their tents and proselytize cadets who had not attended the service, with the declared penalty of not accepting this proselytization being to "burn in the fires of hell."

11. Cadets were encouraged by certain chaplains to "witness" to other cadets in an attempt to convert them to evangelical Christianity.

12. Cadets have additionally been coerced into non-secular prayers during mandatory or otherwise official events at the Academy.

13. In addition to coerced attendance at religious services and prayers at official events, members of the Permanent Party and upperclass cadet staff have encouraged or put pressure on classmates and underclass cadets to engage in religious practices generally, and most especially in evangelical Christian religious practices.

14. Continued violations of the Establishment Clause by the Air Force Academy are severe, systemic and pervasive, and have fostered discrimination and harassment toward non-Evangelical Christian, non-Christian and non-religious cadets and Academy staff.

15. The discrimination and harassment toward non-Christian and non-religious cadets have been manifested within the Air Force Academy by nu-

merous incidents of slurs directed at individual cadets who hold minority religion status or are Jewish or atheists. In addition, Christian cadets who wish to attend Christian religious services have been eligible for "non-chargeable passes" that do not count as regular leave. However, cadets who celebrate the Sabbath on other days of the week have not been able to obtain such non-chargeable passes to attend Saturday services off the Academy grounds.

16. Despite claims by the USAF that it has changed its policies regarding evangelizing at the Academy and throughout the entire USAF, USAF officials have made it clear that they have no intent to actually remedy the unconstitutional practices of the USAF.

17. Shockingly, as recently as July 12, 2005, Brig. General Cecil R. Richardson, the Air Force deputy chief of chaplains, had the audacity to say in an interview carried on the front page of *The New York Times,* "We will not proselytize, but we reserve the right to evangelize the unchurched."

18. Despite being repeatedly asked by Plaintiff to repudiate Brig. General Richardson's statement and to make a clear statement that this is not its policy, the United States Air Force and Defendant Geren have refused to do so, thereby ratifying this policy.

19. Upon information and belief, it is the unwritten policy of many evangelical chaplains to continue proselytizing and evangelizing cadets and staff at the United States Air Force Academy and members of the United States Air Force at large.

Count I—Violatlon of First Amendment Right to Freedom of Religion

20. Plaintiff realleges the preceding Paragraphs as though fully set forth herein.

21. This cause of action is brought pursuant to the First Amendment of the United States Constitution and 42 U.S.C. § 1983.

22. By adopting a formal and informal policy of evangelizing, prosyletizing and otherwise actively challenging the religions of its members, the USAF is violating the Establishment Clause of the First Amendment of the U.S. Constitution, as well as frustrating and hindering USAF members' right to freedom of religion.

23. Such violation has caused injury to Plaintiff as well as members of the USAF.

24. Plaintiff is entitled to injunctive relief as well as the costs of this action and reasonable attorneys' fees.

Count II—Injunctive Relief

25. Plaintiff realleges the preceding Paragraphs as though fully set forth herein.

26. Plaintiff is entitled to the permanent injunctive relief that the USAF, Defendant Geren and its senior leadership adopt and adhere to the following policies:

27. a. No member of the USAF, including a chaplain, is permitted to evangelize, proselytize, or in any related way attempt to involuntarily convert, pressure, exhort or persuade a fellow member of the USAF to accept their own religious beliefs while on duty.

   b. The USAF is not permitted to establish or advance any one religion over another religion or one religion over no religion.

28. There is no remedy in law for the damages caused by the policies and conduct of the USAF.

WHEREFORE Plaintiff respectfully requests a judgment against Defendant giving appropriate injunctive relief, costs of this action, reasonable attorneys' fees, and any other relief that the Court deems just and proper.

APPENDIX E

The Covenant and Code of Ethics for Chaplains of the Armed Forces, from the Basic Chaplains Course (BCC-02C), 20 May–14 June 2002

The Covenant

Having accepted God's call to minister to people in the Armed Forces of our country, I covenant to serve God and these people with God's help; to deepen my obedience to the commandments, to Love the Lord our God with all my heart, soul, mind and strength and to love my neighbor as myself. In affirmation of this commitment, I will abide by the Code of Ethics for Chaplains of the Armed Forces, and I will faithfully support its purposes and ideals. As further affirmation of my commitment, I covenant with my colleagues in ministry and that we will hold one another accountable for fulfillment of all public actions set forth in our Code of Ethics.

The Code of Ethics

I will hold in trust the traditions and practices of my religious body.

I will carefully adhere to whatever direction may be conveyed to me by my endorsing body for the maintenance of my endorsement.

I understand, as a chaplain of the Armed Forces, that I must function in a pluralistic environment with chaplains of other religious bodies to provide for ministry to all military personnel and their families entrusted to my care.

I will seek to provide for pastoral care with ministry to persons of religious bodies other than my own within my area of responsibility with the same investment of myself as I give to members of my own religious body. I will work collegially with chaplains of religious bodies other than my own as together we seek to provide as full a ministry as possible to our people.

I will respect the beliefs and traditions of my colleagues and those with whom I minister. When conducting services of worship that include persons other than my religious body, I will draw upon those beliefs, principles, and practices that we have in common.

I will, if in a supervisory position, respect the practices and beliefs of each chaplain I supervise, and exercise care not to require of them any service or practice that would be in violation of the faith practices of their particular religious body.

I will seek to support all colleagues in ministry by building constructive relationships wherever I serve, both with the staff where I work and with colleagues throughout the military environment.

I will maintain a disciplined ministry in such a way as keeping hours of prayer and devotion, endeavoring to maintain wholesome family relationships, and regularly engaging in educational and recreational activities for professional and personal development. I will seek to maintain good health habits.

I will recognize that my obligation is to ministry to all members of the Military Services, their families, and other authorized personnel. When on Active Duty, I will only accept added responsibility in civilian ministry if it does not interfere with the overall effectiveness of my primary military ministry.

I will defend my colleagues against unfair discrimination on the basis of gender, race, religion, or national origin.

I will hold in confidence any privileged communication received by me during the conduct of my ministry. I will not disclose confidential communications in private or in public.

I will not proselytize other religious bodies, but I retain the right to evangelize those who are non-affiliated.

I will show personal love for God in my life and ministry, as I strive together with my colleagues to preserve the dignity, maintain the discipline and promote the integrity of the profession to which we have been called.

I recognize the special power afforded me by my ministerial office. I will never use that power in ways that violate the personhood of another human being, religiously, emotionally or sexually. I will use my pastoral office only for that which is best for the persons under my ministry.

INDEX